DATE DUE

NOV 0 6 74			
DEC 04 74			
APR 30 75			
NOV 24 88			

Massachusetts Bay: The Crucial Decade, 1640–1650

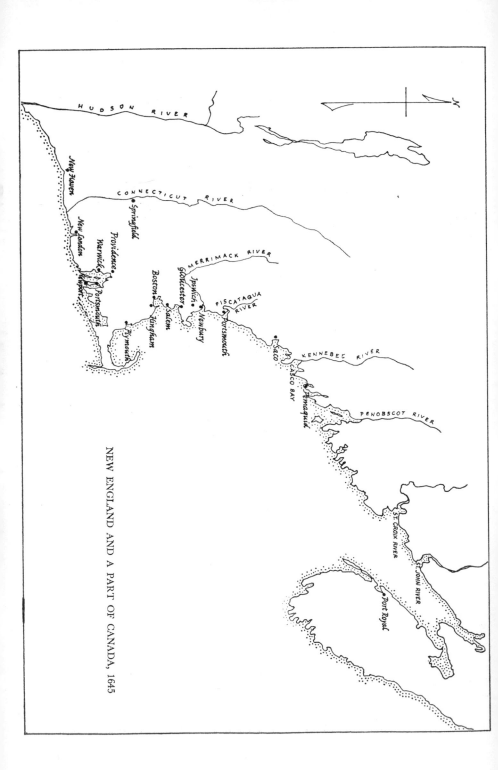

NEW ENGLAND AND A PART OF CANADA, 1645

MASSACHUSETTS BAY:
THE CRUCIAL DECADE, 1640–1650

by Robert Emmet Wall, Jr.

New Haven and London, Yale University Press

1972

Designed by John O. C. McCrillis
and set in Baskerville type.
Printed in the United States of America by
The Vail-Ballou Press, Inc., Binghamton, New York

Published in Great Britain, Europe, and Africa by
Yale University Press, Ltd., London.
Distributed in Canada by McGill-Queen's University
Press, Montreal; in Latin America by Kaiman & Polon,
Inc., New York City; in Australasia and Southeast
Asia by John Wiley & Sons Australasia Pty. Ltd.,
Sydney; in India by UBS Publishers' Distributors Pvt.,
Ltd., Delhi; in Japan by John Weatherhill, Inc., Tokyo.

For Sabina Daly Wall
and
Robert Emmet Wall, Sr.

Contents

Acknowledgments

While researching, writing, and revising the manuscript of this book, I incurred obligations to persons too numerous to thank individually. But there were some whose assistance was so important that it would be a gross oversight if I failed to mention their aid.

As has been true since the first day I met him as a graduate student, I am deeply in the debt of my teacher Edmund S. Morgan of Yale University. His careful reading and suggested revisions of an early draft, combined with a similar reading and suggestions from my former classmate David Hall of Boston University, gave to the finished book a major portion of whatever merit it possesses.

The advice and friendly criticism offered to me over the past several years by Stephen Foster of Northern Illinois University, Kenneth Lockridge of the University of Michigan, Douglas Miller of Michigan State University, Donald Baker of Waterloo University, and Donald Ginter of Sir George Williams University have been most helpful. Together they have again and again prevented me from falling into serious errors and logical traps.

My former colleagues at Michigan State University Robert E. and B. Katherine Brown were constant sources of inspiration in scholarly dedication. Last but certainly not least I wish to thank my own students: Ralph Young, John Van Til, Walter Boston, Stuart Stumpf, Judith Morrill, William Terman, Robert Johnson, Robert Goodman, and Lorena Walsh, who by their questions and criticisms of accepted interpretation forced me to revise some of my own thinking—a fact which eventually led to the writing of this book.

Financial assistance toward the research and technical

preparation of the book was granted by the American Philosophical Society, whose generosity to me is deeply appreciated. Additional funds and time were given by the Humanities Research Fund of Michigan State University and the Committee on Aid to Scholarly Activity of Sir George Williams University.

I would like to thank the *William and Mary Quarterly* for permission to republish the population chart on page 39, which first appeared in that journal in January 1970.

To my editorial advisor, B. Susan Eliot, my deepest appreciation. Invariably at this point one thanks one's wife. My wife has asked me not to.

R. E. W.

Ile des Sœurs, Montreal
April 1971

Prologue: The First Decade

In the spring of 1630, men, women, and children from all over England left their homes to make the long and hopeful odyssey to New England—to John Winthrop's "City on a Hill." Most left their homes with regret but with the firm conviction that they must leave. England was troubled, and in their villages the troubles had been most obvious. Perhaps the vicar of their church was given over to the Prayer Book and to "popish vestments," or perhaps he was shockingly unlearned. If he was the type of clergyman that Winthrop's settlers could respect, then most likely Archbishop Laud's agents were close at hand and ready to remove him from his post. The Church of England needed reforming, yet those in positions of authority and responsible for the reforms were blocking any change.

Winthrop's settlers believed not only that there was trouble within the English church but that the English state had degenerated into an arbitrary tyranny. Englishmen were now ruled and taxed by royal decree and parliaments seemed a memory of the dim past.

Those journeying to the New World were motivated by more material considerations as well. They were convinced that a long rising cost of living, a growing birth rate, a declining death rate, and economic depression were fast reducing their ability to maintain the economic status to which they were accustomed. Land, the most precious possession of these Englishmen, was at a premium. But across the North Atlantic, amid the forests of a new England, they could constitute their churches anew, without bishops, without popish trappings—churches as pure as those of the early Christians; they could organize new governments, more sensitive to their rights as Englishmen and

1

more dedicated to the proper reform of the church. In that same New England, acre upon acre of meadow and woodland lay waiting for these land-starved pilgrims. Although they deserted their homeland with regret, the regret was assuaged by hope for a better future.

Aboard ship and on the high seas Governor Winthrop introduced to his followers his ideas about the government by which they were to be ruled in the years ahead. Winthrop, using the opportunity provided by the close quarters aboard the *Arbella,* preached to his fellow passengers. If they had been educated men, they might have understood that they were hearing a succinct statement of Protestant and, more particularly, Puritan teaching on the state and on man's relationship to it. Winthrop, an apostle of the theologian William Perkins and those others who viewed all of man's relationships with God and with each other in terms of covenants, preached a social covenant—a contract between the settlers under his care and God—a bond which made them a people and commanded them to live by God's law. If obedient, the covenanted people would enjoy the fruits of God's creation in all their abundance. If stiff-necked, the results would be destruction.

Later, Governor Winthrop would elaborate on this concept of civil covenant and speak of its corollary—the bond between ruler and ruled. Man, corrupted by original sin, could not successfully abide by his promises to God without coercion. The people needed judges and kings in the days of Samuel and David, and the people needed judges and kings in the days of John Winthrop and Charles Stuart. The office of ruler was divine in origin—judges were gods. Nor were all men called to be rulers by God. Perkins had written and Winthrop would have agreed:

> Persons are distinguished by order, whereby God hath appointed, that in every society one person should bee above or under another; not making all equall, as

though the bodie should bee all head and nothing else; but even in degree and order, hee hath set a distinction, that one should bee above another. And by reason of this distinction of men, partly in respect of gifts, partly, in respect of order, come personall callings. For if all men had the same gifts, and all were in the same degree and order, then should all have one and the same calling; but inasmuch as God giveth diversitie of gifts inwardly, and distinction of order outwardly, hence proceede diversitie of personall callings, and therefore I added, that personall calling arise from that distinction which God maketh betweene man and man in every societie.[1]

Winthrop was telling his followers that men of birth, wealth, and social standing had been blessed by God and given command to rule, and that it was their obligation as persons covenanted with God to obey and be ruled.

Winthrop did not surprise his "congregation." What he was preaching to them was not distinctly different in practice from what they had experienced all their lives. In their villages the dominant political figure had always been the lord of the manor—the nobleman or gentleman—from whom they held their lands. He settled their disputes and fined their violations of local customs. Invariably the gentry were appointed or elected to the important local posts such as justices of the peace, sheriffs of the county, vestrymen of the parish, and members of Parliament. Usually, the gentry controlled appointments to all local political offices. Those villagers who possessed the franchise voted in elections for the gentry. The gentry expected to rule as their birthright in much the same manner that the villagers expected to be ruled. It is true that when two or more families of the upper classes contested for control, the villager might have his choice, but in either case he was voting for a gentleman and could not conceive of voting for any other kind of man. Winthrop's civil covenant was in many ways merely a New England deification of the political realities of old England.[2]

On June 12 Winthrop's fleet entered Salem harbor after an uneventful journey. Almost immediately after landing, Winthrop and the other leaders of the colony decided to seek another site for settlement. Winthrop planned to settle in one large community located between the Mystic and Charles Rivers, but his plans were upset when not one but several communities were settled. Sickness, lack of good food and water, and fear of French pirates forced the settlers to disperse.[3] One group, under the leadership of Sir Richard Saltonstall, moved four miles up the Charles to the site of Watertown; another, under William Pynchon, founded the town of Roxbury; Winthrop established Boston; Mattapan was renamed Dorchester by settlers coming directly from England under Roger Ludlow. By December, Deputy Governor Dudley and a small group of friends including his magistrate son-in-law, Simon Bradstreet, had established Newtown (later Cambridge), while Increase Nowell presided over those remaining in the base camp at Charlestown. With Endecott remaining at Salem, this left only the small communities of Saugus (Lynn) and Medford without a stockholder of the company presiding. These stockholders would be the new justices of the peace—or magistrates; they would be the great powers within the central government; they would be the New World gentry.

The first task of the stockholders of the Massachusetts Bay Company was the transformation of a trading company into a commonwealth. They brought with them the Royal Charter of 1629—an accomplishment made possible by the failure of the Charter to specify the meeting place of the company. The Charter called for a governor, deputy governor, and assistants to be elected by the stockholders (or freemen) from among the body of the freemen. The governor, deputy governor, and assistants (collectively called magistrates) were to run the company subject to the meetings of the stockholders, which were called General Courts. But in these new circumstances, of course, the only stockholders who could attend the General Courts were that small percentage of the total number of stockholders who had sailed with Winthrop. Since they alone could vote and they alone could serve as officeholders, they alone possessed all effective power in the company and the colony.

Legally, these few stockholders were not bound to share their power. If they abided by the terms of the charter, passed laws congenial to English common law (and to this they would have added a third stipulation—if they did not violate divine law as established in the Scripture), they were in no difficulty. If power were maintained in the hands of a few wealthy, well-born, and just men, the civil covenant would be upheld and Massachusetts Bay could look forward to divine blessings.

Would such an arrangement prove wise, however? Would not such a government be arbitrary? Had not many of the settlers left England because of their distaste for the arbitrary government of King Charles? Winthrop himself would later define arbitrary government as "where a people have men sett over them without their choyce, or allowance: who have power to Govern them, and Judge their causes without a Rule." [4] The government as established in 1630 was clearly, under this definition, an arbitrary one. Was it not courting troubles which might upset the very purpose of the settlement and excite the wrath of God to maintain the status quo?

The solution to this dilemma was achieved in 1630 and 1631. The electoral base of the governorship, deputy governorship, and assistantship would be broadened beyond the governor, deputy governor, and assistants, while at the same time, executive, legislative, and judicial powers were kept in the hands of those destined to rule.

At a meeting of the General Court on October 19, 1630, the magistrates sitting as the General Court of freemen voted to allow the freemen to elect the assistants and that the assistants, in turn, would elect the governor and deputy governor from among themselves. They also voted to grant to the magistrates the power to make the laws—a power which under the charter resided in the freemen. This accomplished, and power safely in the hands of those destined to rule—the magistrates—and beyond the power of the freemen, it would be possible to admit others to the franchise and to give them a voice in selecting their rulers. These changes were assented to by a general assembly of all the settlers then present at Charlestown.[5] At this session of the General Court 109 settlers petitioned the magistrates to be admitted to the rights of freemanship. The following May, 116 adult males—probably a majority of the adult males then in the colony—were admitted to freemanship. To safeguard the future, the General Court also agreed that "for time to come noe man shalbe admitted to the freedome of this body politicke, but such as are members of some of the churches within the lymitts of the same." [6]

In a bold series of moves the magistrates transformed a trading company into a commonwealth and preserved it from becoming an arbitrary state by allowing the settlers to select those who would make their laws and judge them. But so as not to allow later arrivals of sinful men to undermine the purposes of settlement and select unfit rulers and bring down divine vengeance, only church members were to become freemen and, therefore, voters in the future.

The first challenge to the "Settlement of 1630–31" came quickly, and it came from the town of Watertown. In 1631 the assistants had assumed legislative power, and in early 1632 they levied a tax of sixty pounds on the colony for the fortification of Newtown, eight pounds of which were charged to Watertown. Soon after receiving the tax bill, the pastor of the Watertown church, George Phillips, and the Ruling Elder, Richard Brown, called together the people of Watertown and advised them against paying the tax,* asserting that it was contrary to their rights as Englishmen to pay a tax which the people or their representatives had not voted.[7]

A series of events in 1632 brought the Settlement of 1630–31 under further fire. In May the assistants, fearing outbreaks in other towns for the same reasons as Watertown, called for the election of two freemen from each town to meet with them and discuss the question of raising funds by taxation.[8] At the same time, at the Court of Elections' session of the General Court, the freemen proposed that the election of the governor and deputy governor be left to the freemen. The magistrates accepted the suggestion, since the governor and his deputy would always be from among the body of assistants. But in accepting this change, the magistrates made possible further encroachments on the Settlement of 1630–31.[9] Surprisingly, the next assault came from among the magistrates themselves.

Thomas Dudley, Deputy Governor of the colony, was from the beginning Winthrop's chief political rival. Much has been written about Dudley—none of it flattering. He has been called greedy, rigid, belligerent, jealous, and indiscreet. Probably he was all of those things and more. No one would claim that Dudley was ever easy to get along with, and in the summer of 1632 he was as difficult as he knew how to be. He was angry with Winthrop for reneging on his promise to move his residence to Newtown (Dud-

* Sir Richard Saltonstall, the founder of Watertown, had been a member of the body of assistants and would have represented Watertown's interests, but he had since sailed back to England, never to return. Watertown was the only large town without a resident among the lawmakers, and it would naturally react more sensitively to the tax issue than the other towns.

ley's home), which was intended to be the capital of the
colony. He took Winthrop's decision to remain at Boston
as a personal affront. His response to Winthrop, however,
went beyond personality. He called into question Winthrop's conduct of government, his assumption of too much
authority in the application of the laws, and he forced
Winthrop to acknowledge that the fundamental source of
all authority in the colony was the charter. It was only a
matter of time before the inconsistencies of this public
admission and the Settlement of 1630–31 would become
evident to all.[10]

The Court of Elections for 1634 was scheduled to meet
on May 14. On that day the freemen of the colony traveled
to Boston to cast their ballots for governor, deputy governor, and assistants. Prior to the fourteenth, however, the
freemen of the towns, perhaps inspired by Dudley's assault on Winthrop and perhaps inspired by the election of
representatives from the towns to discuss taxation in 1632,
again selected two from each town to discuss items for the
agenda of the General Court beyond the matter of elections.[11]

The representatives of the towns met with Governor
Winthrop. That they had every intention of overturning
the Settlement of 1630–31 is demonstrated by their request for a reading of the charter. Clearly, they had received prior information concerning what that document
stipulated about the power to legislate. After the reading
of those sections granting the lawmaking power to the freemen, questions were asked of the governor. Why did not
the freemen enjoy a right so clearly theirs by the terms of
the charter? Winthrop's answer was to recall to them the
agreements made in 1630–31. But he had already undermined his position on this by his concession of supremacy
to the charter. To the freemen the Settlement of 1630–31
did not satisfactorily protect them from arbitrary government. The attempt of the magistrates to deprive them of

a "fundamental right" in direct violation of the charter was proof enough of a tendency toward arbitrary rule. Winthrop tried compromise:

> He told them, that, when the patent was granted, the number of freemen was supposed to be (as in like corporations) so few, as they might well join in making laws; but now they were grown to so great a body, as it was not possible for them to make or execute laws, but they must choose others for that purpose: and that howsoever it would be necessary hereafter to have a select company to intend that work, yet for the present they were not furnished with a sufficient number of men qualified for such a business, neither could the commonwealth bear the loss of time of so many as must intend it. Yet this they might do at present, viz, they might, at the general court, make an order, that, once in the year, a certain number should be appointed (upon summons from the governour) to revise all laws, etc., and to reform what they found amiss there in; but not to make any new laws, but prefer their grievances to the Court of assistants; and that no assessment should be laid upon the country without the consent of such a committee, nor any lands disposed of.[12]

But it was too late for compromise. The representatives of the freemen insisted upon the freemen's right to legislate. It was of no concern that there were too many of them. That problem could be solved by electing, from the towns, men deputized to act as their representatives. When the General Court of Elections met on the fourteenth, a new rank of official—the deputy—was among those now qualified to sit in the General Court and to legislate for the colony.[13]

John Cotton preached the election sermon prior to this revolutionary session of the General Court. In his lecture, an attempt to save Winthrop from the ire of the freemen, he went far beyond Winthrop, maintaining that a magistrate should be reelected and should not be removed except for violation of the sacred trust of his office.[14]

It is difficult to determine how effective Cotton's sermon was. Winthrop was not returned to private life; he continued to serve as magistrate. But he was not to be governor. The freemen turned to the author (whether directly or indirectly) of the "Revolution of 1634"—Thomas Dudley—with Roger Ludlow serving as deputy governor. As far as the strategic post of governor was concerned, the freemen had rejected Cotton's assertion. The post was to rotate for the next four years: Dudley served in 1634, John Haynes in 1635, Henry Vane in 1636, and Winthrop again in the midst of the great Antinomian crisis of 1637.[15] The freemen believed that Winthrop had deceived them in the Settlement of 1630–31, had robbed them of a "basic right," and had established a political order bordering on arbitrary government. He had been checked, and the freemen would guard against similar threats in the future.

Winthrop and the other magistrates could not fight the Revolution of 1634. They would have to accept the wishes of the freemen and work with their deputies. Dudley's challenge to Winthrop and Winthrop's acceptance of the charter as fundamental law had assured the victory of the freemen. But now a grievous problem existed for the magistrates: imbalance had been created by the freemen's victory. If all were agreed that the magistrates were meant to rule and the people to be ruled, would not the existence of deputies in great numbers in the General Court reduce Massachusetts to the low estate of democracy? The large number of deputies could consistently outvote the magistrates. Those destined by God and by high birth to rule were now in the minority. How could God's law and the covenant be upheld in a democracy? Balance had to be restored, and now it was the magistrates' turn to call upon the charter for support.

In September 1634 a major portion of the settlers of Newtown (Cambridge) petitioned the General Court for permission to leave their town and to settle in the Connecticut valley. A majority of the deputies approved of the move, but a majority of the magistrates disapproved. Immediately, the magistrates asserted, in a rather obscure and not very effective argument, that the charter granted to them the power of a "negative voice"—that a simple majority of the deputies and magistrates sitting together and voting together was not sufficient to turn a proposal into law. A majority of the magistrates, voting as a separate body (although not sitting apart), would have to agree with the deputies.[16]

> Upon this grew a great difference between the governor [Dudley, who favored the Cambridge move] and assistants and the deputies. They would not yield the assistants a negative voice, and the others (considering how dangerous it might be to the commonwealth, if they should not keep that strength to balance the greater number of deputies) thought it safe to stand upon it. So, when they could proceed no farther, the whole court agreed to keep a day of humiliation to seek the Lord, which accordingly was done, in all the congregations, the 18th day of the month; and the 24th the court met again.[17]

This time Winthrop and the major portion of the magistrates called upon John Cotton once again. Apparently Cotton temporarily satisfied all sides in the dispute by asserting that both deputies and magistrates possessed a negative voice.

> He took his text out of Hag. ii. 4, etc., out of which he laid down the nature or strength (as he termed it) of the magistracy, ministry, and people, viz.,—the strength of the magistracy to be their authority; of the people, their liberty; and of the ministry, their purity;

and showed how all of these had a negative voice, etc.,
and that yet the ultimate resolution, etc., with answer
to all objections, and a declaration of the people's duty
and right to maintain their true liberties against any
unjust violence, etc., which gave great satisfaction to
the company. And it pleased the Lord so to assist him,
and to bless his own ordinance, that the affairs of the
court went on cheerfully; and although all were not
satisfied about the negative voice to be left to the magistrates, yet no man moved aught about it.[18]

Cotton's compromise won the day, and the next year his
solution was codified into law.

And whereas it may fall out that in some of these general Courts to be holden by the magistrates and deputies, there may arise some difference of judgment in
doubtfull cases, it is therefore ordered, that noe lawe,
order, or sentence shall passe as an act of the Court,
without the consent of the greater parte of the magistrates on the one parte, and the greater parte of the
deputyes on the other parte; and for want of such
accorde, the cause or order shalbe suspended, if either
partie thinke it so materiall, there shalbe forthwith a
comitte chosen, the one halfe by the magistrates, and
the other halfe by the deputyes, and the comitte soe
chosen to elect an umpire, whoetogeather shall have
power to hear and determine the cause in question.[19]

Yet this issue was not dead. The year the negative voice
was passed into law, there was an attack upon it by a
deputy from Dorchester, Israel Stoughton. But his assault
ended in his being barred for three years from public office. No more was said about it for the time being.[20]

The negative voice had restored balance after the overthrow of the Settlement of 1630–31. The Revolution of
1634 had upset any possibility of arbitrary government,

while the negative voice, on the other hand, had prevented the rule of the "mob." The magistrates had managed to restore good order and to preserve the people's covenant with the Lord.

The magistrates and the freemen could agree on closing the door to an aspect of democracy—universal suffrage. One provision of the Settlement of 1630–31 remained un-attacked: freemen would be selected only from among the church members. More than that, in September of 1635, the General Court acted to close a loophole. In the future only freemen (and therefore church members) would be allowed to vote in local elections.[21] Freemen, deputies, and magistrates, while placing varying emphasis on the dangers of arbitrary rule, were in agreement with the principle that their experiment—their attempt to fulfill God's wishes in church and state—would have to be protected from the ungodly.

The magistrates, after 1631, had little fear of arbitrary government. But they did fear democracy. The negative voice, although for the moment a great and important tri-umph, apparently was not sufficient to satisfy them. Dur-ing the heat of the Pequot war, the Roger Williams's case, and the Antinomian debate, when the colony seemed on the verge of political chaos, the freemen through their dep-uties turned to the tried and experienced leadership of the magistrates and gave in to almost every suggestion the mag-istrates made. With the aid of these pressures, the magis-trates pushed through the General Court in March 1635–36 a law establishing a "Standing Council" of ex-governors who would have magisterial rank for life—whether elected magistrates in a given government or not.[22]

After Roger Williams hurried on his way to seek asylum at Providence and the Antinomians fled into exile in New Hampshire and Rhode Island, many of the freemen and deputies began to regret their hasty actions and the old fears of arbitrary rule returned. Certainly, the Standing

Council was an even greater threat than the Settlement of 1630–31, for under the Settlement the freemen had at least retained the right to choose their rulers, but now they faced magistrates with life tenure.

Not only was it dangerous to have unelected magistrates, but an aroused public feared that an executive official could achieve too much power through reelection. Some attacked what they viewed as budding nepotism as well. John Winthrop, Jr., was annually elected to the magistracy; but when the magistrates nominated Emanuel Downing of Salem—the elder Winthrop's brother-in-law—for election as a magistrate, he was defeated, "though he were known to be a very able man, etc., and one who had done many good offices for the country for these ten years." [23]

The anti-Winthrop faction also found obnoxious the court order reducing the number of deputies to two per town: "This occasioned some to fear, that the magistrates intended to make themselves stronger, and the deputies weaker, and so, in time, to bring all power into the hands of the magistrates; so as the people in some towns were much displeased with their deputies for yielding to such an order." [24] In the next General Court (1639) the freemen through their deputies moved to have the third deputy restored. They argued that the limitation was a violation of their rights. The magistrates answered that the number of deputies had no connection with fundamental rights. The existence of deputies was guaranteed by the provisions of the charter granting legislative power to the freemen, they asserted, but the number of deputies was open to question and should be determined in the interests of good order. The magistrates convinced enough deputies with this argument, and the limitation was upheld despite considerable popular resentment.[25]

Most of the resentment of extensive magisterial power, so discernible in the arguments of 1639, was connected

with the storm brewing over the institution of the Standing Council. And in the May Court of Elections in 1639
the deputies launched a new attack on it: "That, whereas
our sovereign lord, King Charles, etc., had, by his patent,
established a governour, deputy and assistandts, that therefore no person, chosen a counsellor for life, should have
any authority as a magistrate, except, he were chosen in the
annual elections to one of the said places of magistracy established by the patent." [26] Under this barrage the magistrates crumbled. They agreed to the principle announced
by the deputies with only some face-saving word changes.
From then on, the Standing Council was to consist of regularly elected magistrates. In practice the Council was an
executive board consisting primarily of those magistrates
who lived within easy distance of Boston. The Court stated
that it agreed to these changes in order to remove the persis-
tent suspicion of its motives held by many of the people.[27]
There were other reasons as well, which were traceable
to the damaging admission Dudley forced from Winthrop
seven years earlier. The fundamental source of authority
in Massachusetts Bay was the Royal Charter. The deputies
in 1639, secure from the fears of 1637, based their arguments on the charter. The magistrates might complain,
but they had to capitulate. The Standing Council was
unconstitutional. The Council would survive as a source
of magisterial power, but all of its members would be
regularly elected magistrates. No one would serve in it
by right of prior service alone. There would be many
more words wasted on the Council, but the basic issue—
the unelected magistrate, a concept fraught with dangers
of arbitrary government—had been resolved.[28]
    In the 1640 elections for governor, Winthrop was de-
feated by a combination of freemen, who feared his support of the Standing Council, and elders of the church,
who publicly pronounced their fear of one-man rule—no
matter how good the one man. Winthrop was not restored

to the governor's seat until 1642. The freemen were willing
to let the ruler rule, but only as long as his rule did not
jeopardize what they regarded as their fundamental
rights.[29]

John Winthrop's definition of arbitrary government included not only the issue of the choice of rulers but also
the proviso that the ruler must govern according to a code
of law. From the beginning of their participation in the
government of the colony, the freemen worked not only to
guarantee their freedom of choice, but also to force their
elected rulers to abide by established and published laws.
As early as 1635, Winthrop recorded in his Journal:

> The deputies having conceived great danger to our
> state, in regard that our magistrates, for want of posi-
> tive laws, in many cases, might proceed according to
> their discretions, it was agreed that some men should
> be appointed to frame a body of grounds of laws, in
> resemblance to a Magna Charta, which, being allowed
> by some of the ministers, and the general court,
> should be received for fundamental laws.[30]

The next year John Cotton presented a schema for fundamental laws entitled "A Model of Moses, His Judicials,"
which, although respectfully received by the General
Court, was apparently not acceptable.[31]

The years passed and little progress was made. Winthrop, a majority of magistrates, and many of the elders
were opposed to the adoption of a formal code of laws.
The best they could do, however, was to delay.

Winthrop explained in some detail why he and others
opposed a "body of laws":

> Two great reasons there were, which caused most of
> the magistrates and some of the elders not to be very
> forward in this matter. One was, want of sufficient ex-
> perience of the nature and disposition of the people,
> considered with the condition of the country and

other circumstances, which made them conceive, that such laws would be fittest for us, which should arise pro re nata upon occasion, etc., and so the laws of England and other states grew, and therefore the fundamental laws of England are called customs, consuetudines.

2. For that it would professedly transgress the limits of our charter, which provide, we shall made no laws repugnant to the laws of England, and that we are assured we must do. But to raise up laws by practice and custom had been no transgression; as in our church discipline, and in matters of marriage, to make a law, that marriages should not be solemnized by ministers, is repugnant to the laws of England; but to bring it to a custom by practice for the magistrates to perform it, is no law made repugnant, etc.[32]

In September of 1639 the pressure became constant and heavy. It was clear that the freemen would not be put off any longer. At last, John Cotton and Nathaniel Ward presented frames of laws to the General Court for consideration,[33] and the Court established a committee to consider them and prepare them for presentation at the May session of 1640. Winthrop, who was a member of this committee, stated that the frames were "digested with divers alteration and additions, and abbreviated and sent to every town, to be considered of first by the magistrates and elders, and then to be published by the constable to all the people, that if any man should think fit, that any thing therein ought to be altered, he might acquaint some of the deputies therewith against the next court." The freemen would have their frame of laws; the magistrates had finally given in "to satisfy the people." [34] It was not until the December session of 1641, however, that this New England Magna Charta—The Body of Liberties—was finally adopted by the General Court.

The Body of Liberties established once and for all the basic rights of the inhabitants of Massachusetts Bay. Non-freemen, although not legally possessing the vote in either colony or town affairs, were not to be denied attendance at town meetings, where they were to have the right of free speech. The freemen received control of the affairs of their own towns. They were to have the power to govern their own communities, to make laws and try cases not exceeding twenty shillings for any one offense, provided that their bylaws were in no way repugnant to the laws of the colony. They were also to have the right to pick their own select-men, provided they did not exceed nine in number. The freemen of the towns were to have the liberty to choose their deputies to the General Court as long as they chose freemen who had taken the oath of fealty and lived in Massachusetts Bay. They also had the right to elect the general officers of the colony (or magistrates) and remove them without showing cause at election time, and by impeachment during the rest of the year.[35]

By 1641 the freemen of Massachusetts had put an end to the threat of arbitrary government in their colony. It is true that they would agitate in the years ahead for fixed penalties for crimes in an attempt to reduce the discretionary judicial power of the magistrates. This agitation ended with the promulgation of the Book of General Laws in 1648.[36] But in many ways, and despite the hot words of the next decade, the adoption of such a code was less fundamental once the basic rights of the freemen were firmly established.

By the close of the first decade of Massachusetts existence, a proper balance had been attained. The danger of arbitrary government had been reduced, but so too had the possibility of democracy and the "rule of the mob." Although the freemen and magistrates had waged bitter battles, the basic principle—that some were destined to rule and others to be ruled—had been preserved. The freemen shared in the making of laws through their deputies and they chose their own rulers, but the rulers retained power through English tradition and Puritan theology, with the negative voice and the Standing Council serving as their tools.

The freemen of the first decade of Massachusetts history were not seeking to overturn the authority and power of their magistrates. It was the magistrate's function, it was his destiny, and it was divine will that he rule. But his rule was to be limited, and the rights of the ruled were not to be threatened. By 1641 the freemen could look upon their accomplishments in the areas of government with some pride and satisfaction. The people were free and properly governed by qualified men. God's covenant was upheld. The next decade, however, would produce unparalleled assaults on the tranquillity of the colony. The power of Presbyterianism in England, the development of an increased reverence for toleration among English Independents, and the growth of a new power within Massachusetts—a local economic, political elite—all these would have to be met, because failure to meet them could spell the doom of the Puritan experiment.

1 The Rise of the Lesser Gentry

Only the most sanguine of observers could describe the first decade of Massachusetts politics as placid. The harsh struggle for the proper balance of order and liberty in society was fought with bitter words. Yet the second decade of Winthrop's experiment was just as difficult and in many ways more important. The manner in which the leaders of the colony came to grips with each of the problems of this second decade would help to determine the course which Massachusetts would follow; and in most instances the leaders selected the conservative course, protecting their experiment in the reform of church and state, and most assuredly, by their retrenchment and reaction, guaranteeing the failure of all their hopes. The 1640s were the crucial years.

The freemen and the magistrates had resolved their differences by 1641, but their arguments were replaced by even more complex ones between the upper classes, between sections of the colony, and between the colony and the mother country. Probably the most important difference between the first and second decades was the arrival on the political scene of a new force—a group of economically and socially prominent men who used their positions in the towns as platforms to launch political careers in colony-wide affairs. They were men of a higher social status than the freemen and nonfreemen but clearly inferior to the great gentlemen of Massachusetts—the magistrates. This "lesser gentry" would not attempt to unsettle the balance between order and freedom established in the first decade, but rather they would regard themselves as capable upholders of authority and would challenge the magistrates' exclusive reservation of all authority to their office.

The lesser gentry wanted a share of the magistrates' power. The struggle of the second decade was the struggle between the great gentlemen and the lesser gentry.

The magistrates regarded themselves as the divinely appointed defenders of the holy experiment in the reform of church and state. They had been forced to accept compromises with the freemen to protect themselves from charges of arbitrary rule, but the status quo of 1641, after the passage of The Body of Liberties, marked the limits of the magistrates' willingness to share their authority. They would defend the Standing Council of magistrates and the negative voice. To give in on these, they argued, would bring about a state of democracy, jeopardize the holy experiment, violate their covenant with the Lord, and guarantee the destruction of Massachusetts Bay. With few exceptions, they bitterly resented and resisted the pressures of the lesser gentry for a larger role and would accuse them of arousing internal and external forces dedicated to the overthrow of the Massachusetts experiment.

The lesser gentry rejected the magistrates' claims to exclusive power; and although some would strive to increase their economic power and broaden their political base and become magistrates, most would simply attempt to bring greater power to the offices they could hope to attain— those of town selectmen and deputy to the General Court. They would not share the fear of arbitrary government which motivated their constituents, although they would not hesitate to use that fear against the magistrates. In reality, they shared with the magistrates their concern for good order and the preservation of the covenant. They merely wished a greater role for themselves. They would work in the decade of the 1640s to attack the two institutions which they felt gave to the magistrates their excessive powers—the Standing Council of magistrates and the negative voice. These were the institutions which had alarmed the freemen of the first decade also. However, the freemen had feared them as sources of tyranny, while the motivation of the lesser gentry seems very different. They would argue against these institutions because both were used by the magistrates to exclude them from real power. The rhetoric of the debate remained the same, but the realities of it had altered fundamentally.

The lesser gentry were to fail in their efforts to share in magisterial power. Their failure, which itself contributed to marking the second decade as crucial, was partially the result of a miscalculation of the strength they had among the voters of the colony. They thus attempted to destroy the most able and revered of the magistrates, John Winthrop, and in so doing far overstepped what support they had. In attempting to impeach Winthrop the lesser gentry also appeared to be challenging the basic framework of the balance established in the first decade and drove all conservative forces, especially the clergy, into the camp of the magistrates.

Moreover, the lesser gentry as a result of the years of agitation they initiated, managed to convince many external enemies of Massachusetts Bay that there were fundamental differences within the colony. In this manner these enemies of the colony both in New England and in England were inspired to launch attacks on Massachusetts to bring the colony to closer ties with the motherland and to force its leaders to abandon their holy experiment.

With fundamental challenges coming from the outside as a result of the agitation created by the lesser gentry's ambitions, all supporters of the holy experiment, including the lesser gentry themselves, were forced to rally to the cause of the status quo. To do anything else would certainly leave them open to charges of irresponsibility or worse from the magistrates and perhaps actually aid the enemies of the established order. The lesser gentry had no small stake in that established order and could see little gain from its overthrow. In the end they were forced to abandon the attack on the magistrates and to rally to their support in the struggle to preserve Massachusetts's independence. As a result, Massachusetts lost a potentially moderating force in the decades of repression and hostility which lay ahead.

The lesser gentry of Massachusetts Bay were men of economic and social prominence who gradually over the first two decades came to dominate political offices in their local communities. They were not men of the highest social and economic order within the colony, yet they were several steps above the common freemen. Just as the settlers wished to be governed on the colony level by the best men available, so too they wished their towns to be governed by local leaders of high caliber. Obviously there were not enough magistrates to fill all local posts of importance, and so lesser men would have to be picked. In this manner the political rise of a lesser gentry became imperative.

Early in the 1640s effective power in local communities passed from the town meetings to the town executives.[1] And the lesser gentry, because of their domination of the post of selectman, came to power within the towns. A study of the selectmen, therefore, should reveal much about the lesser gentry.

Beginning as early as 1640, a clear pattern of officeholding in the towns developed. In the early years the number of men elected selectmen was large and the change-over rate was heavy. In the second decade, however, it became common practice for the same men to be continually elected and reelected to the same post (the dominance can be observed in table 1). This continuity of officeholding, and the occupation by the same men of the most powerful local office, gave them solid and effective bases for political operations. The towns became a great source of strength for a new group of politicians.

TABLE 1

CONTINUITY OF REELECTION TO LOCAL OFFICE AMONG PRE-1647 SELECTMEN

Town	No. of selectmen	No. of possible posts	No. of 5-term selectmen	% of total no. of selectmen	No. of posts for 5-termers	% of total no. of posts held by 5-term selectmen
Boston	30	155	13	43	123	79
Salem	20	71	6	30	43	61
Watertown	34	97	10	30	57	59
Charlestown	28	96	8	29	57	58
Cambridge	40	93	6	15	39	42
Dedham	13	58	5 (4 term)	38	25	43
Gloucester	15	27	3	20	12	44
Salisbury	16	28	4 (2 term)	25	12	43

Note: These figures are derived from the records of selectmen's elections given in town records. See the Bibliography for a list of the town records.

But who were these men? For one, the selectmen (or townsmen, as they were first called) were freemen of the colony. After 1637 this was required by law and statistics indicate that the law was fairly well observed.[2] Since, after 1631, freemanship required admission to one of the churches of the colony, we may conclude that the selectmen were church members also.

In addition to the prerequisites of religious and political orthodoxy, there were at least two other requirements for election as a selectman—good family and wealth. The selectmen were clearly chosen from among the wealthier freemen, and the fact of their economic superiority is established in a variety of sources—especially tax records, land inventories, and probate inventories.[3]

Clearly, then, town politics in the second decade of Massachusetts Bay were under the control of a new political force. In economic and social power they were found somewhere between the common citizens and the great gentlemen. Since the basis of their power was the town, many of the interests of this lesser gentry must have been similar to those of the freemen who elected them. But it was only natural that having achieved local power, they would strive for more and should ambition to challenge the great gentlemen. The selectmen, however, were not in a strong position to challenge the magistrates. The towns were the creatures of the General Court, and the political leaders of the towns were also, in a sense, creatures of the Court. It was in the General Court itself that the lesser gentry would have to wage their battle in order to achieve power, and they would need a more potent political role. They found it in the post of deputy.

The deputies to the General Court were created as a result of the Revolution of 1634. The large number of freemen made it impossible for them to assemble in one place to conduct the business of government, so a compromise was reached between the freemen and magistrates, and the post of deputy was created. They were to be the proxies of the freemen of the towns—casting ballots on specific issues coming before the General Court. However, they did not remain proxies. There is no evidence for asserting that the deputies were under strict instructions from the town meetings in the seventeenth century. Instructions to delegates have survived for the eighteenth-century period, but there are none from the period of the 1640s. In all likelihood, given the dominance of the town by the selectmen in the seventeenth century, and given the similarity of personnel between the selectmen and deputies to the General Court, the deputies were more representative of the desires of the local elite than they were representative of, or controlled by, the mass of freemen.

The laws of the colony clearly stated the prerequisites for election to the post of deputy. In 1636 the General Court stated "no person shall henceforth bee chosen to any office in the commonwealth, but such as is a freeman." [4] The deputies, therefore, were freemen. Other than this, however, there were no other legal qualifications. There was no resident requirement, and frequently a citizen of one town would sit as a deputy for another town. This occurred most frequently when remoter towns requested residents of Boston or some other Suffolk or Middlesex town (usually relatives of a leading political figure of the remote town) to sit as their deputy. The towns were, however, limited in the number of deputies they could send to any one session of the General Court. Those towns with fewer than ten freemen would have no deputy, while the others were to have no more than two after 1639.

Despite the lack of more than a freemanship qualification for election as a deputy, there were unwritten qualifications. Although there were no property requirements, for instance, almost all the deputies came from among the ranks of the wealthy local elite; and in those towns which have extant lists of selectmen and deputies, it is clear that most of the deputies served as selectmen before their election to the General Court.

From the beginnings of the post of deputy in 1634 until the change in the local franchise law in 1647, 237 men sat as deputies to the General Court. Two hundred twenty-seven of the total of 237 were definitely freemen. The other 10 may or may not have been freemen.[5]

Of the twenty-three towns which sent deputies to the General Court there are extant records indicating the election of selectmen for thirteen. Ninety-three of the 131 deputies from these thirteen towns served as selectmen before their election to the General Court. Of the remaining 38, many served as selectmen after serving in the General Court. Rarely did a deputy fail to serve some time on the board of selectmen of his home town, and a majority continued to serve simultaneously as selectmen and deputies.[6] But the deputies were generally chosen from the ranks of not only the selectmen but the wealthier selectmen (see table 2).

TABLE 2

COMPARISON OF ESTATE INVENTORIES FOR TOWN SELECTMEN
AND TOWN DEPUTIES

Town	Deputies' inventory average	Selectmen's inventory average
Boston	£1756	£926
Dedham	500	484
Dorchester	893	947
Watertown	430	373
Charlestown	942	813
Salem	1085	362
Ipswich	1307	933
Salisbury	799	344

Note: See the Bibliography under the various counties and towns
for the sources of these statistics.

More than wealth, however, it was family connections
which helped to create and then distinguish the lesser
gentry. While not as prestigious as those of the magistrates,
such connections were nevertheless significant. Frequently
the lesser gentry married within their own group, but the
more fortunate and more ambitious of them were able to
marry either themselves or their children into the first
families of the colony and in this way advance their own
careers.

In Boston the lesser gentry included such figures as
Thomas Leverett, William Hutchinson, and Robert
Keayne. Keayne's son, Benjamin, was married briefly and
disastrously to the daughter of Deputy Governor Dudley.
John Newgate was related by marriage to the Olivers of Boston. Both Newgate and his in-laws served as Boston selectmen and deputies to the General Court. Anthony Stoddard,
Boston selectman and deputy, town clerk, and town commissioner, was related to Governor Winthrop through his
marriage to Mary Downing, Winthrop's niece.

In Dedham the Lushers and Fishers were the dominant
families. Anthony Fisher, Sr., Anthony Jr., Joshua Sr.,

Joshua Jr., and Daniel served 55 out of a possible 324 terms as selectmen for Dedham from 1639 to 1686. John Aldus, brother-in-law of Joshua Fisher, Jr., served twelve terms as a selectman. Eleazur Lusher was co-owner of the Dedham sawmill with Joshua Fisher. Lusher was a Dedham selectman for thirty terms. Altogether this group served 97 of a possible 324 Dedham posts, and had a similar grasp on the deputies' posts. There were 92 possible Dedham deputies' posts to the General Court during the Old Charter period. Thirty-eight of the 92 were filled by Fishers, 1 by Aldus, and 17 by Lusher—a total of 56 of the possible 92 seats.

In Braintree, Moses Paine, Sr., married the widow of Edmund Quincy, Sr. The two leaders of town politics in the years that followed were Moses Paine, Jr., and Edmund Quincy, Jr. The widow Quincy, after the death of the elder Paine, married Robert Hull of Boston, the father of the goldsmith-mintmaster-magistrate John Hull. John Hull then married Judith Quincy, his stepmother's daughter, the sister of Edmund Quincy, Jr., Henry Adams of Braintree, founding father of the Adams clan, later one of the leading politicians of Medfield, was married to Elizabeth Paine, sister of Moses Jr.

The Hobart Family dominated the church and town of Hingham. Peter Hobart was pastor of the Hingham church, while his father, Edmund Sr., and his brothers Joshua, Edmund Jr., and Thomas held a large percentage of the town's elective posts. The Hobarts were also leaders of a large migration of settlers from Old Hingham in Norfolk, England.

James Blake of Dorchester, a deputy to the General Court and selectman, was married to the daughter of Deacon Edward Clap. She was also the niece of Roger Clap, deputy and selectman for Dorchester. Blake's brother, William, represented the town of Milton in the General Court, and his brother-in-law, John Capen, was captain of

the Dorchester militia and a deputy to the General
Court.

While the leading family in Roxbury was the Dudleys,
among the lesser gentry were the Denisons, William and
his sons Edward and Daniel. Both William and Edward
Denison represented Roxbury in the General Court. Daniel Denison moved to the town of Ipswich, married one of
Thomas Dudley's daughters, and became a leader not only
in his new town but in the colony as well. He served as
a selectman and deputy for Ipswich and finally was elected
to the magistracy.

In Charlestown, William Stiltson was a deacon of the
Charlestown church and served as a deputy to the
General Court. He was elected a Charlestown selectman
twenty-two times in his long career. His daughter married
Francis Norton, who then rose to the position of deacon
of the church, and was ten times a selectman and fifteen
times a deputy to the General Court.

In Salem one finds examples of the lesser gentry raising
themselves through marriage. Thomas Gardiner, founder
of one of the most important eighteenth-century Salem
families, was also connected to the Winthrops after the
marriage of his son to Governor Winthrop's niece. George
Corwin, a leading Salem merchant and later a politician,
had the good fortune to arrange a marriage between his
son and John Winthrop Jr.'s daughter, while another of
his children—a stepdaughter—was married to Thomas
Gardiner's son.

One of the leaders of the lesser gentry in Salisbury was
Robert Pike. Pike was elected a selectman ten times,
served eleven terms as a Salisbury deputy to the General
Court, and was eventually elected a magistrate. The second most important politician in town was Thomas Bradbury, who was a selectman twenty-nine times and a deputy
six times. The Pike and Bradbury families were related
after Pike's daughter married Bradbury's son. Through-

out the seventeenth century, family ties were important
for social prestige, which was an essential prerequisite for
political power for the lesser gentry.[7]

It is quite clear that despite many interests in common
with both freemen and nonfreemen, the local political
elite constituted a distinct economic and social group. It
is also clear that they were inferior both economically and
socially to the leaders of the colony.

The magistrates were without exception the great gentlemen of the Bay Colony. The original group had been
the source of all political authority and had assumed the
role of the English country gentry in their New England
environment. Most were men of high social standing and
considerable wealth in the motherland and had managed
to transfer successfully to the New World both their
wealth and their prestige. Those that followed the original
group were men of the same caliber.

The thirty magistrates who served from 1630–50 were
men of excellent family connections in England and in
America. Moreover, many were related to each other.
Isaac Johnson and John Humphreys were the sons-in-law
of the Earl of Lincoln, while Thomas Dudley held the important post of steward to this same nobleman. Simon
Bradstreet was Dudley's son-in-law. Herbert Pelham was
the grandson of Lord de la Ware, while Richard Bellingham and Atherton Haugh were high officials in the city
of Boston, the Earl of Lincoln's major town. John Endecott was married to a cousin or a niece of Matthew Crad-
dock, the first governor of the Massachusetts Bay Company. Roger Harlakenden was of the Essex gentry and a
close friend of the Reverend Thomas Shepard. Harlakenden's brother-in-law was John Haynes, governor and magistrate in Massachusetts and later governer of Connecticut.
Sir Henry Vane was the son of the comptroller of the king's
household and the king's good friend. There were two sets
of father-son magistrates from 1630 to 1650. The Salton-

stalls, Sir Richard and Richard Jr., were Yorkshire gentlemen. Sir Richard was the nephew of the Sir Richard Saltonstall who served as Lord Mayor of London during the
reign of Elizabeth. The Winthrops, John Sr. and John
Jr., were Suffolk gentry and the only father and son to
serve simultaneously in the magistracy.

In addition to good family, magistrates as the gentry of
the New World were expected to be men of wealth. In the
vast majority of cases the expectations were fulfilled. The
county courts frequently requested inventories of estates
after death as part of the probate procedures. There are
extant inventories for ten of the thirty pre-1650 magistrates. These estates average £1,363, which is far higher
than the estates of nonmagistrates.[8] In divisions of lands
based on already held land ownership, the magistrates invariably received the largest portions.[9]

The lesser gentry and the great gentlemen were distinct
orders. True, some might, with time, pass from one order
to the other. Massachusetts Bay was a frontier society and,
as a result, a socially fluid one. But during the 1640s these
two groups would come into conflict and each would regard victory by the other in any debate as distinctly opposed to its own best interests.

In addition to the magistrates and the lesser gentry,
there was a third important group in the politics of Massachusetts in the 1640s—the elders or ministers. Their
position was a good deal more complicated, since they had
no official political role and were actually barred from holding political office. Yet church and state in the seventeenth
century were intimately related, and it would have been
impossible for the clergy to remain aloof from the affairs
of state. The ministers would naturally ambition for the
maintenance of properly reformed churches, the lack of
which had driven them to oppose the governing authorities of the Church of England, and to resist the force of
the English state. Now, having achieved a proper reform

in New England, they would rigorously oppose any threats to that establishment.

In England one of the greatest obstacles to proper reform had been the church itself; in New England the elders supported Congregationalism, not only because they thought it a proper polity, but because the independence of each church guaranteed that no hierarchical authority could undo the reforms they had achieved. The Presbyterian "hierarchy" in England could prove as dangerous to good reform as any episcopal structure. Presbyterianism in New England, therefore, would be carefully restricted, even routed out, if this would not antagonize too many on both sides of the Atlantic. At the same time, the ministers could not tolerate heretical enthusiasm. To tolerate Anabaptists, Antinomians, and Familists was to toy with the fickle anger of God and to make inevitable a mighty fall for the colony. In addition, the elders were anxious to prove a point. The opponents of Congregationalism had incessantly, and apparently successfully, equated Congregationalism's belief in independence with separatism. The word *separatist* usually held the connotation of enthusiasm with overtones of the horrors of continental radicalism. The New England Congregationalists, who insisted they were not separatists and not heretics, were extremely anxious, therefore, to disprove the charges leveled against them by Anglican and Presbyterian alike, and would punish harshly enthusiasts who happened to stumble into their hands.[10] The New Englanders had solved the obstacle of a hostile hierarchy by migrating, and they were determined to keep both the hierarchy and the sectarians in check.

The English state, by demanding conformity within the English church, had also blocked proper reform. Yet this was a function which the New England elders would not deny to the state. They would insist, in fact, that the essential function of the state was to guard and assist the reformed churches of Christ. The elders knew that the ministers of the state—the magistrates—had a large and significant role in God's scheme, and it was in the interests of the church and its elders to support a powerful Christian magistracy dedicated to the furtherance of the churches. Therefore the elders would feel compelled to support the magistrates when they confronted demands from either freemen or deputies to the General Court which in the elders' opinions might undermine the fundamental powers of the magistrates. On the other hand, their most recent experience with the state had been unhappy. The magistrates of England had upheld a view of the nature of the church quite different from that of the New England ministers. Yet because of their view of the function of the state and the sacred role of the magistrate, the clergy had found the state difficult to deal with. How did one combat erring magistrates without harming the church itself? Moreover, the magistracy of England, and especially the office of the chief magistrate, was hereditary. Once in power, only revolution or the intervention of God would prevent an "evil-minded" king from working his will and creating havoc within the fold.

Their English experience did much to color the attitude of the elders in New England. They would support the magistrates on the fundamentals, but they would fear and work against the accumulation of too much power in the hands of one man, one family, or any one power grouping. They would support the freemen when it seemed the magistrates would usurp their basic rights and establish an hereditary magistracy; and they would seek to use the ambitions of the deputies to balance those of the magistrates and keep the state on its proper course as the defender of Christ's churches on earth.

Thus far, emphasis has been placed upon social status in an effort to explain the distinctions and divisions of the

political scene in the second decade, but there is evidence
for asserting that geographic differences played an equal
role in the struggle. The people of Essex County and old
Norfolk County were different: they were further removed from the seat of the central government than were
those of Suffolk and Middlesex; they were more exposed
and thus more sensitive to the possibility of foreign attack; they were poorer on all levels and jealous of the
prosperity of Suffolk-Middlesex residents; and, later, during the economic distresses of the forties, Essex-Norfolk
residents were probably hit harder, since they were poorer
to begin with. One result was that the Essex-Norfolk region developed different political attitudes from the very
beginning.

The southern region (Suffolk-Middlesex) was dominated by the magnificent harbor of Boston, and by 1640
all roads led there. An economic setback occurred in the
middle of the second decade of settlement, but Boston and
her sister town on the harbor, Charlestown, were important commercial centers, looking seaward and initiating an
important trade with the West Indies. Within the great
towns retail merchants were developing thriving trade
with the local citizenry and with storekeepers in the in-
terior towns, which were agricultural but still within the
commercial orbit of Boston and Charlestown. It was from
these ports that they received their supplies, and it was to
these ports that they sent their produce for trade.

None of the Essex-Norfolk towns, with the exception of
Lynn, were very close to Boston harbor. Essex had ports of
her own in Salem, Marblehead, Gloucester, and Newbury,
while Norfolk towns on the Merrimack made use of Newbury's port, and the northern Norfolk towns on the Piscataqua sent their goods to the tiny town of Portsmouth
or Strawberry Bank, as it was then called. But none of
these ports were rivals of Boston-Charlestown. Marblehead and Gloucester contained fishing fleets of some eco-

nomic importance, but had little or no overseas trade. Newbury had only begun to develop as a town. Originally, the settlers located themselves on the Parker River, a small stream leading nowhere. Later, shrewder minds in the town talked the settlers into moving to the northern boundary of the town, the Merrimack River. A port could be established there which could drain the whole Merrimack hinterland. In the eighteenth century this move paid dividends, and the separate town of Newburyport became a major New England port. In the seventeenth century, however, these developments were only dreams. Salem was the only real commercial center interested in overseas trade north of Boston harbor. But Salem suffered from serious disadvantages. Its harbor was not nearly as good as Boston's, and it was very much smaller. Most of the migrants to New England set foot in the New World for the first time at Boston and were inclined to stay there or in the nearby towns, allowing Boston and Suffolk-Middlesex to grow rapidly, while the population of the north lagged behind. The remoteness of the northeastern regions prevented the development of a wealthy, commercial population. Salem had its merchants in the seventeenth century, and, of course, it would develop important commerce in the eighteenth century, but in the early periods her merchants were fewer, poorer, and quite jealous of their counterparts to the south.

The terrain of Essex County prevented the development of thriving agriculture. Most of the towns of the county were built in coastal areas. Lynn, Salem, Marblehead, Manchester, Wenham, and Gloucester dotted the coastline north of Boston, along the north shore of Massachusetts Bay to Cape Ann. The northern towns of the county—Ipswich, Rowley, and Newbury—were located on the the coast and along the tidal rivers which cut the country from west to east. The land in the southern part of Essex was rocky, and the interests of the people ran toward commerce and fishing. In the north the land was low-lying and swampy; there was abundant meadowland, not the champion land so sought after by the early settlers, but saltmarsh, useful for pasturing livestock, which was the major source of income for the first settlers, but absolutely useless for the growing of any crops. After the halt of migration from England, the livestock business collapsed since there were no longer any newcomers seeking livestock, and the saltmarsh of northern Essex lost much of its value. In the towns of Suffolk-Middlesex, the meadowland formerly used to feed the now unwanted cattle could be profitably turned over to the growing of corn and wheat. The Essex towns could not convert as readily and were more deeply hurt by the depression of the second decade.

In the 1640s the people of Essex-Norfolk were poorer than their fellows to the south. There are several statistical indications of this. In the colony tax rate of 1645 the Suffolk-Middlesex towns which contained about 60 percent of the population of the towns paid 68 percent of the total tax. Throughout the whole of the seventeenth century, Suffolk-Middlesex estate inventories averaged about one hundred pounds higher than Essex-Norfolk inventories.

No doubt the settlers left behind at Salem by Winthrop in 1630 felt keen disappointment. They were probably relieved that they would not have to support such a crowd, but they must also have been aware that they were being left in the backwaters and that the center of the colony's life and the political capital of the colony would move with the governor to the Charles River region. The settlers of Salem must also have felt bitter over the treatment their town received at the hands of the General Court in the Williams case, when the town was refused a grant of land in Marblehead until the church reformed its ways. As the years passed and the northeastern counties developed, with new towns coming into existence, their remoteness from Boston and the General Court allowed them to develop their own political procedures with very little interference from the central government. For one thing, there were not nearly as many freemen in Essex and Norfolk as in the other counties, as can be seen from table 3. The percentages of freemen to total population were much higher for the areas around the capital in Boston than they were in Essex-Norfolk and in the remote Springfield. This cannot be explained by a failure to record the names of freemen in the remote areas, since after 1642, the names of freemen could be enrolled in the county court records, and the Essex-Norfolk lists have survived fairly complete and have been used in composing this table. At the same time, it cannot be said that the remote areas were controlled more completely by the local elite than the Boston area, since there is very good evidence that even before 1647, nonfreemen were allowed to vote in local elections at least in the remoter towns. In several of the Essex-Norfolk towns nonfreemen were serving in the important post of selectman, and if allowed to hold office, they most surely were allowed to vote.

Essex and Norfolk developed separate practices and attitudes in their towns during the seventeenth century which helped to constitute them as a separate power bloc in the decade following 1640. The deputies, and occasionally the magistrates, of these two counties would combine with the lesser gentry politicians of Suffolk-Middlesex to challenge the authority of the Boston magistrates whenever it suited the interests of their section.

In 1642 these forces of social status and region began their clash within the General Court. The men of Essex-Norfolk (no matter what their status) and the lesser gentry of the south would call into question the institutions cherished by the magistrates—the Standing Council and the negative voice. These were the struggles of the crucial decade, and their resolution would determine the future course of the colony. It is to the story of those struggles that we must now turn our attention.

TABLE 3

ADULT MALE POPULATION OVER 21 AND FREEMEN IN 1647

County & Town	Population in 1647	No. of freemen	Percentage
Suffolk	936	507	54
Boston	389	208	53
Dedham	107	64	60
Dorchester	103	65	63
Roxbury	94	59	62
Braintree	87	37	43
Hingham	79	32	41
Weymouth	68	37	54
Hull	9	5	56
Middlesex	599	316	53
Watertown	150	62	41
Charlestown	129	84	65
Cambridge	121	68	56
Sudbury	61	30	50
Concord	55	36	65
Woburn	55	27	49
Reading	28	9	32
Essex	788	309	38
Salem	246	104	42
Ipswich	227	67	29
Newbury	115	51	44
Rowley	77	42	56
Gloucester	58	15	26
Wenham	30	16	53
Andover	20	9	45
Manchester	15	5	33

(continued)

TABLE 3 (*Continued*)

County & Town	Population in 1647	No. of freemen	Percentage
Norfolk	177	71	40
Hampton	73	25	34
Salisbury	68	30	44
Haverhill	36	16	44
(Hampshire)			
Springfield	43	7	16

Note: See Bibliography for a description of the town, selectmen's, proprietors', church, and county records used to arrive at these figures. Lynn and Medford had to be omitted from the study because they have no records for this period. Dover, Exeter, and Portsmouth, since they had just been annexed to Massachusetts Bay and were atypical towns, quite antagonistic to Massachusetts orthodoxy and political practices, were purposely excluded. See Robert Emmet Wall, Jr., "The Massachusetts Bay Colony Franchise in 1647," *William and Mary Quarterly,* 3d ser., 27 (1970): 136–44.

2 The Standing Council and the Negative Voice

The two issues over which the power struggle between the "great gentlemen" and the "lesser gentry" would be fought were those of the Standing Council and the negative voice. They were the obvious issues, since one involved the power of the magistrates to exclusive rule when the General Court was not in session, and the other involved their ability to dominate even when the Court was sitting. If the lesser gentry were to extend their role and to share power effectively with the magistrates, these two institutions would have to be abolished or at least drastically modified.

There were many indications throughout 1640 and 1641 that the deputies, as the spokesmen of the lesser gentry, were about to launch programs beneficial to the interests of their own group, but the first major jurisdictional fights of the second decade did not come until 1642.

In the past the magistrates had proved most vulnerable on the issue of the Standing Council, since in its inception the magistrates had envisaged a council of former governors with life tenure. This had not only disturbed the freemen, but even the elders had looked upon such a body with deep suspicion as a possible source of arbitrary government contrary to the interests of both church and state. The Council, even as modified, had remained suspect ever since. In the session of May 1642 the deputies raised the issue once again.

Earlier, the Standing Council question may have involved the fundamentals of liberty and order, but after 1641 this was no longer quite so clear. In 1642 the question had become a political issue between the deputies,

who wished a legal recognition beyond that of mere
spokesmen for the freemen, and the magistrates, who
wished to keep to themselves the right of governing the
colony and the sole authority to rule when the Court adjourned. In addition, the Standing Council, because of its
emergency nature, consisted not of all the magistrates but
only of those whom the governor could call together
quickly; in effect, this meant the magistrates of Suffolk-
Middlesex. The Standing Council issue therefore involved
not only the antagonisms between deputies and magistrates but also the rivalries between Boston and the men
of the northeastern counties.

One man who was intimately connected with the cause
of the lesser gentry and the cause of Essex-Norfolk was
Richard Saltonstall, Jr., of Ipswich. In 1642 Saltonstall
was only thirty-two years old and by far the youngest of
the magistrates, even though he was then serving his fifth
term. Despite the fact that his father, Sir Richard, had
been a leader in the establishment of the Massachusetts
Bay Company, Saltonstall was not one of the ruling inner
circle. He belonged, rather, to that group of young men
who had served as deputies and who had risen to popularity and the magistracy by criticism of the high-handed
tactics of the great gentlemen. This group included, in
addition to Saltonstall, Israel Stoughton, the most forth-
right opponent of the negative voice, and Richard Bellingham, who in 1641 had defeated Winthrop for the governor's post after a campaign against the accumulation of
too much power in any one man's hands. All three had
served as deputies prior to their elections as magistrates,
and all three had strong support among their former colleagues.

As a leader who drew much strength from his ties with
the deputies and the lesser gentry in general, Saltonstall
consistently worked to increase the powers of the deputies.
He was an ardent opponent of the Standing Council, since

it put too much power into the hands of an unchecked
and possibly arbitrary "extra legal" body when such power
"rightfully" rested in the General Court of deputies and
magistrates together.

As a magistrate from Essex-Norfolk, Saltonstall had
other grounds for criticizing the Standing Council. Prac-
tically speaking, the Council consisted of Suffolk-Middlesex magistrates only because they alone lived close enough
to the capital to respond to calls for emergency sessions.
Yet Saltonstall could foresee occasions when the interests of
Boston would differ from those of the frontier regions,
and in such circumstances he had no doubts whose interests would be served.

Sometime before the May session of 1642 Saltonstall decided to put his objections to the Standing Council into
writing and to begin an assault on the institution by circu-
lating his writing among the deputies. Possibly fearful
the fate of Israel Stoughton, who, when a deputy, authored an attack on the negative voice and was barred from
holding public office as punishment, Saltonstall kept
identity as the author of this new manuscript secret.

During the May 1642 session Saltonstall's manuscript
tacking the Council was passed around until it came
the notice of the magistrates. They took immediate
ception to its contents. Saltonstall had posited three p
ciples:

1. In a commonwealth rightly and religiously co
   tuted, there is no power, office, administratio
   authority, but such as are commanded an
   dained by God.
2. The powers, offices, and administrations tha
   ordained of God, as aforesaid, being giver
   pensed, and erected in a Christian common
   by his good providence, proportioned by he
   to their state and condition, established as

> power against all opposition, carried on and accom-
> panied with his presence and blessing, ought not to
> be by them either changed or altered, but upon
> such grounds, for such ends, in that manner, and
> only so far as the mind of God may be manifest
> therein.
>
> 3. The mind of God is never manifested concerning
> the change or alteration of any civil ordinance,
> erected or established by him as aforesaid in a
> Christian commonwealth, so long as all the cases,
> counsels, services, and occasions thereof may be
> duly and fully ended, ordered, executed, and per-
> formed without any change or alteration of gov-
> ernment.[1]

Arguing from these principles, Saltonstall went on to declare the Standing Council an alteration of existing procedures, which had been ordained by God and needed no
altering. The Standing Council, since its membership was
not extended to all the magistrates, was a disruptive force
in the government which produced disunion and factions
among the freemen. In terms not very flattering to the
existing Council, the manuscript concluded that the Council should be abolished.[2]

Governor Winthrop introduced a motion in the General
Court that the book be carefully examined and its author
tracked down. The deputies would not agree. Many of
them already knew who the author was, and eventually the
fact of Saltonstall's authorship became common knowl-
dge.

Winthrop, undaunted by his first rejection, again moved
at the contents of the book be studied. He hoped for a
ndemnation and an immediate halt to any effort by the
puties to deprive the magistrates of their power to rule
colony when the General Court was not in session.

he deputies refused to consider Winthrop's call for an
stigation unless the magistrates agreed beforehand that

the author would suffer no censure as a result of the investigation. Winthrop thought the guarantee unwarranted. He suggested asking the elders of the churches if the author should be protected. The deputies countered by suggesting that the whole matter—the guarantee of immunity, the contents of the book, and the institution of the Standing Council itself—be sent to the elders for their consideration and advice. They must have trusted that the elders were hostile to the Standing Council and felt confident that the results of the elders' arbitration would favor Saltonstall's interpretation. In the end the deputies had their way. The book would be investigated; Saltonstall would be protected; and the ministers would meet to consider the institution of the Standing Council.[3] Within a short time, however, the magistrates also felt the need of a little protection for themselves: "It was voted by the Cort to vindicate the office of the standing counsell, as it is now ordered, and the persons in whom it is now vested, from all dishonor and reproach cast upon it or them in Mr. Saltonstalls booke."[4]

Winthrop was angry with the way the Court had handled, or rather failed to handle, the case of Saltonstall's book. The way the case seemed to hang on must have been a source of additional anger. Rumors spread throughout the colony that the magistrates had plotted to take away Saltonstall's life or at least to censure him heavily and remove him from the government, so enamored were they of their powerful posts on the Standing Council. Saltonstall would be dead or banned from government were he not protected by the deputies. Winthrop found it necessary in a letter to an anonymous "Rev[erend] and Dear Sir" to deny these charges.

> For the Office of C[ouncillor] I am no more in love with the honor, or power of it, then with an olde friese coat in a summers daye; therefore, when it was propounded to have the power taken away, I never op-

posed, but presently drew up the order for it, and
shalbe as ready to doe the like for the abrogation of
it, if it be so dissolved. Neither will those speeches I
used in the Court about the book or the author (if I
might be justly dealt with to be heard before I were
censured) argue any indulgent affection in me towards
the Office, or disaffection to the Author for I professed
my concurrence with those that cleared him; only I
differed in this that I would have it done in an orderly
way. I would have had the book first read and the
Court to have determined of the matter of it, before
they had meddled with the author but finding the
court to be bent the contrary way I drew up an order
for his clearing as full and safe for him as himself
could have drawn. As for any conspiracy against his
life or etc. I never heard it (to my best remembrance)
so much as propounded by any of the magistrates for
that or any other Censure but only that he might be
questioned for it.[5]

After considerable debate and deliberation, the elders
meeting at Ipswich in October announced their approval
of the basic principles posited by Saltonstall in his book.[6]
But in the application of the principles they found Saltonstall in error. A Standing Council which had tran-
scendent power over the magistrates would be wrong, the
elders asserted. But a Standing Council distinct from the
magistrates was necessary for the colony and not produc-
tive of divisions among the magistrates or freemen. Saltonstall himself was fully exonerated as merely trying to promote the best interests of the colony. Then the elders
turned their attention to the Standing Council, laying
down four rules for perfecting it:

1. That all the magistrates, by their calling and office,
   together with the care of judicature, are to consult for the provision, protection, and universal
   welfare of the commonwealth.

2. Some select men taken out from the assistants, *or other freemen* [italics mine], being called thereunto, be in especial, to attend by way of council, for the provision, protection, and welfare of the commonwealth.

3. This council, as counsellors, have no power of judicature.

4. In cases of instant danger to the commonwealth, in the interim, before a general court can be called, (which were meet to be done with all speed,) what shall be consented unto and concluded by this council, or the major part of them, together with the consent of the magistrates, or the major part of them, may stand good and firm till the general court.[7]

The elders had taken the middle ground, justifying the existence of the Council, since it seemed essential for the proper functioning of the state. But then, as if fearing too powerful a magistracy, they undermined the magistrates' claims. The Standing Council should consist of all the magistrates, or failing that, it should consist of selected magistrates and "other freemen."

Although Perry Miller, the great historian of New England, found the ministers to be the firm supporters of the magistrates in all disputes, it seems that just as good a case can be made for the opposite view.[8] The ministers had sided with the deputies and with the Essex faction on the question of the accumulation of too much power in the hands of one man. Here at the Ipswich meeting, while upholding the institution of the Standing Council and finding it a necessary institution, they opened the possibility of the admission of nonmagistrates to membership. It was a golden opportunity for the deputies to extend their power and seek participation in the executive function of ruling Massachusetts Bay outside of the General Court; and it was a chance to force the magistrates to

share their power. To convince the magistrates to concur
with this decision of the elders would become one of the
driving ambitions of the deputies in the years ahead. The
ministers performed no favors for the magistrates at the
Ipswich conference.

Despite a mild beginning, the year 1643 did witness an
intensification of the basic disagreements between the deputies and the magistrates. The opening given the deputies
for sharing power outside of the General Court was not
immediately exploited—most probably because of pressing business and new opportunities. In 1643 a civil case
between Robert Keayne, a Boston merchant, and Goodwife
Sherman over a missing sow would reopen the whole issue
of the negative voice with a renewal of all the charges of
arbitrary government and the countercharges of democracy which had characterized the issue in the past. In addition, Governor Winthrop was to become involved in the
disputes of the French in Nova Scotia, arousing legitimate
fears in the minds of Essex-Norfolk men of the possibility
of foreign invasion. By his involvement the governor also
opened the Standing Council to attacks by the Essex-Norfolk magistrates and deputies, since by aiding the French,
the Council seemed to be acting in the interests of one
section (Suffolk-Middlesex) at the expense of the remote
and exposed sections of the colony. The year was also one
in which Massachusetts Bay became involved in a dispute
with the arch heretic Samuel Gorton of Rhode Island,
which led to a small war with Gorton and the possibility
of a much greater one with the Narragansetts of Chief
Miantonomo.

Before the September 1642 Court adjourned, it confirmed an earlier order that prior to the next Court of Elections (May 1643), a committee of freemen would meet in
Salem in Essex County to consider nominations for the
magistracy.[9] Winthrop informs us that the majority of this

committee was to be composed of the newly elected deputies for May 1643.[10] The number of magistrates had averaged only eight or nine since 1637, and the deputies, apparently with the magistrates' agreement, were determined to increase the number of magistrates. Given the method of election during this period—a list of nominees presented to the electorate for their vote of yes or no—anyone nominated by this committee stood a good chance of election. We do not know whom the committee nominated, but no effort was made to unseat any of the incumbents. A ruler was a ruler, and even if the deputies were unhappy with the magistrates, the latters' prestige and the reverence in which they were held by the freemen was so great that they could not have been unseated even if the committee had wished to bring about such a revolution.[11] All of the incumbent magistrates were reelected in 1643. The only change affected by the Salem meeting was the nomination of two new candidates—Samuel Symonds of Ipswich and William Hibbens of Boston. Both men were former deputies and perhaps more sympathetic to the deputies' point of view since they had served in the post themselves. The Salem committee took it upon itself to call upon another Essex leader, the Reverend Ezekiel Rogers of Rowley, to preach the election sermon in 1643.

The magistrates were surely ill at ease about the Salem meeting. The procedure for nominating magistrates was not specified in the charter, and the freemen (or, more accurately, their deputies) did seem to be within their rights in making nominations. The only vocal complaint concerning the Salem proceedings, however, was about the nomination of the election preacher by the committee:

> Mr. Rogers, hearing what exception was taken to this call, as unwarrantable, wrote to the governor for advice, etc., who returned him answer: that he did account his calling not to be sufficient, yet the magis-

trates were not minded to strive with the deputies
about it, but seeing it was noised in the country, and
the people would expect him, and that he had advised
with the magistrates about it, he wished him to go
on.[12]

The General Court of Elections for 1643 assembled in
Boston on the tenth day of May. Seventeen of the thirty-
eight deputies present were men who had served in the
last session (September 1642). In all, twenty-four of the
thirty-eight had participated in the recent disputes between
the deputies and the magistrates.

Mr. Rogers's sermon was in the tradition of recent election sermons. He described the type of man the voters
should elect as governor, and perhaps he knew that Winthrop best fitted his description, because he then launched
into a vehement condemnation of the practice of naming
the same man as governor for two terms in succession. The
alliance of ministers, who were afraid of one man rule, of
Essex County leaders, who were fearful of Boston domination, and of deputies, who were challenging the rule of
the magistrates, was back in operation once again.[13] Nevertheless, Winthrop was reelected governor. Endecott was
elected deputy governor, and all the incumbent magistrates were returned to power with the addition of the
two new men, Symonds and Hibbens.

The major controversy between the deputies and the
magistrates in 1643 concerned the negative voice. The dispute was a holdover from the earlier decade, but now it
was taking on a different meaning. The initial argument
over the magistrates' veto power and its use as a possible
source of extending magisterial power arbitrarily had been
successfully resolved by the extension of a similar veto
power to the deputies. What, then, was the purpose of
the renewal of the agitation? If the veto was denied both
magistrates and deputies, then by the sheer weight of num-

bers, the deputies would dominate in the General Court. The case which the deputies used to argue their cause was made to order—a poor woman "cheated" of her "rightful possession" by one of Boston's wealthiest and most unpopular men who was "protected" because of his wealth and position by the "haughty and arbitrary" magistrates.

In 1636 the wife of Goodman Richard Sherman of Boston—along with many other Boston residents—placed her swine on Deer Island in Boston harbor to forage. In November of that same year, with winter approaching, many of the pigs were brought back to town. The Shermans did not recover their sow, while Robert Keayne picked up a stray. Keayne was one of Boston's most prominent merchants, related to Thomas Dudley by the marriage of his son to Dudley's daughter. But he had an unsavory reputation. Later, in 1639, he was hauled into court, fined two hundred pounds for overcharging his customers, and severely admonished by the Boston church for the same reasons.[14]

Despite Keayne's reputation, in the case of the stray sow he seems to have acted honestly. He advertised it several times, and almost everyone who had a missing sow came to Keayne's pens to view this particular stray, but no one laid claim to it. "Goody" Sherman let it be known about the town that the stray sow held by Keayne was hers, although she did nothing about claiming it for a whole year. In October of 1637 Keayne slaughtered his own sow, and no sooner had this been accomplished when Goody Sherman visited Keayne's pens to identify hers. She loudly proclaimed then and later throughout the town that the sow in Keayne's pens was not hers. Hers was all white except for a black spot under one of the eyes about the size of a shilling and had a ragged ear. She claimed that Keayne had slaughtered her sow and preserved his own. Goody Sherman complained to the Boston church, where a full hearing was held and Keayne exonerated completely.

During the next three years, while Keayne's reputation went from bad to worse and he suffered humiliations at the hands of both church and state, the bad blood between the Shermans and the Keaynes deepened. Goodman Sherman traveled to England, leaving his wife alone in Boston. She took a boarder into her home—the young merchant George Story. Keayne complained to the governor that this arrangement was highly suspicious. Keayne was having his own troubles concerning his profits and perhaps he thought that if others could be hypercritical of him, he should be free to react the same way.

In 1640 Goodwife Sherman, with the backing of George Story, brought suit against Robert Keayne in the Boston inferior court. A jury trial was held, and after a full investigation of the facts of the case of the missing sow, the jury found in favor of the defendant, Keayne, and awarded him three pounds in court costs. Keayne, often found guilty both before his brethren in the church and before the bar of justice, perhaps in a fit of righteousness—an emotion so rarely allowed him—decided to pursue the matter further and sued George Story and Goodman Sherman and his wife for spreading malicious stories that he had unlawfully deprived them of their rightful property. He once again emerged victorious. This time the Boston court awarded him twenty pounds damages for defamation.

Now it was the opposition's turn. Story scoured Boston for witnesses who would swear in court that the sow killed by Keayne in 1637 was white with a ragged ear and with a black shilling-sized patch under one eye. He found several who would testify to this, but fearing to bring suit in the Boston court and desperately desiring to get the case to the General Court, Story turned elsewhere.

Keayne, despite his troubles with the authorities in the past, was intimately connected with the gentry. A Boston merchant and a former member of the Merchant Adventurers of London, he had prospered mightily in Boston. His son, Benjamin, had wooed and won Sarah Dudley, daughter of the magistrate Thomas Dudley and sister-in-law of the magistrate Simon Bradstreet and the future magistrates Daniel Denison and John Woodbridge. It is true that the marriage ended in disaster and divorce, but that lay in the future. With such connections as these, Keayne's position might be weaker in a court outside Boston than in the capital. In Essex, men hostile to the dominance of the Suffolk gentry might listen sympathetically to the case of an "oppressed" goodwife who in her attempts to restore her "rightful property" had been cheated and mercilessly fined for her efforts. Story took his case and his new witnesses to the Salem inferior court, where his witnesses testified and the court granted his request of appeal to a higher body—to the General Court.[15]

In May 1642 the General Court received the Story-Sherman petition and agreed to hear the case, although Winthrop pointed out that the proper procedure was to hear the appeal first in the Court of Assistants. The General Court listened to seven days of testimony. Story's witnesses claimed that the sow killed by Keayne in October of 1637 had a black spot under the eye and some "cutts and ragges on the eare." Keayne, in return, had several witnesses who swore that his own sow, which he claimed to have slaughtered, also possessed this kind of black spot on its skin but that it was not too clearly visible when its hair grew long. In addition, Keayne had six or seven witnesses who swore that the sow slaughtered by Keayne was the one which he had purchased from a Mr. Houghton.

A vigorous debate followed the completion of the testimony. Winthrop argued in favor of Keayne, asserting that all the witnesses could be telling the truth and still Keayne would not be guilty. The plaintiff's witnesses offered evidence of probability only, while Keayne's witnesses "gave a certain evidence upon their certain knowledge and that upon certain grounds."[16] Yet, obviously, not everyone in the General Court agreed with Governor Winthrop. After long debates a vote was taken and the Court was split. Two magistrates and fifteen of the thirty deputies found for the plaintiffs—Story and the Shermans; seven magistrates and eight deputies favored the defendant—Keayne; seven deputies abstained.* Therefore no decision could be reached, which in itself was a pro-Keayne decision, since the Shermans were seeking redress from the decision of a lower court. The negative voice blocked any decision for the plaintiffs. If there had been no negative voice, the Shermans and Story would have won seventeen to fifteen. A majority of both magistrates and deputies was required for approval of any petition, and the magistrates and deputies had taken opposite sides. There are no extant division lists for this vote, but considering their actions in the past, it seems fairly certain that Bellingham and Saltonstall had again deserted the other magistrates and voted with the majority of the deputies.[17]

Winthrop called the case a difficult one and explained the large vote for the Shermans among the deputies by "prejudices (as one professed) against the person [Keayne] which blinded some men's judgments that they could not attend the true nature and course of evidence." [18]

It was at this point that the case moved from the realm of petty dispute to that of serious struggle between the lesser and greater gentry. The deputies were determined to challenge the negative voice. If they failed to overturn it, they were determined to place upon the magistrates the burden of upholding arbitrary institutions. In the months after the deadlock in the General Court, public opinion was aroused against Keayne and against the magistrates for supporting him. Winthrop described Keayne as being of

> ill report in the country for a hard dealer in his course of trading, and having been formerly censured

---

* There were 35 deputies to the General Court in May 1642. Winthrop implies that only 30 were present and voting when the decision was called for.

in the court and in the church also, by admonishion
for such offences, carried many weak minds strongly
against him. And the truth is, he was very worthy of
blame in that kind, as divers others in the country
were also in those times, though they were not detected as he was; yet to give every man his due, he
was very useful to the country both by his hospitality
and otherwise. But one dead fly spoils much good oint-
ment.[19]

Story had worked hard to build up the general hostility
toward Keayne; and when Keayne was not found guilty,
the instrument used to acquit him, the negative voice,
came under harsh attack. There was talk of putting magistrates out of power and abolishing the negative voice.[20]
Winthrop and the other magistrates felt that they would
have to offset the bad publicity they were receiving with a
statement explaining their position. Winthrop, meanwhile,
insisted in July 1642 that the alternatives in the case had
not been exhausted by the split vote,

> yett was there noe necessitye, that the cause might not
> have bene brought to an issue, for eyther the Court
> might have Argued the Case againe by which meanes
> some who were doubtfull might have come to a
> reasolucion or others might have changed there Judg-
> ments and soe have proceeded to a new voate, or else
> committyes might have bene Chosen, to order the
> Cause according to Lawe.[21]

Before adjourning the General Court, Winthrop tried to
pass a resolution stating that the members of the Court,
despite their disagreements, parted with much affection
and great charity toward each other. The resolution was
rejected.[22]

The deadlock in the General Court and the row over the
negative voice continued. In October 1642 the issue was

raised at the Ipswich meeting of the elders (the primary concern of this meeting was, of course, Saltonstall's book and the Standing Council). Winthrop, in a letter to the elders, attempted to answer all possible objections to the negative voice. He had heard them all and most recently in the debates over the sow case. What if the magistrates should grow corrupt? Their powers through the negative voice would lead to grave abuses. Winthrop countered that this was no more to be feared than the deputies growing corrupt, since they too had a negative voice; and what if all the rest of the people became corrupt?—"then it was all beyond remedy." What if the Court of Assistants committed an injustice? They and the magistrates in the General Court were the same persons. Through the negative voice they could perpetuate their injustice. Winthrop responded by asking what if the General Court should err or commit injustices? In this case the negative voice could prevent the commission of injustice, Winthrop's final argument was telling. If the magistrates committed injustices and failed to harken to the better advice of the General Court, then the people had the ultimate remedy. They could elect new and better magistrates.[23]

Winthrop insisted on the retention of the power of veto against those who insisted it was a pernicious doctrine. He attacked those who advocated the abolition of the power. He asserted that since the opposition knew the present magistrates would block such a move, those who advocated it were in reality calling for the turning out of the old magistrates and urging the election of new ones. Winthrop found such a position dangerous and dishonorable, since they had not been guilty of any injustices.[24]

Winthrop, still smarting over the failure of his suggestion of a resolution of mutual affection, as well as the defeat of his brother-in-law, Downing, went on to comment to the elders in strong tones which he was sure they would endorse:

The last thing that I will trouble your patience with at the present is about a position maintained in the Countrye (and those none of the worst) that it should be dangerous for the Com[mon]w[wealth] to have the magistrates united in love and affection, therefore care to be had, that there be no kindred, affinity, or close amity betweene them: but that they should rather be divided in factions etc: If this past for good doctrine, then let us no longer professe the Gospell of Jesus Christ, but take up the rules of Matchiavell and the Jesuits, for Christ saythe Love is the band of perfection, and a kingdome or house devided cannot stand but the others teache (or rather the Devill teacheth them) divide et imperia etc.[25]

The ministers, after receiving Winthrop's letter, went on to suggest solutions to the problem of the Standing Council and Saltonstall's book, but almost nothing was stated concerning the negative voice. It was as if they hoped by ignoring the messy problem, it would go away of itself. Yet the sow case and the problem of the negative voice would not be solved that simply.

In the spring of 1643 another meeting of the elders was held. Winthrop insists that the deputies and the two magistrates who had supported Goody Sherman and George Story presented their case to the elders without mentioning any of the evidence supporting Keayne. The elders transmitted this account of the events to the rest of the magistrates, and then they presented their account of the case.[26] By this time, the clergy were as befuddled as everyone else. A meeting of deputies, magistrates, and elders was held just prior to the Court of Elections (May 1643) in an effort to settle the question. At this meeting the ministers declared "that notwithstanding their former opinion, yet, upon examination of all the testimonies, they found such contrariety and crossing of testimonies, as they did not see any ground for the court to proceed to judgment in the case, and therefore earnestly desired that the court might never be more troubled with it." [27] The magistrates quickly agreed to drop the matter, and so apparently did the deputies present at the meeting. As for the ministers, they agreed to bring pressure on the deputies from their own towns to end the case. Bellingham and Saltonstall still held out. After much persuasion by the ministers, Saltonstall finally agreed that many of the things in his treatise on the Standing Council had been unfortunate and he "was brought to see his failings in that treatise, which he did ingenuously acknowledge and bewail and so he was reconciled with the rest of the magistrates." This reconciliation apparently led to his agreeing with the majority of the magistrates on the sow case as well. This left only Bellingham, who, still insisting that the magistrates should be divested of their veto power, would not budge from his position. The ministers tried to dispel the bad feeling between Winthrop and Bellingham, but Bellingham would have no part of any reconciliation, "whereby it rested in a manner as it was." [28]

When the Court of Elections met on May 10, 1643, the magistrates felt that at least the sow case and the attack on the negative voice had been settled. They were mistaken. George Story petitioned the Court for a new hearing, and the deputies agreed to receive his petition. Those deputies who had attended the meeting with the magistrates and elders now claimed that they could not let the case drop. Their constituents were angry, particularly because a rich merchant had been awarded twenty pounds from a poor woman. Winthrop cited this as an example of the "democratic spirit" represented by the deputies, but we must remember that it had been the deputies who had reported the facts of the case to the voters. Most had opposed the decision of the Court and probably had done little to assuage the anger of the freemen.

Winthrop, the most ardent defender of the negative voice, found it necessary once again to write in its defense.

He published a discourse on the institution in which he insisted that its origins were in the Royal Charter, which was the fundamental source of all authority in the colony. Next, he proceeded to show that the General Court had perceived the validity of this claim when they established the institution by law in 1634: *

> and whereas it may fall out that in some of theis General Courts, to be holden by the magistrates and deputies, there may arise some difference of judgment in doubtfull cases, it is therefore ordered, that noe lawe, order, or sentence shall passe as an act of the Court, without the consent of the greater parte of the magistrates on the one parte, and the greater number of deputyes on the other parte, and for want of such accorde, the cause or order shalbe suspended, and if either partie thinke it so materiall, there shalbe forthwith a comitte chosen, the one halfe by the magistrates, and the other halfe by the depytyes, and the committee soe chosen to elect an umpire, who togeather shall have power to hear and determine the cause in question.[29]

Furthermore, Winthrop argued that if the negative voice were taken away, the freemen (and here he meant the deputies) would become absolute masters of the colony and the state would be reduced to a mere democracy. If the covenant with God, the charter, and the "mixed aristocratic-democratic" nature of the government were to be upheld, then the negative voice was fundamentally necessary.[30]

Someone of the magistrates (probably Bellingham) undertook to answer Winthrop. The answer has not survived, and all that we know of it is Winthrop's comment

---

* Winthrop's memory failed him here. The principle of the negative voice may have been established at the sessions of 1634, but the law he cited to support his contention was passed at the session of March 1635/6.

that "it avoided all the arguements both from the patent and from the order etc." Yet it must have been convincing since "the deputies made great use of it in their court, supposing they had now enough to carry the cause clearly with them so as they pressed earnestly to have it presently determined." [31] The magistrates fought back. They were not about to change so fundamental an institution that had operated well without any inconvenience or apparent mischief for many years, and they argued that since the elders had been consulted before the negative voice was adopted, then they should be consulted before it was repealed.

Finally, another compromise was worked out. The opinion of the ministers of the colony would be sought again. If they agreed that the negative voice was "inconvenient, or not warranted by the patent and the said order, etc.," then the magistrates would consent to abolish it. The deputies agreed to this suggestion. They had received support from the ministers before on the question of reelection of governors and had received their endorsement for participation in the Standing Council the previous October. They had no reason to think the ministers would be prejudiced against their cause. The magistrates, on the other hand, seem not to have been acting in good faith. Their major concern was the popular support the deputies were getting. Winthrop frankly admits that the magistrates were playing for time—so that hotheads could cool off, so that they might win away from the deputies some of their outraged constituents, and so that voters might forget about Goody Sherman. [32]

Also, as part of the compromise, the General Court ordered that all of its members should seek advice; that it would be no offense for any, either publicly or privately, to state their conclusions; and that the opinions of the ministers would be sought before the next General Court. Meanwhile, Winthrop was busy preparing another statement on the negative voice—his reply to Bellingham. He wrote a long treatise attempting to prove that the negative voice was reserved to the magistrates by the charter. He quoted that document to the effect that the governor, deputy governor, and seven of the assistants constituted a full and sufficient court. The governor, deputy governor, and the freemen could admit freemen and make the laws as long as the governor, deputy governor, and six of the assistants, "to be allways seven," were part of the court. Winthrop, continuing to quote similar selections from the charter, concluded that not only was the presence of the governor or deputy governor and six assistants necessary for a quorum, but that their approval was necessary for a measure to pass into law. Bellingham had contended the opposite, that these sections of the charter referred to quorum regulations only.

In the second section of his treatise Winthrop undertook to answer the question whether the negative voice "be a fundamental part of our Government." His answer was an emphatic yes! It was based on the charter, and the charter was the fundamental basis of government in Massachusetts Bay. He went on to argue that if the negative voice was dropped, the essential nature of the government would be altered, from a mixed aristocracy to a democracy. Anything which, when altered, changes the essential nature of a thing is fundamental to it.

In this last argument Winthrop did his best to discredit the deputies. He was aware of their ambitions, and to thwart them he made every effort to equate them with the freemen. They had no power, he asserted, other than as the voices of the freemen, and of themselves they were nothing. He could therefore claim that if they were to dominate the magistrates (as they certainly would if the negative voice were abolished) then Massachusetts was reduced to the status of mere democracy.

> Now if we should change from a mixt Aristocracy to a meere Democratie: first we should have no warrant in scripture for it: there was no such Government

in Israell. We should heerby voluntaryly abase our selves, and deprive our selves of that dignity, which the providence of God hath putt upon us: which is a manifest breach of the 5th Com[mandmen]t and for a Democratie is, among most Civill nations, accounted the meanest and worst of all formes of Government.[33]

This argument had a twofold effect. First, it was meant to preserve the power of the magistrates, while secondly depriving the deputies of any claim to magisterial dignity. If fundamental power rested with the deputies, it rested with the freemen, and the colony was a democracy, deprived of good government and the rule of the best qualified men. In his answer he totally ignored the deputies' claim to be more than the voice of the freemen. If he accepted that claim, if he admitted the deputies to magisterial dignity, then the abolition of the negative voice would not reduce the colony to "a meere democratie."

Later on in his work Winthrop turned to this most fundamental question: What was the role of the deputies and what were their powers? The deputies wished to share in magisterial power and dignity; they also wished to participate in the functions of the Standing Council. Winthrop would not bend before these ambitions. The deputies had the same position and authority that the charter gave to the freemen. When the General Court was in session, the deputies with the magistrates held all the legislative power and certain judicial powers. But they had no function in and of themselves. On this point Winthrop would not yield. The deputies were merely the voices of the freemen, and the freemen were not magistrates.[34]

The proposed mediation of the elders recommended by the General Court in the May 1643 session took place in September. We know from the testimony of the Reverend Richard Mather of Dorchester that a convention of the elders was held at Cambridge in September 1643.[35] Yet there is no record that this meeting did anything outside the realm of the church. Essentially it was an effort to win away from Presbyterianism the two Newbury clergymen, Thomas Parker and James Noyes.[36] Perhaps the elders found time to discuss the question of the negative voice outside the regular debates of the convention. The General Court records for September 7, 1643, state that "three conclusions were delivered in by Mr. Cotton, in the name of himselfe and other elders about the negative voyce." [37] We do not know what the elders suggested, but considering that no more is heard about the issue of the negative voice, and that it remained in effect, it seems safe to conclude that their arbitration favored the magistrates' interpretation. It is also logical that they should have sided with the magistrates on this issue. Their driving motivation was to protect their reformed churches and to thwart any potential arbitrary power which might interfere with the reform. The negative voice presented no threat of arbitrary power after 1635, when both deputies and magistrates were granted similar veto powers. To abolish the negative voice might in fact weaken the magistrates to the point where they could no longer freely accomplish their main function—the preservation of God's law and the protection of the churches. To side with the deputies on the negative voice issue would create the very imbalance the elders ardently wished to avoid.

Had the decision of the elders supported the deputies and called for the abolition of the negative voice, there is good evidence that the magistrates still would have resisted. To them the May compromise resolution was only an effort to gain time for tempers to cool and for Winthrop to publish and distribute his answer to Bellingham's attack on the negative voice.

The last move by the deputies was a feeble one, but nevertheless important constitutionally. At the special Court session of March 7, 1643/4, the deputies moved that the two groups, deputies and magistrates, sit apart in the future. In effect, it was a surrender, an admission that the magistrates' claim to a separate existence within the General Court was valid. It was a guarantee of the continued existence of the negative voice. But the deputies tried to make the most of a bad thing. They too would now have a separate existence, without the domination of the great gentlemen's physical presence. The magistrates accepted the deputies' proposal. It was a small price to pay for a victory as important as the one they had just achieved.[38]

Throughout the whole period of debate on the Standing Council and the negative voice, the major source of divisions was the ambition of the deputies and the magistrates' resistance to it. In 1643, however, the sectional differences between the leaders of Essex-Norfolk and Suffolk-Middlesex became very pronounced. Political sentiment in the north had consistently run counter to the policies of the magisterial group. John Winthrop was in constant debates with Essex leaders during the whole period. This Essex group—including some of the Essex magistrates (Saltonstall and occasionally Bradstreet), as already noted, sided with the deputies rather than with the magistrates on most issues.

In the 1640s there was economic and political discontent in the Essex-Norfolk region. It manifested itself in efforts to lessen the power of the Suffolk-Middlesex based magistracy. The discontent in Essex-Norfolk combined with that of the lesser gentry of the whole colony and with the fears of leading ministers that one man might gain too much power in the office of governor by consecutive elections. These three elements, if added to the ingredient of a generally unpopular policy adopted and upheld by the magistrates, could bring about the election of someone other than John Winthrop as governor. In 1644 the discontent of the lesser gentry, the fears of the ministers, and the jealousies of Essex-Norfolk men were present on the political scene. It was Winthrop who provided the unpopular policy.

The events which were to bring about the downfall of Winthrop in 1644 began as early as 1633, when Winthrop recorded in his Journal that Charles La Tour had attacked a Plymouth Colony trading post in the northern regions, killed two of the five factors on the scene, and carried off all the others and their goods. La Tour had a commission from the Chevalier Rasilly to govern the province of Acadia from the St. Croix River eastward (present day New Brunswick and Nova Scotia), while a rival and soon bitter enemy, Charles d'Aulnay, governed western Acadia (present-day Maine). When in 1635 Plymouth authorities reached La Tour's headquarters at Port Royal and demanded the return of their men and their goods, La Tour refused to comply, saying that he would seize any English vessels or trading facilities found east of Pemaquid (some fifteen miles east of the Kennebec River in Maine). Apparently La Tour had an exaggerated notion of the extent of his domain, for before long he and d'Aulnay were at each others throats and in 1641 actually waged war against each other.[39]

La Tour's attitude toward the English changed abruptly after he became involved in hostilities with the stronger d'Aulnay. In November 1641 La Tour sent an agent (a Protestant) to Boston to present proposals. He suggested freedom of trade between the "Bostonais" and his domain of Acadia. The Boston-Charlestown merchants would have gladly agreed to this. Rochett, La Tour's agent, also requested the assistance of the Bay Colony in La Tour's war with d'Aulnay, whose station was now located on the Penobscot. In addition, Rochett requested freedom for La Tour "to make return of goods out of England by our merchants." Winthrop states that the first proposal—that of free trade—was agreed to but that the others were not because Rochett did not bear a commission from La Tour. The implication, of course, was that they would be approved, or at least seriously considered, if the agent returned with a commission. Winthrop does not state who made these decisions, but presumably it was the Standing Council—which in practice meant the Suffolk-Middlesex magistrates, who would normally handle business such as this if the General Court were not in session.[40]

No more was heard from La Tour until October 1642. In that month a French shallop bearing fourteen men and commanded by La Tour's lieutenant arrived at Boston. The French brought letters from La Tour to Winthrop requesting his support against d'Aulnay. La Tour was shrewd enough to offer one obvious inducement to the Puritans—the chance to open a new trade with northern neighbors and this at a time when Massachusetts was in the throes of a depression. Her merchants, in the first enthusiasms of their calling, were eager for any opportunity for trade.* At the same time, La Tour offered a more subtle inducement. The sending of a Protestant agent in 1641 had implanted a favorable impression in the minds of the Puritan leaders, and in all likelihood a similar impression was made on the minds of the powerful clergy. In 1642 the Frenchmen who arrived in Boston were admittedly Catholics, but they agreed to attend services in the Boston church. They had nothing but high praise for the services and for the manner in which Boston was run. One of the elders gave the lieutenant a French Bible with notes by the Huguenot theologian Augustin Marlorat, which he promised to read. There was developing in the relationship of La Tour and Massachusetts the hint of a possible evangelistic coup for the Puritans, the conversion

---

* Not all Massachusetts merchants would welcome La Tour's invitation. Those of Essex-Norfolk who ambitioned to open an English trade in furs in the northern areas would not appreciate the presence of Suffolk merchants in the northern territories.

of French Acadia, or at least La Tour's Acadia, to Protestantism. The price for such an opportunity was, of course, the elimination of the Papist d'Aulnay.[41]

In November 1642, in reaction to the free trade agreement, some Boston merchants sent off a pinnace to trade with La Tour. He received them kindly and sent home with them a letter to Winthrop explaining his controversy with his countryman. On the way home the pinnace put in at the trading post at Pemaquid, where apparently a meeting was arranged with d'Aulnay. He showed the New Englanders a copy of a decree issued by authorities in France outlawing La Tour and warned the English that if they returned to trade with La Tour, d'Aulnay would regard them as subject to seizure.[42]

It was not until 1643, however, that the relations of Winthrop with La Tour took on significance for Massachusetts politics. On the twelfth day of June in that year La Tour himself appeared in Boston. He arrived on a 140-ton ship which had sailed from the Protestant stronghold of La Rochelle with a Protestant in command and a Protestant crew working her. The ecumenism of La Tour was displayed by the presence of two friars aboard. While in Boston, however, he attended the services of the Boston church and kept his priests conveniently out of the way. La Tour sailed into Boston harbor past the guns of Castle Island, which had been abandoned the year before. The fact that he surprised the town and did not take advantage of its defenselessness was taken by Governor Winthrop as a mark of his good intentions. A meeting between the Standing Council members and La Tour was arranged at the home of Captain Gibbons of Boston, one of the merchants who had become involved with La Tour the year before.

La Tour told his story. The Rochelle ship had been sent from France to supply his post on the Saint John River, New Brunswick, but had not been able to reach him because the mouth of the river was blockaded by d'Aulnay's naval forces. La Tour had slipped out of his post past the blockade and had joined the ship. He then sailed straight to Boston to seek aid.

No decision was reached on June 12, but on the next day another meeting was scheduled. For this second meeting, Winthrop called together "such of the magistrates as were at hand, and some of the deputies" (but apparently not all the deputies "as were at hand"). They met with the governor, La Tour, and the captain of the Rochelle ship, who presented his commission dated April 1643, bearing the seal of the Vice Admiral of France, and calling upon him to supply La Tour. The captain referred to La Tour as "His Majesty's Lieutenant General of L'Acadye." The conclusion reached at the governor's meeting was that d'Aulnay had lied when he declared that La Tour was a rebel and that La Tour was all that he claimed to be. When it came to assisting him against d'Aulnay, however, the magistrates and those deputies present grew more cautious. They agreed that they could not join any hostilities against d'Aulnay without consultation with the Commissioners of the United Colonies. But neither would they leave La Tour friendless. No barriers would be placed in his way if he wished to hire men and ships from among those of Boston harbor. Apparently, the Suffolk-Middlesex magistrates, and certainly the merchants, were anxious for booty. They saw a chance to get rich quickly at the expense of d'Aulnay, and many of them, led by the merchant Gibbons, became involved in the Acadian war. Winthrop apparently did not think (nor did he feel he had any need) to consult with any of the other magistrates much less any of the other deputies. In the days that followed, the French were entertained and allowed to train and drill with the Boston militia company, but this was the lull before the storm.[43]

Before long, word of these remarkable events in Boston began to find its way to the remoter towns, and the reaction against Winthrop and the Suffolk-Middlesex magistrates and merchants was swift and violent, especially in Essex County. Winthrop probably received his first inkling of this anger when he received a letter from his good friend John Endecott of Salem, which was dated June 19.

Endecott, who had not participated in the events of the thirteenth, expressed to the governor his satisfaction that La Tour was not to receive any official aid from Massachusetts Bay, and he forcefully stated the case against allowing him to hire mercenaries from among the English:

> His [La Tour's] Father and himselfe as I am informed, have shed the blood of some English already, and tooken away a pinnace and goods from Mr. Allerton [a Plymouth Colony merchant]. It were (I think) good that that business were cleared before hee had either ayd or libertie to hire shipps yea or to depart.[44]

La Tour was not to be trusted. Endecott made it clear that Essex men were indeed disturbed by the news from Boston:

> Sir it is not the manner abroad to suffer strangers to view Forts or Fortifications, as it seems theise French have done. I must needs say that I feare we shall have little comfort in having any thing to doe with theise Idolatrous French. The Countrie heerabouts is much troubled that they are so intertayned and have such libertie as they have to bring their souldiers ashore and to suffer them to trayne their men. And great Jealousies [suspicions] there are that it is not Dony [d'Aulnay] that is aymed at, seeing such a strength will neither sute such a poore designe, and La Tour a man of weak estate as it is said. Wherefore other mens hands are imployed, and purses to for some other service.[45]

Endecott argued what became the basic position of the Essex men. Massachusetts should keep out of the affairs of the French. As long as they fought each other, they remained weak and Massachusetts had nothing to fear from them. Should one French faction conquer the other or should they unite, then the English settlements were in danger. The closest English settlements to the French—the most exposed, the most defenseless—were those of the northeastern counties of Essex and Norfolk. The men of Essex felt that Winthrop had put them in grave danger merely to satisfy the greed of Boston and Charlestown merchants.

Winthrop took only part of the Salem magistrate's advice. He raised with La Tour the matter of the assault on English traders in 1633. While the Frenchman acknowledged his participation in those events, he denied he was guilty of an intentional wrong and agreed to submit the case to judgment and make satisfaction if he lost.

The governor, apparently satisfied by this answer, agreed to La Tour's request to leave Boston on the fourteenth day of July. Four New England ships (one of them carrying sixteen guns) and seventy soldiers and volunteers sailed with La Tour. The expedition returned to Boston on August 20 after breaking d'Aulnay's blockade, killing several of his men, and seizing what supplies d'Aulnay had left there during his occupation of La Tour's fort on the Saint John River. The English also seized one of d'Aulnay's pinnaces bearing four hundred moose skins and four hundred beaver skins. With two-thirds of this loot in tow, the English mercenaries returned to their home port.[46]

Meanwhile, the reaction to Winthrop's allowing La Tour to leave with hired English support was angry. The leaders of Ipswich and Rowley, lay and clerical, agreed to compose a letter to Winthrop and the other magistrates and elders of Suffolk-Middlesex challenging their actions. The letter written by Richard Saltonstall is dated the same day that La Tour sailed—July 14, 1643. It was signed by Saltonstall and two other Ipswich magistrates, Simon

Bradstreet and Samuel Symonds, and by the elders—
Ezekiel Rogers of Rowley and Nathaniel Rogers and John
Norton of the Ipswich Church. Another signer of the letter
was Nathaniel Ward of Ipswich. They opposed the policy
adopted in the case for a variety of reasons. Wars, they asserted, should be just and necessary. How could Massachusetts Bay decide between La Tour and d'Aulnay when the
French courts could not? Secondly, Massachusetts had no
business conducting wars against the agents of a foreign
state without consultation with the mother country. In
addition, since wars should be holy, they failed to see how
God's glory would be proclaimed by a looting expedition
by greedy merchants. The last point in the Essex letter
stressed a grave fear among the leaders, and apparently
among the masses of the northeastern counties, that d'Aulnay would retaliate and would fall upon them as the most
exposed and defenseless portions of the English settlements.[47] Wars should be feasible; moreover, d'Aulnay, they
reminded Winthrop, was said to be strong.[48]

Winthrop responded quickly to the Essex letter. From
his answer we can conclude that the letter from Saltonstall
and the others had been made public. Winthrop treated
the letter as a dangerous public appeal with political overtones, viewing it as an attempt to stir up opposition to his
reelection:

> We are condemned in Court in Country, by private
> letters and by publik edict, and never asked why have
> yow done this? and all this so carryed on, and un-
> seasonably dispensed as no man can tell (nor do your-
> selves propound) what yow whuld have or how it may
> tend to any publik good or prevention of that great
> danger which you suppose to hang over us: except it
> may be conceaved that, either D'Aulnay will be paci-
> fyed with a protestation; or the people stirred up to
> sacrifice some of us to make their owne peace.[49]

Winthrop complained that it was clearly within the power of the magistrates of the Boston area to act without consultation with the Essex magistrates because of the emergency created by the sudden arrival of the French. He did not argue the wisdom of his actions; and in his Journal he listed the hastiness of his decision, and failure to consult, as one of the most important errors of judgment in the case.[50] But there was no such admission in his public statement. In fact, he used the clever device of turning the argument upon his critics and found them neglectful of their duties in their failure to consult with *him* on the issue. In addition, their very protestations were clear evidence to d'Aulnay of division within Massachusetts Bay and would jeopardize the colony far more than any actions taken by the Suffolk-Middlesex magistrates. Winthrop's answer to Saltonstall is in fact one of the most clever political maneuvers of his career.

Winthrop's arguments apparently split the unity of the Essex group, at least temporarily. Endecott of Salem had not been party to the Saltonstall letter, although he had been one of the first to criticize Winthrop's actions. On July 26 he wrote to Winthrop, stating that he was much satisfied by Winthrop's reports of his dealings with La Tour. We do not know what Winthrop told him, but in his Journal the governor clearly states that the mercenaries hired by La Tour were merely an escort to see justice done and were in no sense a war party. He later expressed his unhappiness when he learned of their belligerent actions against d'Aulnay.[51] Perhaps Winthrop argued in this manner with Endecott in his letter. We do know, however, that he converted him. The Salem magistrate warned Winthrop of the great ill will toward him developing in Essex County, and stated that he was doing his best to reestablish the good names of Winthrop and the other Suffolk-Middlesex magistrates. At this stage Endecott was clearly more worried about the possible internal political upheaval which might occur as a result of the La Tour decision than he was of possible outside attack by an enraged d'Aulnay: "I see no good use of such protestation as I heare of, but they may prove more dangerous then the french business by farre if our God hinder not." [52]

Of the rebellious Ipswich magistrates, Simon Bradstreet was the most moderate. In August he responded to Winthrop's letter (as well as to one from his father-in-law, Thomas Dudley). Apparently he had wished to have another joint letter composed, conciliatory in tone, but he had failed to get the other signatories of the Essex letter to agree. He therefore decided to respond on his own. Bradstreet expressed his love for Winthrop and the other magistrates, and denied any intention of casting dishonor on any of his friends. But, he argued, Essex men were angry and frightened by the "unwarrantable" actions of those in charge in Boston. The purpose of the letter, Bradstreet insisted, had been "a staying of aid for La Tour." His only hope had been to caution the mercenaries against hasty belligerency. But none of the signatories had intended any condemnation of the actions of the magistrates.[53]

Bradstreet's statement concerning his motives for signing the letter is probably true; but as for not intending condemnation, clearly the letter of July 14 challenges the decision reached by the other magistrates and casts doubt upon the validity of that decision. Now, however, the whole matter would be given over to the voters for a decision.

The year 1643 had been one of alienation. The struggle over the negative voice had embittered the deputies and had finally seen them withdraw and constitute themselves as a separate house of the legislature. Essex County's jealousies had been transformed into anger and fright by the handling of the La Tour-d'Aulnay disputes by the magistrates of Suffolk-Middlesex; and 1644 was to see the continuation of this alienation and the renewal of the debate on the Standing Council. Yet some advances had been made by the deputies in 1643. When the General Court of 1643 reconvened in September, its membership was the same as that of the May session. Unlike previous years, there was no call for new elections. The deputies were to be elected for the year. In October the Court voted to continue the procedure of deputies serving year-long terms from Court of Elections to Court of Elections. And the deputies were to have the same tenure of office as the magistrates.[54] This would lend continuity to the membership of the General Court and seemed to give the deputies an existence outside of the Court. The man elected for the May Court would also be a deputy in the fall. During the months between, the magistrates might not wish to recognize any special role for the deputies, but no longer could they be regarded as mere freemen either. Psychologically, annual elections were an important step forward in the deputies' quest for magisterial status.

One further gain was made by the deputies in the fall of 1643. The magistrates, frightened at the prospect of war with the Narragansetts and desiring a united front for the defense of the colony, agreed to establish, until the next session of the General Court, a joint council of war. This council was to be composed of the magistrates of Suffolk-Middlesex and the deputies from the towns of Boston, Charlestown, Cambridge, Roxbury, and Dorchester.[55] Apparently the deputies and magistrates of Essex-Norfolk agreed to this proposal, or disagreeing, were outvoted. But, in all likelihood, they too were worried about a possible Indian war in addition to their fears of a French war. This council of war was also made more palatable to the Essex-Norfolk deputies by the inclusion of men of their own rank, even if they were from the southern towns. It is true that the council of war was not the Standing Council of the colony and that it had only a temporary existence, but the creation of the war council and the participation of the deputies was the first occasion in which the magistrates had been willing to share executive power with the deputies. It was the first time they had been willing to admit that the deputies had an existence outside the General Court. Despite its temporary nature, the council of war of 1643–44 was viewed as an important precedent for the future which the deputies might exploit.

Winthrop informs us of one more development of importance coming before the 1644 Court of Elections. "Those of Essex" had adopted a provision that the deputies from the different shires elected for the May session of 1644 would meet in their shire towns to discuss matters for presentation to the Court. The order calling for this action gives as a reason the length of General Court sessions. Hopefully, a planned agenda could cut the time and expense of holding General Courts. But the Essex men had other things in mind as well. They wanted a meeting in Salem to organize a united front for an assault on Suffolk-Middlesex dominance: one sure way to achieve these ends was to elect an Essex man as governor. The Salem meeting had as a goal, then, a concerted effort to unseat John Winthrop.[56]

Winthrop relates none of the details of the Court of Elections held in May 1644, other than to state that John Endecott was elected governor, and himself deputy governor. Apparently the anti-Winthrop factions had triumphed again. Endecott was a compromise candidate. Surely Winthrop's foes would have preferred Saltonstall or even Bellingham if they could have been elected. Although Endecott was normally in the Winthrop camp, his opposition to Winthrop's actions in the La Tour case and the possibility that he might be able to defeat Winthrop, considering the latter's recent unpopularity, probably prompted the anti-Winthrop forces to support him. Ende-

cott also had the advantage of being an Essex man. Another indication of the opposition strength in May 1644
was the election of Simon Bradstreet and William Hawthorne as Commissioners to the United Colonies. Both
were Essex men and one was only a deputy. Winthrop
found their elections in some ways more unpalatable than
his own defeat. He found fault with their ages (they were
relatively young men—forty-one and thirty-eight respectively), and he thought Massachusetts would be at a disadvantage in commissioners' meetings, since the other
colonies sent only their most prominent men.[57]

The deputies were plotting even more significant steps
when the General Court assembled in May 1644. Thirty-
nine deputies from twenty-five towns attended the Court of
Elections' session, twenty-one of whom had served in the
March special session which had split the legislature into
two houses. Another four elected for May 1644 had served
in the 1643 Courts and had participated in the debates on
the negative voice. Only ten of the deputies of 1644 were
serving their first terms in the General Court.

The deputies of Essex County meeting in Salem before
the elections decided on a program to end Suffolk domination. They would demand in the General Court (after
Endecott was elected) that the capital of the colony be
moved to his home—Salem—and that the General Court
move to that town also. This, of course, would mean that
the Essex magistrates would of necessity become the Standing Council. The Court of Assistants should also meet in
Salem, and probably in the other shire towns as well. Still
nervous about the possibility of a French raid, the Essex
deputies agreed to push for the transferral of part of the
colony's weapons stock to Essex. But most of all, they wished
to extend the precedent established when the General Court
had appointed a council of war consisting of magistrates
and deputies to handle military emergencies between sessions of the Court. They desired that the Standing Council—the permanent governing body between sessions—be

constituted in the same manner. This was the Essex program; and certainly for the last proposition—concerning the composition of the Standing Council—they had the support of the deputies of the other shires.[58]

When the General Court met on May 29, 1644, the deputies, sitting by themselves for the first time, elected a Salem deputy, William Hawthorne, as their Speaker. One of the first pieces of business that the new House of Deputies ordered was the establishment of a committee consisting of Hawthorne of Salem, George Cooke of Cambridge, John Glover of Dorchester, Nathaniel Sparhawk of Dorchester, and Edward Rawson of Newbury "to examine the French business, and to state the case, to draw the bills, to lay the charges, to produce the testimonye and to present it to the house." [59] From this point on, the Standing Council would have its acts during the interim carefully checked by a separate agency—the House of Deputies.

On June 5 the lower house passed the first part of the Essex program. "It is ordered, that the Courte of Elections for the yeare next ensueinge shall be att Salem." The magistrates rejected the proposal. That same day, June 5, the deputies passed and sent on to the magistrates the second part of the Essex program:

> It is ordered, that all the countrys stocke (except greate artillary) shalbee divided into the three sheires (Norfolke to bee layd to Essex) accordinge to the last country rate, (the Castle being first provided for,) and the small artillary to bee kept in one place of each sheire, allways ready fixed, and that some men of each sheire bee deputed to see to the performance of the order and to give security for the stock and to bee accomptable for it as the Courte shall require.[60]

This proposition was also rejected by the magistrates. The deputies called for a committee of both houses to recon-

sider the matters. In the committees the magistrates refused to compromise and the vetoes stood.[61]

The major effort made by the deputies, however, was in
the realm of extending their power beyond the General
Court. They passed a resolution, which they sent to the
magistrates, calling for the General Court to commission
seven magistrates, four deputies, and the deputies' favorite
preacher and compiler of laws, Mr. Nathaniel Ward of
Ipswich, to act as a Standing Council for the governing of
Massachusetts Bay when the General Court was not in
session. The deputies had guaranteed the magistrates control of the Standing Council, perhaps in an effort to lull
them into acceptance. In reality, it would take but two
magistrates' votes to throw control of the Standing Council
to the deputies, if they in turn remained united. The magistrates would have nothing to do with the plan. They took
the strongest exception to the concept of the General Court
commissioning the Standing Council. They argued that
their right to govern the colony in the absence of the
General Court was fundamental to the charter. Any change
in this matter would undermine their government and the
rights of the freemen.[62] The deputies, who were keenly
disappointed at the magistrates' reactions to their proposals, visited them as a body to protest their obstruction-
ism—to no avail.

The magistrates, according to Winthrop, rejected the
deputies' plan for three reasons. They argued that general
officers—such as those the deputies wished to commission
as the Standing Council—could be chosen only by the freemen in the general elections held in May. Some magistrates
elected to their posts by the freemen would not be members of the Standing Council according to the deputies'
plan and would therefore be unconstitutionally deprived
of the rightful powers granted them by the fact of their
elections. Last, and most importantly, the magistrates refused to accept by commission from the General Court

those powers they already had from the charter and from the freemen by the very fact of their elections as magistrates.[63]

The deputies responded that there already existed a precedent for allowing them to share in the government of the colony outside the General Court. They reminded the magistrates of the council of war of 1643 and of other variations from the charter. Constitutionally, the deputies took the position that the governor and other magistrates were the creatures of the General Court and had no powers other than those which the Court granted to them. The magistrates, on the other hand, denied that the council of war was any precedent at all. They argued that it had been contrary to the charter to begin with and was not a precedent but an error. In those areas where practice had varied from the demands of the charter, none of those other variations concerned fundamental matters. To the charge that the governor and assistants were the creatures of the General Court, the magistrates replied

that the governour and assistants had power of government before we had any written laws or had kept any courts; and to make a man a governour over a people, gives him, by necessary consequence, power to govern that people, otherwise there were no power in any commonwealth to order, dispose, or punish in any case where it might fall out, that these were no positive law declared in.

It was consented to that this court had authority to order and direct the power of these magistrates for time, place, persons etc., for the common good, but not wholly to deprive them of it, their office continuing: so as these being chosen by the people, by virtue of the patent to govern the people, a chief part whereof consists in counsel, they are the standing council of the commonwealth, and therefore in the

vacancy of this court, may act in all the affairs thereof
without any commission.[64]

The fundamental issue between the deputies and the
magistrates is exposed in this exchange. The deputies' ambition was to share not only in the legislative power of the
magistracy (as they already did in the General Court) but
also to share in its executive and judicial functions—in
short, to be magistrates. The magistrates argued that the
deputies would undermine the doctrine of the calling and
the divine sanction of the magistrate and would eventually
establish mob rule. In the past, whenever the magistrate
defended what they regarded as their legitimate rights under the charter, the deputies responded by dragging out
the "bloody shirt" of arbitrary government in an effort to
stir up the freemen against the magistrates. In 1644 the
the magistrates waved their own "bloody shirt": they accused the deputies of attempting to establish a democracy.

Their major proposal rejected, the deputies attempted
to salvage it by compromise. They suggested that the commission for a Standing Council specifically include all the
magistrates, that the deputies and Mr. Ward participate in
the governing of the colony only on matters of warfare,
and that this special council on war be the only council
which needed the commission of the General Court. All
the other matters of importance arising between sessions
of the General Court would be handled by the uncommis-
sioned Standing Council of magistrates, as in the past. But
the magistrates were unbending and rejected this proposal
too. They would accept nothing from the deputies which
attempted to commission them for any reason and which
did not include a statement to the effect that this authority
granted them by the General Court was one which they
also had by virtue of the charter. They would agree to
adding three or four nonmagistrates to participate in the
Council as the elders had earlier recommended if the deputies would agree that the magistrates served by virtue of

fundamental rights stemming from their election to office.[65]

At this point the deputies were angry. Although they probably should have accepted this offer, they did not. They wanted more than the magistrates were willing to give, and they were not about to accept the few concessions of the magistrates when they might gain more by appealing to the voters. The House of Deputies resolved that nothing should be done on the matter of the Standing Council until the Court met again in October. The magistrates agreed, but asserted that if an emergency arose between then and October, they intended to act upon it as they always had. To this, the Speaker, William Hawthorne, responded bluntly and menacingly, "You will not be obeyed." [66]

The magistrates were now quite certain that the deputies were about to engage in a massive propaganda campaign against them among the freemen, accusing the magistrates of attempting to effect an arbitrary rule over the colony.[67] To offset the deputies' efforts, all the magistrates but two (probably Saltonstall and Bellingham) agreed to sign a declaration maintaining their authority and denying their intention of creating a tyranny. They sent the declaration to the deputies and fully intended to publish it so that it might come to the attention of the freemen. They fully intended, also, to place squarely upon the deputies full responsibility for any collapse of authority in emergencies arising while the Court was not in session. The deputies requested that the magistrates withdraw their declaration and that another conference committee meet to compose formally and jointly a statement of the differences between them. The magistrates agreed and the conference committee stated the case as follows:

> whether the magistrates are by patent and election of
> the people the standing council of the commonwealth
> in the vacancy of the general court, and have power

accordingly to act in all cases subject to government, according to the said patent and the laws of this jurisdiction; and when any necessary occasions call for action from authority, in cases where there is no particular express law provided, there to be guided by the word of God, till the general court give particular rules in such cases.[68]

Actually, two different issues were raised in this statement—and one for the first time in this particular debate. The argument had been up to this point over the questions of who was to constitute the Standing Council and what were the origins of its power. But the conference committee raised the issues of how the Standing Council was to act—of what guidelines the Council was to follow in the absence of specific laws, and for that matter, what guidelines the magistrates in the Court of Assistants or in the inferior courts were to follow in the absence of law and specific penalties for violation of the law. In the months and years ahead the deputies would realize that this was a far more potent issue than the one they were now pursuing. It became more and more difficult to hold that the magistracy was dependent upon the General Court, and apparently the deputies had little success convincing the voters that it was the magistrates' tyrannical ambition which caused them to refuse to accept the deputies' interpretation. But limiting the discretionary powers of the magistrates by the establishment of set penalties for set crimes was a popular program which had much support among the freemen. The magistrates' efforts to block this was exploited by the deputies as another example of the tyrannical ambitions of the great gentlemen of the colony.[69]

The court session of May–June 1644, however, could not solve the issue of the Standing Council. All that could be done was to state the issue and to agree to a temporary arrangement for the handling of emergencies until the next session.[70]

During the summer of 1644 there occurred further developments in the struggle between deputies and magistrates. La Tour, now at a serious disadvantage with d'Aulnay, returned from France with reinforcements and an official declaration outlawing his rival. He hoped to obtain more aid from Massachusetts Bay, and arriving in Salem harbor, he asked for a conference with Governor Endecott. The governor had no desire to repeat Winthrop's mistakes. He had no intention of becoming further involved with the French if he could help it, but neither did he intend to take any steps without consulting the other leaders of the colony. He called together all the other magistrates and many of the elders of the colony for a special conference in Boston. Perhaps by bringing into the meeting the prestige of the elders, he could blunt much of the criticism he expected from the deputies. Endecott called the meeting for July 23.

The governor's meeting discussed the question of aid to La Tour, aid to belligerents in the war then raging in England, and the responsibility of masters toward their servants. Finally, Endecott arose and addressed the magistrates and ministers on a subject dear to his heart. He stated that he was deeply concerned over the constant fighting in the General Court between magistrates and deputies. The sources of these disputes, he felt, were ill-founded suspicions in which the ministers sometimes participated. He berated them for not handling them in a way of God, referring to the fact that it was frequently the clergy who stirred up opposition to the incumbent governor no matter who he was. They created by their attitudes deep suspicions among the voters. In addition, they did nothing to uphold the dignity of the magistrates in their towns. This was particularly pressing during that

summer, for apparently the deputies were doing their best
to blacken the names of their opponents. Endecott accused
the ministers of "hearing them reproached and passing it
in silence: also their authority questioned, as if they had
none out of court but what must be granted them by commission from the general court, etc." [71]

Endecott, even if he had been elected by those opposed
to the magistrates, was no Bellingham. His break with
Winthrop had been short, and he had made his peace with
his friend as soon as he was convinced that he had done his
best in the La Tour case. On all other issues they were
of one mind.

In his speech Endecott was taking the ministers to task.
They were quick enough to jump in against the magistrates when they had the slightest suspicion that the magistrates were taking too much power, but in this case it
was the deputies who clearly sought to undermine the
constitution of the colony by depriving the magistrates of
their power, while the elders looked on in silence. By their
mediation in October 1642 on the issue of the Standing
Council and Saltonstall's book, the elders had opened the
door to participation by the deputies in the Standing
Council. It was they who had opened the Pandora's Box.
Endecott's call was clear: do your duty; redress the present imbalance!

The elders responded by agreeing to meet together before the next session of the General Court and to attempt
to bring about a reconciliation between the magistrates
and the deputies. The magistrates present at the Boston
meeting went home content except for Bellingham and
Saltonstall, who voted against this interference by the
elders.

When John Winthrop returned to his study after meeting with the magistrates and ministers, he returned to a
labor he had set for himself and had diligently pursued
for the whole period between sessions of the General

Court. It is not absolutely certain why Winthrop decided at this time to write a discourse on arbitrary government and a defense of the Massachusetts system. Perhaps he hoped to offset the propaganda the deputies were indulging in that summer. Endecott referred to increased agitation by the deputies when he took the elders to task for not checking it. No matter what the reason, it was apparently necessary in the summer of 1644 to deny categorically any tyrannical intentions on the part of the magistrates.

Winthrop began his treatise with a definition of arbitrary government. A government was arbitrary "where a people have men sett over them without their choyce, or allowance: who have power, to Governe them, and Judge their Causes without a Rule." Such absolute power belonged solely to God. For man to usurp these divine prerogatives was "Tiranye and impietye." Winthrop went on to conclude: "Where the people have Libertye to admitt or reject their Governors; and to require the Rule, by which they shalbe governed and Judged, this is not an Arbitraye Government." [72] In the light of this definition Winthrop declared that Massachusetts Bay was no tyranny. It was protected by the charter, by positive law and common custom.

Winthrop proclaimed that under the charter the body politic was reduced to two kinds of members—the governor, to whom were added the deputy governor and the assistants and in whom rested the power of authority, and the company or the freemen, in whom rested the power of liberty. The liberty of the freemen was not merely passive freedom but a liberty of action—the liberty to elect and to counsel. Winthrop, despite the years of agitation, was still unwilling to grant any role whatsoever to the deputies other than a carrying out of some of the freemen's responsibilities. His treatise, therefore, was not calculated to bring peace to the colony. If anything, it would frustrate the deputies all the more.

Massachusetts was not only ruled by men of the free-men's choosing; it was also governed according to a rule. For some time, there had been talk of forcing a compila-tion of the laws with penalties established for stipulated crimes. Many asserted that unless such a compilation were made and published, the magistrates would have too great a discretion in punishing crime. A lack of uniformity would lead to a lack of justice, and the colony would be on its way toward tyranny. Winthrop had admitted that without a rule of law a government would become arbi-trary, but in his treatise he tried to show that Massachu-setts Bay was governed according to a rule without any compilation of laws. Apparently he was alarmed when this new issue had been raised (at the previous session of the General Court). In his new work he hoped to quiet it for good. Winthrop asserted that the laws of the colony provided a rule. The law of May 25, 1636, stated: "It was Ordered, that untill a bodye of Fundamentall Lawes (Agreeable to the word of God) were established, all causes should be heard and determined accordinge to the Lawes allreadye in force: and where no Lawe is, there, as neere the Lawe of God as may be." [73] Winthrop offered further proof of his assertions by citing The Body of Liber-ties, which guaranteed the basic rights of freemen and nonfreemen alike, and which was a sufficient compilation. In Winthrop's eyes, they had rule enough to preserve the government from any charge of arbitrary power. The laws of the colony, The Body of Liberties, and the word of God were their rule.

To his own satisfaction, the deputy governor had proved that Massachusetts was not an arbitrary government be-cause the people chose their officers and lived by a rule. This was the first goal of his treatise. Secondly, he had attempted to blunt the propaganda of the deputies, whom he still refused to recognize as anything but spokes-men for the freemen. He tried to show that a lack of prescribed penalties for specific crimes did not constitute a lack of a "rule."

The arguments seemed convincing to Winthrop, but he must have known they would be unacceptable to the deputies—if only because he ignored them totally. He must have known, also, that two years before, the elders had rejected his viewpoint and had suggested the participation of the deputies in the Standing Council. Perhaps Winthrop hoped that his long, logical discourse would win converts among the elders and help to put an end to any further agitation.

Winthrop does not immediately inform us concerning reaction to his book. But one year later, in 1645, in discussing the events which led to the Court dispute over the Hingham militia, he states that the year before he had received poor treatment. Apparently, during the summer he showed a draft of the work to several deputies. He found approval from some and silence from others. After he showed it to the other magistrates and most of the elders, he expanded it, completed it, and intended to present it formally to the General Court when it returned to Boston in October. But on the first day of the session some of the deputies read a copy of the document in the Court and proclaimed it a "dangerous libel of some unknown author." [74] They were well aware of the author's identity, but Winthrop speculated that they were afraid he would receive the same immunity that their friend Saltonstall had received when questioned about his book on the Standing Council. If no one knew the author was a magistrate, there was no need not to pursue the matter with the utmost vigor. The deputies, discouraged by the ambivalent attitude of the elders in their mediation, and perhaps realizing that a commissioning of the magistrates would never get through the General Court, found in Winthrop's discourse a new weapon and a new cause. His denial of the need for set penalties could be construed as

an attempt to prevent uniform and equal justice. It
smacked of high-handed arbitrary law and could be used
against him and the other magistrates by the deputies.
It became the issue which the deputies fought to exploit
from 1644 until, in 1648, they achieved victory with the
publication of the Book of General Laws.

In the meantime the deputies organized a special committee to investigate Winthrop's book. The committee's
findings were unfavorable, and the House of Deputies
voted approval of the committee's work, describing Winthrop's definition of arbitrary government as defective,
although why they found it so they did not reveal. The
deputies had no hesitation about giving their opinion of
Winthrop's distinction between the power of liberty and
the power of authority. The committee reported, and the
house approved a condemnation of that point of view as
unsupported by the charter. They accused the author of
the book of attempting to deny legitimate authority and
power to the freemen—even in the General Court. Concerning Winthrop's assertion that Massachusetts was governed by a rule—although a general one and thus free
of any charge of arbitrary government—the deputies listed
this view "a dangerous position" and labeled in the same
manner another of the deputy governor's positions that
"Judges ought to have Libertye to varye from suche generall Rules when they see Cause." [75]

The deputies picked up the author's denial of a need
for set penalties and accused him of perpetrating "per-
nitious and dangerous reasons and consequences." They
insisted that if the judges were not bound by an exact and
carefully prescribed rule and set of penalties, then the
possibility of arbitrary government would exist, with the
implication that resistance to their point of view was nothing more than the magistrates attempting to force tyranny
upon Massachusetts Bay. Perhaps they were sincere in
their accusations, but no doubt they found the charge of

tyranny a highly effective and useful weapon against the power of the magistrates.

The findings of the House of Deputies were sent to the magistrates with a request that they condemn the book and censure the "unknown" author. Winthrop claims that their ultimate ambition was to remove him from office, and considering the events of the next year, he may have been correct. But as events were to prove, that was no easy thing to do. The magistrates had no intention of approving any such move. Most likely, the deputies only hoped to reduce the prestige of the greatest of all the magistrates and in so doing reduce the prestige of magistrates in general. The magistrates, however, refused to go along with the deputies' report. Winthrop composed an answer to their charges against his book, but the matter was for all practical purposes dropped temporarily.[76]

Winthrop's troubles with the deputies over his book were the first fruits of the Standing Council mediation efforts of the ministers—an indication that the suggestions of the elders did not necessarily carry great weight with the deputies.

When in October 1644 the ministers met in Boston to consider the major questions dividing the magistrates and deputies, the question presented to them for answering was "whether the magistrates are, by patent and election of the people, the standing council of the commonwealth in the vacancy of the general court, and have power accordingly to act in all cases subject to government, according to the said patent and the laws of this jurisdiction." [77] This is not the same question formulated by the joint committee of the Court in June. It merely seeks to solve the basis for the authority of the Standing Council. The June question also called for a ruling concerning the procedures by which the Standing Council should act.

On the day after the elders went into consultation—October 31, 1644—they asked to meet with the General

Court to give their answer. The report of the elders was
delivered by John Cotton. Perhaps friendly elders had revealed the thrust of Cotton's intended remarks to the deputies beforehand, since they did not attend this extraordinary meeting in a body, but sent a committee of four as
their representatives. Winthrop reported this as a deliberate insult to the elders, considering that some had traveled
as far as thirty miles to attend the session. All we know of
Cotton's remarks is that they were "affirmative on the
magistrates behalf." [78] The elders were consistent to principle in their decision, however. They had determined
that that the Standing Council was a necessary adjunct to
the powers of the magistrates, and they would not agree
to allow the deputies to dominate it. But domination and
participation were two different things. The elders had
not reneged on their opinion that the deputies should participate. The deputies had been offered participation.
They should have accepted it.

The deputies were not finished with the elders, however. They had lost the first round only. They pushed the
elders for an answer to the second part of the original
question: Should the magistrates be guided by a set code
of law? And they wanted an answer to help determine
whether or not the magistrates needed commissions from
the General Court, and whether in fact the deputies had
any magisterial functions. The ministers answered that the
magistrates should be bound by an express rule and thus
came out in support of less discretion for them—a position
distinctly opposed to that held by Winthrop but consistent
with the elders' desire to check all magisterial power
which they deemed over and above their necessary powers. On the rest of the points raised by the deputies, their
answers were closer to the positions held by the magistrates. Magistrates were magistrates by right of the charter,
not by any commission from the General Court. If they
needed commissioning, then the General Court would

have the right to leave some magistrates elected by the people out of the magistracy, thus frustrating the intention of the freemen. The implication is, of course, that the elders did distinguish between deputies and freemen even if Winthrop refused to. Authority, according to the patent, lay in the governor and assistants; to the freemen was given the right to name the governor and assistants.

The ministers then went on to define the role of the General Court. It was the highest civil authority in the colony. It had executive, legislative, and certain judicial powers—those of impeachment of general officers and receiving appeals in civil and criminal cases provided that such appeals were from cases tried first in inferior court and then in the Court of Assistants. Whatever magisterial functions the deputies had, they had as part of the General Court. The magistrates now probably had no intention of sharing magisterial power outside the Court, and on this point the elders were now silent.

The magistrates then put questions to the elders. They wanted a clarification of their position on the need for fixed laws and fixed penalties. They asked "whether we may warrantably prescribe certain penalties to offenses which may probably admit variable degrees of guilt." The answer given was not altogether clear, but the elders seemed to say that the punishment should fit the crime. The magistrates questioned further "whether a judge be bound to pronounce such sentences as a positive law prescribes in case it be apparently above or below the merit of the offense." The elders, who seemed not to want to be pinned down on these specifics, continued to insist that positive law should fix the penalties although the judge should have the power to lessen the punishment but never to increase it.[79]

What had the mediation of the elders accomplished? The power of the magistrates—to be magistrates and to be a Standing Council without a commission from the Gen-

eral Court—had been upheld. These were powers essential
to the magistracy if the magistrates were to function duti-
fully. On the other hand, the elders had reaffirmed the
General Court's position as the supreme authority in the
colony and had reaffirmed to the deputies through their
participation in the Court a limited judicial function. The
right of the deputies to serve in a Standing Council had
not been resolved, but considering both the elders' failure
to speak on the subject and the growing opposition of the
magistrates, it did not seem likely that the deputies would
ever participate in the Council. To a certain extent, however, this was balanced by the elders' support of the need
for a book of laws. The magistrates must have been
alarmed by any indication of support for the magisterial
pretentions of the deputies, and they must have been unhappy with the elders' opinions on a book of laws. But still
the magistrates probably emerged stronger and the deputies weaker.

The deputies' efforts to advance their powers had been
thwarted. It is not surprising, therefore, that they would
attempt to exploit what small advantage they gained from
the mediation of the elders. The ministers had granted judicial powers to the deputies as part of the General Court
in cases of appeal and in cases of crimes in office by high
officials. One way to attack the Standing Council was to
check on the activities of its members, and if they exceeded their powers or rendered justice in an arbitrary
fashion, then the General Court and particularly the deputies could exercise the judicial powers granted them by the
elders, which even the magistrates would not dare to challenge. In 1645 the deputies gained the opportunity to act
as judges as one result of an incredibly involved and angry
dispute in the town of Hingham, and in their desperation
the deputies leaped at the chance. It was to be the cul-
mination of their struggle for recognition.

3 The Hingham Militia Case

Bare (or Bear) Cove—a site about equal distances between the old fishing stations of Weymouth and Hull—was settled by Norfolk men in 1633. The place was renamed Hingham in honor of the settlers who had come from Hingham in Norfolk. A second influx of Norfolk men arrived in 1635 and included Edmund Hobart, Sr., and his sons Edmund Jr., Thomas, Joshua, and the pride of the family, the Reverend Peter Hobart.* From 1635 on, the Norfolk group dominated life in this new Hingham, with the Hobarts dominating the Norfolk group. Between 1639 and 1641 Edmund Sr. served as a Hingham deputy five times. His son Joshua served as a deputy twenty-six times between 1643 and 1681 and was Speaker of the House of Deputies. The board of selectmen in Hingham was also Hobart-influenced. Peter Hobart was chosen pastor of the Hingham church in 1635 and ruled his congregation firmly until his death in 1679—so firmly, in fact, and with so little consultation with his congregation that Winthrop accused him of being of a "Presbyterial spirit." [1] Among other Norfolk men who held positions of power was Bozoan Allen from Lynn in Norfolk, whom Peter Hobart described as his "very good friend" upon Allen's death in 1652,[2] and who served eight terms as a deputy from 1643 to 1652 and was second in command of the town militia. John Beal of old Hingham was twice deputy to the General Court in 1649 and 1659, and his son Nathaniel also served as a Hingham deputy. Daniel Cushing, born in old Hingham in 1619 and who migrated to new Hingham in 1638 with his father, mother, and five broth-

* Peter Hobart attended Magdalen College, Cambridge. He received his A.B. in 1625 and his M.A. in 1629.

ers and sisters, served as town selectman, as town clerk from 1669 until 1700, and twice as deputy to the General Court under the old charter. Jeremiah Howchen of Halleston in Norfolk, although he never lived in Hingham and was a resident of Boston, was nevertheless called upon by his former Norfolk neighbors to represent them in the General Court six times from 1651 to 1659. Nicholas Jacob, who came from old Hingham to the new town in 1633, represented the town in the Court in 1648 and 1649. Stephen Paine from Great Ellingham in Norfolk, who came to new Hingham in 1638, served in the General Court in 1641 but left the town for Plymouth Colony shortly afterward. Joseph Peck was born in Beccles in Suffolk, but he too can be classified as a Norfolk man, since he migrated to old Hingham to enjoy the preaching of his brother, the Reverend Robert Peck, who was vicar of the old Hingham church. Joseph Peck spent many years in old Hingham, migrated to New England in 1638, and served as a deputy eight times between 1638 and 1642. Robert Peck came also to new Hingham and joined Peter Hobart as teacher of the new Hingham church. Henry Smith, a Norfolk man, was deacon of the new Hingham church and served once as deputy to the General Court. In all, eleven Norfolk men served as Hingham deputies, holding sixty-seven of a possible one hundred seats in the General Court from 1636 to 1686. In addition, they held a large number of the selectmen's posts, although the records on this matter are only fragmentary and do not particularly lend themselves to valid generalizations. The Norfolk men, however, and more particularly, the old Hingham men, were the most powerful political force in new Hingham affairs. Those who did not fit in with the Hingham clique held few, if any, political offices.[3]

The one exception to this Norfolk domination was the commander of the town militia—Lieutenant Anthony Eames, a West Countryman who arrived in Hingham in

1636 after the two influxes of old Hingham settlers. Eames became a freeman of the colony in 1637, and a member of the Hingham church. He served several times as deputy to the General Court, but only once after 1639. He was a respected citizen of the town and a man in whom his fellow citizens put considerable trust. In 1645 the militia band of Hingham was raised to the dignity of a company, and its commander, Lieutenant Eames, seemed the logical candidate for the post of captain. The militia band met, Eames was elected, and his name was presented to the magistrates, acting as a Standing Council, for approval.

Just what happened in the interval between the presentation of Eames and the next meeting of the Hingham militia band is unknown. Perhaps the other leaders of the community saw an opportunity to remove the "outsider"; perhaps Eames acted in some manner which antagonized his fellow townsmen. When the Hingham militia band met again, the members determined to change their nomination of Eames and substituted Bozoan Allen as their choice for the post of captain. Since the magistrates had not yet acted upon Eames's nomination, the Hingham band obviously felt that they were well within their rights in changing their minds. They submitted Allen's name to the magistrates for approval.

The magistrates refused to consider Allen's nomination, since they felt it would injure Eames's legitimate claims. He had been lieutenant for many years, and since Allen did not seem to possess any qualities superior to Eames and "had no other skill, but what he learned from Eames," the magistrates advised both Eames and Allen supporters to return to Hingham and maintain the status quo, stating that Eames should train the Hingham band for the time being.[4]

It is clear not only that Eames initially had some support in Hingham, but that the refusal of the magistrates to agree with the decision of the majority of the Hingham train band was regarded by many in the town as a violation of their rights to choose their own leaders. It was a clear-cut interference in the affairs of their town and another example of magisterial high-handedness and the danger presented by the Standing Council. Many, who perhaps earlier were willing to support Eames, now switched to support Allen's candidacy.

Eames was present when the Standing Council gave its official decision, after which the maverick magistrate, Richard Bellingham, took Eames aside and advised him that the best thing he could do was "to goe home, goe into the field, and honorably lay doune his place."[5] Either Bellingham said the same thing to others at the meeting, or other interested parties were present at his conference with Eames. In any case, Bellingham's words were used against him.

One of the messengers of the militia band present at the meeting of the Standing Council in which the magistrates found for Eames was Joshua Hobart, a supporter of Allen. When he returned to Hingham, he called a meeting in a private home and reported to the train band that the magistrates had decided to continue Eames in office for the present. But he also reported that Bellingham, a magistrate, and therefore a person in authority, had told Eames to resign. The implication was that Eames should and would follow Bellingham's advice.

On the next day Hobart ordered a drill session for the train band. When it assembled on the field, the lieutenant was missing. But rather than this being a sign of his intended resignation, it was the result of failing to inform him of Hobart's call for a drill. Eames received word of the assembly and rushed to the training field to take command. In a very dramatic moment the lieutenant faced his troops and barked his first command, only to be met with silence and stillness: no man moved a muscle. Eames, no doubt slightly flustered, repeated his command. This time the response was a demand from Joshua Hobart that he show some order from authority granting him the right to train the band. Eames answered that he had the authority of the magistrates' recent decision. When Hobart demanded to see the written order of the magistrates and Eames refused to show it, Hobart asserted that Eames was lying and that he had heard a magistrate advise him to resign.

After Hobart had finished, there were rumbles of approval from the ranks. Someone shouted that even if some magistrates had found for Eames, it was only three or four of them and they had no authority to overrule the train band, even if all of them had been present. Another shouted, "What had the magistrates to do with them?" Still another militiaman proclaimed his willingness to die for his right to pick his own officers. At this point the clerk of the band called for an immediate vote of all the citizens of Hingham present at this confrontation to determine whether or not they would support their train band. Once they had given their endorsement, Joshua Hobart called upon his friend Bozoan Allen to assume his "rightful" post as captain, but Allen refused, saying he would not assume the post unless a new vote for captain were taken. This was agreed to, the train band was polled again, and Allen won easily. Allen was now convinced of the legality of his election, took command, and continued to train the band for the next two or three days. Eames left the field in a huff, muttering (according to John Folsom, an opponent of his) that he would never lead the Hingham militia into the field again.

Eames, however, was not without friends in Hingham. Winthrop says that about a third of the band refused to train under Allen and followed Eames off the field.[6] But on the next Sunday the full power of the old Hingham group, and particularly of the Hobart family, was brought to bear upon poor Eames, who was accused by his brethren in the church of lying when he had denied that authority had advised him to lay down his position. When Eames denied the charge, witnesses who had been trainband messengers to the Standing Council, and present at the meeting with the magistrates, were called upon to testify. One of these, John Folsom, a native of old Hingham, testified in the church that he had heard both Governor Dudley and Deputy Governor Winthrop say that they had given no order to Eames to train the militia band, nor could they have given such an order. Winthrop and Dudley later denied having uttered those words, and Folsom, when called upon to testify under oath that they had, refused and was jailed. Then Joshua Hobart, who was called upon to answer Eames's charge that he had lied, testified that Bellingham had advised Eames to resign. Bellingham was a magistrate and therefore in a position of authority. He had thus not lied when he asserted that authority had told Eames to resign. John Tower, another native of old Hingham and also a messenger, corroborated Hobart's story.[7]

Pastor Hobart had now heard enough. He called upon Eames to repent his sins, and when he refused, the pastor —who, as a Presbyterian, tended to allow himself far greater powers as pastor than most of his colleagues in Massachusetts Bay would have approved of—had a mind to cast him out of the church. However, several members of the church objected to such haste and demanded that any further action be delayed until tempers cooled. Those in favor of delay prevailed.[8]

The next few days brought the first outside intervention in the Hingham case. When Lieutenant Eames appealed to the magistrates for redress, they responded by requesting several elders from nearby churches to write to Hobart in an attempt to prevent his excommunication of Eames and to forestall any schism in the Hingham church. The only effect of this intervention was to delay further, by a few days, Hobart's plans for expelling Eames. Seeing that a majority of the church would in all likelihood agree to Hobart's plan, Eames and twelve of his friends formally stood up in the congregation and withdrew from communion with the rest of the church.[9]

These interventions were ordered by a minority of the magistrates, the Standing Council—those magistrates who happened to be in Boston at the time. When Eames made his complaint, Winthrop, John Endecott, Increase Nowell, and William Hibbens were available. These four then summoned five of the Hingham ringleaders, especially Joshua Hobart and his brothers Thomas and Edmund, and told them to be prepared to find "surities" for their appearance before the next General Court. The Hobarts came to Boston accompanied by their brother, Peter. The pastor attacked Eames and his supporters, calling them talebearers, and complained that his brothers should be summoned before the magistrates like criminals. Hobart was a hothead and his speech apparently soon grew into a tirade which the magistrates found offensive. They finally halted him and told him that the only thing keeping him out of the Boston jail for contempt was their respect for the cloth. When the Reverend Hobart's brothers were questioned concerning Eames's accusations, Winthrop claims that they denied most of them and were then bound over to the next Court of Assistants.[10]

The magistrates followed this action by summoning five men who had testified concerning the magistrates decision, and against Eames, in the Hingham church. These five came to Deputy Governor Winthrop, apparently at his home, when he was alone. They demanded an explanation of the charges against them and demanded to know the names of their accusers. Winthrop, unprepared for this attack, told them as much of the accusations as he could remember and referred them to Secretary Nowell for a written copy. As for their accusers, Winthrop told them they knew the men and the matter. Perhaps, then, in an effort to regain his dignity in front of these brash defendants, Winthrop haughtily asserted that he had no intention of revealing the names of their accusers. The five Hingham men later said that he based his refusal on the law of God and man. The deputy governor denied saying this. Winthrop then ordered the five to give bond for their appearance before the courts. They refused. Trying to be reasonable, Winthrop argued with them to show them their errors and then dismissed them to give them time to reconsider. Perhaps he also realized that he had gone a little too far in his claims for his powers concerning the concealment of the accusers. Finally, two weeks later, he spied two of the five, Folsom and Tower, at a session of the Suffolk inferior court. He again requested that they give bond, and again they refused. Winthrop felt compelled to commit them to jail.[11]

Now it was the turn of Hingham to react. A petition signed by eighty-one persons was drawn up for presentation to the General Court: *

> To the Honoured, the Generall Court, consisting of the Magistrates and Deputies of the Country now assembled in Court at Boston: The humble Petition of the greater part of the Inhabitants of the Township of Hingham
>
> Whereas there hath fallen out some agitations amongst us concerning the choice of our chief Mili-

* This figure of 81 probably represents the vast majority of the males over 16 years old (the minimum age for service in the militia). The adult male population (21 and over) in 1647 was only 79. This figure is lower than Waters's estimate of total population for Hingham in 1640, although his figure of 131 families does not seem to consider those which settled in Hingham and then left to settle other towns. See John J. Waters, "Hingham, Massachusetts, 1631–1661 . . . ," *Journal of Social History* 1 (June 1968): 352.

tary Officers, which by Order of the Court we have
power to choose (as we conceive) So it is that we did
elect and present to the Generall Court for their con-
firmation, Mr. Bozoune Allin for our Chieftain: but
the Court not having time to finish that business at
that time, some other things and overtures have happened since, whereby it hath so fallen out that some
of us have been compelled to appeare before some of
the Magistrates, and to give Bonds for appearance at
a Quarter-Court which is to be holden after this
Generall Court; and some for not giving Bond to answer there, are committed to prison, and remain there
at present: the matters of accusation (as we conceive) is
for certain words spoken by some, concerning the liberty and power of the Generall Court, and our own liberty granted to us by the said Courts, and to the Country in generall; and also it doth concern the Liberty
of an English free-borne Member of that State, and
further it hath occasioned such disturbance and
schisme in our Church, and trouble to some of our
Members for witness against a Delinquent: whereby
the power of the Ordinances of Jesus Christ in his
Church is slighted, and the free passage thereof
stopped, to the endangering of the liberty of the
Churches amongst us, if timely remedy be not by
your Wisdoms provided. Now seeing the matters in
hand doth concern the generall liberty of the whole
Country, and the peace of the Churches, and glory of
God, as we are ready upon the hearing of the Court
to make it appeare; We humbly sue to this honoured
Court to be pleased to grant us an honourable and
free hearing, and that we may have liberty to plead
our common Liberties in this Court, together with
the liberties of the Churches of Christ maintained.
And we shall ever pray for your peace and prosperity
long to continue.[12]

The leaders of Hingham had taken a new course. They were appealing to the lower house of the General Court for redress against the usurpations and high-handed applications of power by the magistrates. They were identifying their cause with the cause of the local leadership in their struggle for power with the magistrates. At the same time, two Hingham citizens, Joshua Hobart and John Folsom, registered complaints against the deputy governor, one for binding him to the Court of Assistants and the other for committing him to prison when he failed to post bond. The issue of magistrates versus deputies would be reduced to Winthrop versus Hingham.

Perhaps it appeared the obvious thing to do considering the struggles of the years preceding, as well as the animosity which existed between deputies and magistrates. On the other hand, the appeal to the deputies may have been part of a carefully organized plot to bring about reforms granting greater liberties to those who disagreed with the established order in Massachusetts Bay. It may have been the work of one prominent enemy of the established order.

William Vassall was one of the original assistants of the Massachusetts Bay Colony. He had accompanied Winthrop in 1630, but had returned to England and never again held public office in Massachusetts Bay. He returned to the New World but settled in Plymouth Colony rather than in Massachusetts.

It is difficult to label William Vassall's convictions. Winthrop was not overly fond of him, but has left one of the few evaluations of him:

> One Mr. William Vassall, sometimes one of the assistants of the Massachusetts, but now of Scituate in Plymouth jurisdiction, a man of a busy and factious spirit, and always opposite to the civil government of this country and the way of our churches, had practised with such as were not members of our churches

to take some course, first by petitioning the courts of the Massachusetts and of Plimouth, and (if that suceeded not) then to the parliament of England, that the distinctions which were maintained here, both in civil and church estate, might be taken away, and that we might be wholly governed by the laws of England.[13]

Winthrop's description and Vassall's association with Presbyterians have prompted observers to classify him as a Presbyterian. Further support is given to this classification by Vassall's founding of the second Scituate church after breaking with Charles Chauncy, the pastor of the first church. The second church apparently had very liberal policies about admitting persons to communion.[14] Vassall seems to have been dedicated also to overturning the power of the political elites of Plymouth and Massachusetts Bay. He may have wished to see greater extensions of English law and may have felt that the concepts of the leaders of Massachusetts Bay in particular were a danger to his enjoyment of his basic rights as a freeborn Englishman, or he may have been a demagogue who wished a share of their power for himself. Nevertheless, he was a lifelong opponent of those who ruled Massachusetts Bay— the New World agent of those in England who denounced the New England Way. Many of those who condemned Massachusetts Bay were Presbyterians, while many others were Independents who had accepted the solution of religious toleration.

No matter which group Vassall belonged to, his intentions were clear. He hoped to upset the status quo in both Plymouth and Massachusetts. Perhaps he correctly understood the struggle between the magistrates and the deputies as a power struggle within the structure but hoped to take advantage of the disagreements within Massachusetts to further his own ambitions. Perhaps he thought his goals would be advanced by a reduction in magisterial power or by discrediting the most magisterial of the magistrates— John Winthrop. Or he may truly have miscalculated the events in the Bay Colony, viewing them as a fundamental struggle between tyranny and freedom, and hoped for a victory by the deputies. Whatever, the Hingham case seemed like a golden opportunity to further the cause of the deputies and to further the cause of William Vassall.

In 1645 Vassall was living in the Plymouth Colony town of Scituate, which bordered the Massachusetts town of Hingham. He must have been aware of the disturbance in Hingham shortly after it began, and must have noticed how the Hingham case could be translated into another struggle between the deputies and the magistrates if the Hingham leaders could be induced to appeal to the deputies. Edward Winslow in his *New England's Salamander* asserts that at this point Vassall's interventions were the decisive factor: "But our Salamander [Vassall] living too neere them, and being too well acquainted with them, blew up this to such a height by his continuall counsell and advise which the major part of the Toune followed to their owne smart, and the great griefe and trouble of Church and Commonwealth." [15] Now it is true that when he wrote those words Winslow was Vassall's bitter enemy, but there is no reason to doubt that Vassall would consult with the Hobarts and Bozoan Allen in a case so sure to further his own plans. Winslow also claims that in the events that followed, it was Vassall who masterminded the Hingham assault on the power of the magistrates: "our Salamander was got to Boston, where though hee would not openly show himselfe, yet kept close in a private roome where they [the Hinghaam petitioners] had recorse to him many dayes, yea many times a day for advice, and followed it to the utmost, to the great charge of the countrey." [16]

The election of 1645 continued the predominance of the anti-Winthrop faction. It was able to prevent his election as governor, and Thomas Dudley succeeded Endecott, who was elected sergeant major of the militia. Dudley was not an Essex man but at least he wasn't Winthrop. Although he was known in the past to have opposed Winthrop, the differences between them were personal rather than ideological and were clashes of personalities and ambitions. Dudley's popularity with the freemen and support from Essex from the lesser gentry and the clergy combined to overcome the heavy support which Winthrop could be expected to receive in every election. Winthrop retained his position as deputy governor and in this capacity confronted the most serious assault on his power and prestige he had ever faced.

The other participants in the 1645 debates would be the same magistrates as those of 1644, with the addition of Herbert Pelham of Cambridge. Richard Saltonstall, who had requested his removal from the lists of magistrates, was denied his request and was reelected.[17] The magistrates remained divided as they had been in the past. Bellingham and Saltonstall, occasionally joined by Bradstreet, stood in opposition to magisterial prerogative and were opposed by the rest of the upper house. Opposed to the majority of the magistracy were the deputies. In 1645 they numbered thirty-six. Sixteen of the total number had served in 1644, and twenty-six of the thirty-six had served in the General Court since the beginning of the struggles between deputies and magistrates. The deputies from Hingham were Joshua Hobart and Bozoan Allen. It was obvious that Hingham had every intention of pushing its cause with the deputies.

On the first day of the Court of Elections—May 14, 1645—the petition of the eighty-one inhabitants of Hingham was presented to the deputies. The deputies regarded

the Hingham case as a ready-made opportunity to recover
from the disappointments of the elders' mediation. It offered them the opportunity to demonstrate that it was the
excessive powers of the magistrates which presented the
greatest dangers to the country—a theme which had been
useful in rallying support to the deputies in the past. It
offered them the opportunity to act as a check on the proceedings of the Standing Council and to embarrass the
leading magistrate in the colony, to portray the deputy
governor as an abuser of popular liberties. It was an opportunity the deputies eagerly took up. They agreed to
receive the Hingham petition and complaints against Deputy Governor Winthrop, but unfortunately for them,
they did this without heeding the proverbial admonition
about looking before leaping.[18]

After entertaining the petition, the deputies were then
faced with the problem of what to do with it. How were
they to proceed? They submitted it to the magistrates and
asked their concurrence that the cause be heard. The magistrates expressed shock that any such petition should be
allowed by the deputies without a conference with them
first, but they agreed that a hearing could be held as long
as the Hingham petitioners would single out the magistrates they charged and stipulated exactly what they were
charged with.[19]

Hobart and Allen spoke for their fellow townsmen.
They named Winthrop as the defendant for having summoned the Hobarts before him and having had them
bound over to the Court of Assistants, and for having
others imprisoned for failure to give bond. Apparently several of the magistrates thought there were grounds for refusing to entertain the petition. Winthrop was accused for
doing what he had every right to do, and the charges
against him were ridiculous. Winthrop disagreed. He was
anxious to clear his name and by so doing to uphold the
authority of his fellow magistrates, "knowing well how

much himself and the other magistrates did suffer in the cause through the slanderous reports wherewith the deputies and the country about had been possessed." [20]

Winthrop was shrewd enough to realize that the deputies had gone too far. The magistrates were insisting on criminal charges being brought against Winthrop. If the deputies accepted this in their thoughtless quest to embarrass the magistrates, they would in effect be calling for an impeachment trial of the most important and probably most consistently popular magistrate in the colony, and they were demanding his removal for his insistence on following his conscience. Even the most bitter enemy of the magistrates among the deputies, if he stopped and thought, must have realized he was falling into a trap. The impeachment of Winthrop was an impossibility. If the deputies succeeded, they would have to face the ire of the impeached magistrate's numerous supporters among the freemen. If they failed, the deputies would suffer a defeat of far more staggering proportions than the October mediation by the elders. Their only hope was to drop the whole issue, using it only as anti-Winthrop propaganda. The deputies, however, failed to see the trap. They accepted the magistrates demand for a public hearing on specific charges involving specific individuals.[21]

The day set for Winthrop's trial was in the second week of June 1645. The General Court met in the Boston meetinghouse in joint session. A large number of the citizens of Boston and the surrounding towns jammed into the building to witness what was clearly the most spectacular event since the downfall of Sir Henry Vane and Ann Hutchinson in 1637. As the magistrates entered the room and seated themselves in the high places of judgment, Winthrop left them and stepped down into the seat of the accused and removed his hat. It was a dramatic gesture and an emotional one, but above all, a calculated one. Immediately, a murmur of opposition ran through the Court and the crowd. The deputy governor was being treated like a common criminal. When these objections were voiced, Winthrop responded that, on the contrary, he was accused of criminal actions and therefore could not sit in judgment on himself; furthermore, he had no intention of jeopardizing his own defense by remaining in the supposedly impartial judgment seat.[22]

Joshua Hobart and Bozoan Allen, the deputies from Hingham, then proceeded to present the case of the Hingham petitioners against Winthrop. They asserted that he had acted illegally in binding Hobart and his brothers over to the Court of Assistants, and that he had acted illegally in imprisoning Folsom and Tower for standing on their rights and refusing to post bond for witnessing in a church matter.

Then it was Winthrop's turn to speak. The deputy governor began by stating that he felt no disgrace at being called upon to defend the cause of the magistrates, and that he could have based his defense on the intrinsic weakness of the petition itself. Winthrop claimed that his actions were totally justifiable. There were clear reports of mutinous actions in Hingham. He had sent for the accused offenders, and finding good cause for their standing trial for their actions, he bound them over and imprisoned those who had contemptuously refused to post bond. All of his actions were justifiable under Massachusetts law and custom of the past fifteen years, as well as under English law. He denied ever saying that it was against the law of God and man for justices to reveal the names of accusors to the accused before the trial. He admitted saying that judges can at their discretion conceal the accuser from the accused to protect him from harm, but he did not base this opinion on any law of God or man. Furthermore, were accused criminals themselves adequate witnesses to what a magistrate had said or not said?

Winthrop, in short, denied all wrongdoing. His actions

were those proper to a magistrate. If the deputies condemned him, then they condemned him for doing his
duty and with him they condemned all judges. Without
judges there was no law. To condemn Winthrop was to
invite chaos into Massachusetts Bay.[23]

Both sides had been heard, and now it was the turn of
the General Court to deliberate and reach a decision. For
two days deputies and magistrates argued publicly without
even agreeing on how to state the case. Again and again
the debate returned to the fundamental question of whether
the magistrates had too much authority or whether authority was much slighted in the colony. Finally, the deputies and the magistrates each named three men to a joint
committee whose function it was to state the case as it appeared from the charges and from the evidence given. Yet
even the committee spent a great deal of time debating the
issues—although this time in private.[24]

Finally, the magistrates withdrew to their separate meeting place, leaving the deputies to argue the case among
themselves. But now they were divided more than they
had been in the past. Winthrop's defense of himself was
superb, and fewer and fewer of the deputies were willing
to participate in any attempt to impeach him. On June 16
the deputies turned to the magistrates and asked them to
render their decision in the case.[25]

What they received back from the upper house certainly
could not have been to their liking. The magistrates now
held the advantage and were not about to let the deputies
off easily. Their first opinion was that Lieutenant Eames
was the chief officer of the militia company at Hingham
when the company rejected his authority. The election of
Allen had been invalid, and the company was guilty of
mutiny. To accept this finding, the deputies would have
to abandon Hingham unless some other loophole was
found. Some had argued that since Eames had resigned at
one point before all the agitation began, the election had

been valid. To cover this point, the magistrates asserted, "Wee finde that though he laid downe his place, it was of no validity, it being never allowed by authority; and if it were, yett he was chosen againe by the company of Hingham and confirmed at the last General Courte, by the Counsell for life, with the consent of the magistrates and the warrant of the major generall, to trayne them as their left."

The deputies agreed to accept that Eames was properly lieutenant at the time of the dispute on the training field by the vote of eighteen to twelve. Then, in a clear contradiction, they refused to accept that Eames's earlier resignation had been of no validity by the vote of seventeen to sixteen. They went on to reject the idea that even if his resignation had been valid, he had been reconfirmed by the votes of the Standing Council, the magistrates, and the major general of militia by the vote of fifteen to fourteen, with four not voting. The only explanation of these contradictory votes was that although the deputies were willing to concede that Eames was properly in command of the Hingham militia, the wording of the next two propositions embellished the power of the magistrates, and particularly the Standing Council, and enough deputies were opposed to that to bring about the defeat of the magistrates' second and third opinions.

After establishing Eames's position, the magistrates went on to conclude that Joshua Hobart had been guilty of sometimes reporting the advice and directions of the magistrates falsely, or at least in doubtful terms, especially when he met with the company in the meeting the night before the company attempted to drill without Eames. They also asserted that his carrying away the colors and putting forward of Allen's name for election on the drill field were all blameworthy. Finally, when Eames had responded that the magistrates had advised him to keep his command, Hobart had falsely accused him of lying. The deputies agreed to accept this characterization of Hobart's actions.

The magistrates then named Joshua Hobart, Daniel Cushing, Thomas Hobart, Edmund Hobart, William Hersey, and Bozoan Allen "the chief actors and occasoners of this disorderly and mutinous carriage, though some more guilty therefore than others." They also found that Edmund Gold was worthy of censure. The deputies agreed to these accusations by the vote of eighteen to fifteen, with most of the fifteen objectors disagreeing with the use of the word "mutinous."

Next, the magistrates turned to the happenings in the Hingham church. They found that John Tower had supported Hobart in his story that authority had ordered Eames to resign and that John Folsom had gone even further and quoted Dudley and Winthrop as saying that they gave Eames no order to exercise the company, which words Dudley and Winthrop denied. Finally, the magistrates concluded that the charges of Folsom and Tower against Winthrop were causeless and unjust. With regard to Folsom, the deputies, obviously influenced by his refusal to repeat his story under oath, agreed fourteen to thirteen, with six abstentions. They would not agree with the findings on Tower by the vote of seventeen to fourteen.

The magistrates concluded that the petition of the eighty-one Hingham men contained some false and scandalous things for which the petitioners should be censured. The deputies agreed sixteen to twelve that it contained false and scandalous things, but disagreed, eighteen to twelve, that the petitioners should be censured.

Now the task would be to iron out the differences. The magistrates had achieved much in the first actions, but this time they were determined to gain a complete victory. Winthrop was to be exonerated and the Hingham leadership was to be punished.

The deputies were probably surprised by the strong stand taken by the magistrates. After receiving their opinions and voting on them, they were now required to submit counterproposals for those aspects of the magistrates' document they had voted down. The deputies declared that Eames had retired from his post as commander of militia. The magistrates asserted that if the deputies meant "in so far as it was in his power to lay-down his post," they dissented, but if they meant "legally resigned," they assented.

The second point the deputies wished to make was to claim that Bellingham had legally advised Eames to resign. The magistrates responded that whether or not Bellingham was within his rights to advise Eames was not pertinent to the case. The advice of the entire body of magistrates took precedence over Bellingham's advice.

The deputies further stated their long-standing desire to curtail the powers of the Standing Council. They insisted that it was not within the power of that Council or the major general to confirm officers while the General Court was sitting. To this the magistrates returned a rather sharp rebuke:

> To the third, wee answer that wee formerly sent unto you two lawes, (viz.) in 1636, 7 mo.; the other in 1636, 10 mo., whereby power was given to the counsell to confirm military officers in their places without restraining them from so doing at any time or in any place. If any lawe or order can be shewed to take this power from them, wee desire it may be produced, and we shall rest satisfyed. But if there be none, (as wee believe there is not, because wee have searched and cann finde none,) wee then desire that you would be satisfyed.[26]

The deputies still seemed determined to pin something on Eames and found him guilty of provocative action in refusing to show his orders from the magistrates to the Hingham company. Although the magistrates agreed that his refusal may have occasioned some disturbances, they found him blameless of any wrongdoing, since those who demanded to see his orders were in no position to demand them of him.

Finally, still trying desperately to find some illegal action by the deputy governor, the deputies insisted that his expression (that it was against the law of man and God for the accused to know his accusers before the trial) was blameworthy. The magistrates responded to this charge by going back to the testimony of Winthrop, who had admitted refusing to name the accusers, claiming that it was common practice to protect the accusers from pressures from the accused, and had denied asserting that this action was ordered by God or English law. They declared that Winthrop had not offended criminally with his words, that even if he was mistaken and had used them, he already had confessed that he did not believe that it was against the laws of God and man to reveal the accuser to the accused.[27]

Thus far the magistrates still had the upper hand. The case against Winthrop had collapsed completely. The deputies would no longer even suggest that he was guilty of anything other than a verbal indiscretion. Certainly, they had no recourse but to acquit him. The deputies had also admitted that the Hingham militia company had mutinied against their legitimate commander and that their petition to the General Court was erroneous and scandalous. The only small gain the deputies had made was to get the magistrates to admit that Eames had erred in resigning his post by walking off the training field. This point the deputies would magnify in the days ahead.

The magistrates sensed an important victory within their grasp and they pushed ahead vigorously. They thought the time was ripe to force the deputies to agree to censures and fines for the Hingham petitioners. And in an effort to hurry the deputies along, they suggested that the petitioners be forced to pay the costs of this prolonged session of the General Court.[28]

The deputies were faced with a dilemma. They could reject the magistrates' determination to fine the Hingham petitioners by use of the negative voice, which would, of course, be highly objectionable in principle, considering the deputies' long-standing opposition to the very concept of a negative voice. But another factor entered their considerations at this time: the last suggestion of the magistrates that the petitioners bear the expense of this marathon session of the General Court, which touched a sore point. The colony coffers were almost empty and someone would have to pay for the Court's expenses; if it was not the Hingham petitioners, then it would have to be the deputies' constituents. There seemed to be no alternative but to acquiesce in the fining of the Hingham petitioners. Once again the deputies gave in, insisting only on lower fines than those recommended by the magistrates and insisting on fining Eames also.[29]

The deputies, however, had not reckoned with the stubbornness of the magistrates. They returned an answer to the deputies which made it quite clear that they would veto any attempt to fine Eames. They would compromise and allow him to be admonished, but no more than that. As far as the rest of the deputies' proposals were concerned, the magistrates had achieved another victory in forcing the deputies to agree that the fines were proper, even if rather small, considering the offenses. They also stated they would consent to the deputies proposals, but only "if . . . the Dept Gounr may be pronounced innocent in what hath binn chardged upon him, and the petcconers enjoyned to make publicq acknowledgments for the injury donne him, wee shalbe content to yield to the Depts in the rest." The magistrates, now supremely confident, suggested that if the deputies could not agree with these demands, the whole issue could be brought before impartial arbiters, in other words, mediation by the ministers.[30]

The deputies were obviously annoyed with the magistrates. They had gone as far as they felt they could go. They would not remove Lieutenant Eames's fine nor would they exonerate Winthrop anymore than they had already done. Nor did they feel they could force the petitioners to acknowledge publicly the wrong done to the deputy governor.

But the deputies' cause was hopeless. Since this controversy was a serious matter, and since the two houses were deadlocked, the law required arbitration, and the magistrates had no hesitation in calling upon some of the elders to mediate. They knew that Peter Hobart and the Hingham church were unpopular with more orthodox clergymen. In addition, many elders had visited Hingham in an effort to heal the schism in the church, and most were convinced that Hobart and his party were in the wrong.[31] And clearly, the elders would not agree to the proceedings against Winthrop. The deputies realized that the magistrates intended to call upon the elders, and properly concluded that they would gain more from compromise with the magistrates than they would gain from the elders. They asked the magistrates for a joint conference of the magistrates and a committee of six deputies.

The conference committee finally reached a compromise on the first day of July. The deputies would insist on fining Lieutenant Eames £5. The magistrates, in turn, would insist on vetoing that fine. They did agree, however, that he might be admonished for laying down his post without authority. In this the deputies concurred. Joshua Hobart was fined £20, Edmund Hobart £5, Thomas Hobart £2, Peter Hobart £2, Edmund Gold £1, John Folsom £5, Daniel Cushing £2.10, William Hersey £4, and Bozoan Allen £5. The rest of the petitioners were to pay equal shares of a £53.10, with the exception of John Tower, whose punishment was to serve out his imprisonment. All were to pay their fines within three months. Finally, the deputies agreed to the following exoneration of the deputy governor:

> This underwritten was agreed on to be openly read to the whole assembly.
>
> The Generall Cort haveing very largely hard and debated a complaint brought against John Winthrope, Esq. by certeine persons of Hingham do judge tht the Deputy Governor is legally acquited of those things that have bene complained of, or layed to his charge, and have therefore, and for their other offences, punished the said complainants by severall fines to be paid the country the sume of £46.10s, and for charges of the Generall Cort £53. 10s and for the Deputy Governor his clearing wee desire the country will hereby take notice.[32]

The Hingham militia case was over. One more joint meeting of the General Court would be necessary to read the verdicts and exonerate the deputy governor from any charge. On July 5 the magistrates and deputies again took their places in the Boston meetinghouse. Once again Winthrop took his seat in the accused's place and removed his hat. Thomas Dudley, governor of the colony, read the formal sentence, and the deputy governor was requested to return to the magistrates' bench. Once Winthrop was seated and properly covered, he requested the opportunity to speak.

He then delivered his famous speech on liberty. The first half is a familiar defense of magisterial authority. Paraphrasing the opinions given in his earlier writings on the negative voice and arbitrary government and those given by the ministers in the mediation of October 1644, Winthrop preached:

> It is yourselves who have called us to this office, and being called by you, we have our authority from God, in way of an ordinance, such as hath the image of God eminently stamped upon it, the contempt and violation whereof hath been vindicated with examples of divine vengence.[33]

This is about as strong a statement of his belief in the divine sanction of the magistracy as Winthrop ever delivered. The deputies, with their emphasis on defense against arbitrary rule and the aggrandizement of their roles, had been routed, and the deputy governor, in a moment of triumph, was making very clear just what the doctrines of the victors were.

Winthrop agreed that once a ruler was elected and allowed to receive his powers from God, the people should not be without recourse to remove a bad ruler. But they must not ever again mistake human frailty and honest error for crimes:

> I entreat you to consider, that when you choose magistrates, you take them from among yourselves, men subject to like pasions as you are. Therefore when you see infirmaties in us, you should reflect upon your own, and that would make you bear the more with us, and not be severe censurers of the failings of your magistrates, when you have continual experience of the like infirmaties in yourselves and others.[34]

The only time a magistrate is to be called to account for his actions is when he violates his oath and covenant. With the rights and duties of those in authority unmistakably settled, the deputy governor went on to speak concerning what he felt was a very misunderstood subject—liberty:

There is a twofold liberty, natural (I mean as our nature is now corrupt) and civil or federal. The first is common to man with beasts and other creatures. By this, man, as he stands in relation to man simply, hath liberty to do what he lists; it is a liberty to evil as well as to good. This liberty is incompatable and inconsistent with authority, and cannot endure the least restraint of the most just authority.[35]

Winthrop was implying that those who constantly challenged the legitimacy of just authority and humiliated magistrates with impeachment charges without grounds for such charges, forcing them to place themselves before the bar of justice like criminals solely for attempting to fulfill their obligations, were leading the colony toward a disastrous confusion of true liberty with natural liberty. True liberty was the proper end and objective of authority, and it withered without authority:

This liberty is maintained and exercised in the way of subjection to authority; it is the same kind of liberty wherewith Christ hath made us free. The woman's own choice makes such a man her husband: yet being so chosen, he is her lord, and she is to be subject to him, yet in a way of liberty, not of bondage; and a true wife accounts her subjection her honor and freedom, and would not think her condition safe and free, but in her subjection to her husband's authority. Such is the liberty of the church under the authority of Christ, her king and husband . . . Even so brethren, it will be between you and your magistrates.[36]

The people of Massachusetts Bay would be free and safe from tyranny only by striving for true liberty, and this liberty would seek safety in obedience to just magistrates with whom the people are covenanted.

The deputies had hoped to avoid this lecture. They had an agreement with the magistrates that there would only be the reading of the verdict at this session.[37] But Winthrop would not be denied. He said nothing this day that he had not said before. Most of the deputies had fought his interpretation of the extensive powers of the magistracy for years and were not converted to his views on this July day of 1645. But he had cleverly associated them with the opponents of the very framework of the government. He equated them with those who would upset the balance between liberty and authority by too broad an interpretation of liberty. In reality, the deputies had not wished to destroy authority as Winthrop claimed; they had only wanted some of the authority for themselves.

At this moment, however, all the fight had been taken out of them. They had been foolish to undertake the Hingham cause and make ill-prepared, ill-conceived assaults upon the deputy governor. The best they could hope for was to get the business over with, go home, and hope the matter would soon be forgotten. Next year would be a new year. The mistake they had made in 1645 was to be caught up in particulars and in the prosecution of an incredibly weak case against the very proper and very popular magistrate. In the past the deputies had had success by sticking to general charges, by playing upon the fears of arbitrary government prevailing among freemen and nonfreemen alike, by speaking of excessive powers and magisterial discretionary powers.

The Hingham militia case was an enormous setback for the deputies and for the lesser gentry as a group. Their ambitions to share in the power of the magistracy were routed. In addition, events were occurring simultaneously to the great debate in the General Court, which would further force the lesser gentry to cease their attacks on the magistrates.

It has already been asserted that the lesser gentry and

the deputies in particular had no quarrel with the fundamental framework of the government of Massachusetts Bay. They only desired to share power within the framework. Beginning in 1643 and continuing to almost the end of the decade, however, external forces began an attack on that fundamental framework. Samuel Gorton of Shawomet in Rhode Island was able to call into question the freedom from English control under which Massachusetts was operating, and the even more formidable forces commanded by William Vassall and Robert Child attempted to force England to take over complete jurisdiction of the colony by appointing a governor general. Under these pressures the lesser gentry had no alternative but to rally to the support of the magistrates for the duration of the troubled years. No one could miss the obvious fact, during those years, that the most serious threats to the independence of Massachusetts had been encouraged by the arguments within the General Court. Further arguments would only encourage further external intervention. In this way the careers of Gorton, Vassall, and Child were just as responsible for ending the power struggle within Massachusetts Bay as was the fiasco of the Winthrop impeachment.

4 Massachusetts versus Samuel Gorton

In the decade of the 1640s the most pronounced differences between English and New England Puritanism lay in their attitudes toward heresy. In England there had never been the unity in the Puritan movement which isolation and common opinions made possible in Massachusetts Bay. Its leaders in England were compelled by theological diversities to live in peace with all who were willing to join in the struggle against the Crown. Later, the Independents needed the support of fringe groups to bring about the overthrow of the Presbyterian majority in Parliament. Toleration became a necessity among the Puritan Independents.

After English Puritans turned necessity into virtue, they began to find fault with New England intolerance. Those in the New World who were determined to work for the overthrow of the New England Way in church and state could therefore expect assistance from orthodoxy's closest counterparts in England. But the experiences of one man, the Rhode Island heretic Samuel Gorton, did more than the growth of English tolerance to encourage the enemies of Massachusetts Bay to seek their solutions in England. William Vassall, defeated in his efforts to seek victory by use of the deputies' debate with the magistrates, could not have failed to observe and learn from Gorton how Massachusetts Bay could be humbled.

Samuel Gorton, sometimes "gentleman," sometimes "citizen of London," sometimes "clothier," and sometimes "professor of the mysteries of Christ," is one of the most difficult of all the early religious leaders of New England to understand. His enemies, who included nearly everyone in New England at one time or another, called him at worst an atheist (which he was not) and at best a familist. He possessed a fine grasp of Scripture, a rudimentary knowledge of theology, a sharp wit, and an even sharper tongue. While his charm and personal magnetism made lifelong devoted followers, his arrogance made dedicated and brutal enemies.

Gorton arrived in Boston in 1637 and proceeded immediately to Plymouth Colony. This move was completely voluntary, but he must have known after even the most cursory observation that a man of his religious mentality would not be welcome in the Bay Colony. He was not in Plymouth very long before he was in trouble with the very tolerant magistrates of that colony. In 1639 he was fined eighteen pounds and given fourteen days to leave the colony for actions contemptuous of the courts and magistrates of that colony.[1] He moved his residence to Portsmouth, on the island of Rhode Island, along with a convert, John Weeks. Once again, Gorton involved himself in a dispute with the magistrates and was finally banished from Portsmouth after being publically whipped.[2] His friends, now including Randall Holden, Richard Carder, Sampson Shotton, and Robert Potter, in addition to Weeks, subsequently followed Gorton to Mr. Williams's settlement at Providence.

Gorton had not been in Providence long before Williams expressed his opinion of him in a letter to John Winthrop:

> Mr. Gorton having foully abused both high and low at aquednick, is now bewiching and madding poor providence both with his unclean and foule sensurs of all the ministers of this Countrey, for which my self have in Christs name withstood him: and allso denying all vizable and entarnall ordinances, in depth of familisme, against which I have a littell disputed

and written and shall the most high assisting mee to
death: as paul said in asia, and I of providence (all-
most) all suck in his poyson as at first they did at
aquednick: sume few and my self doe withstand his
inhabitation and towne privelidges without confession and reformation of his unsivell and inhuman
practises at portsmouth: yet the tyde is to strong
against us and I fear if the framer of hearts help not
it will force me to littell patience, a littell iland next
to your prudence, Jehuoa himself bee pleased to bee
a saintuarey to all whose hearts are perfect with him;
in him I desiar unfainedly to bee Your worships true
and affectionate.[3]

Before Gorton arrived in Providence the town was
badly divided over land distributions. To these disputes
he soon added arguments over his theological beliefs and
his views on oaths, the magistracy, and the sacraments.
Winthrop reports that the disputes would have led to
bloodshed had it not been for the intervention of Williams.[4]

At the time these events occurred, Gorton was leading
the majority faction in Providence, although neither he
nor any of his Plymouth or Rhode Island followers were
ever admitted to freemanship in Providence.[5] His actions
finally drove the minority in Providence to a drastic step.
These refugees from Massachusetts Bay intolerance petitioned their former oppressor for aid in a desperate attempt to control Gorton's following. On the seventeenth
day of November 1641, a petition signed by thirteen men
(but not including Roger Williams—contrary to Morton's
account) appealed to Massachusetts Bay.[6] In this petition
Gorton and his friends from Rhode Island, along with the
Providence inhabitants John Greene and Francis Weston
and six or seven others, were accused by the petitioners

of "insolent and riotous carriages." They were also accused
of planning "to have no manner of honest order or government."

> If it may, therefore, please you, of gentle courtesy,
> and for the preservation of humanity and mankind,
> to consider our condition, and lend us a neighborlike
> helping hand, and send us such assistance, our neces-
> sity urges us to be troublesome into you, to help us
> to bring them to satisfaction, and to ease us of our
> burthen of them at your descretion; we shall ever-
> more own it as a deed of great charity, and take very
> thankfully, and diligently labor in the best measure
> we can, and constantly practise to requite your loving
> kindness, if you should have occasion to command us
> or any of us in any lawful design. And if it shall
> please you to send us any speedy answer, we shall take
> it very kindly, and be ready and willing to satisfy
> the messenger; and ever remain your loving neighbors
> and respective friends.[7]

Although Massachusetts Bay refused to enter the affairs
of Providence, the magistrates did leave a possible opening. The Bay Colony leaders reasoned that physical assistance would be an act of war which they could not undertake without the approval of the General Court, which
was not then in session. Nor would the leaders offer the
Providence petitioners any help unless the petitioners submitted themselves to the jurisdiction of either Plymouth
Colony or Massachusetts Bay. This last proposal was made
in the hope that the Providence settlers would respond
favorably. Massachusetts Bay was in an expansionist mood
in the 1640s, and nowhere did the magistrates desire ex-
pansion more than in that hotbed of heresy, Narragansett
Bay.[8] The idea was planted and quickly bore fruit.

On September 8, 1642, four men—two of them signers
of the petition of the previous November, and one, the

father of a signer—took up the offer made in the rejection message and submitted themselves to the jurisdiction of the Bay Colony. The four were William Arnold, Robert Coal, William Carpenter, and Benedict Arnold,[9] all residents of the district of Pawtuxit, which was claimed by the town of Providence.

Massachusetts agreed to accept the submissions of the Pawtuxit men partly to rescue them from the unjust violence of the Gortonists and "partly to draw in the rest of those parts, wither under ourselves or Plymouth, who now lived under no government, but grew very offensive." [10] Gorton in his account agrees with the second reason and explains the actions of Massachusetts in terms of her general intolerance.[11] Winthrop, however, explicitly states that Massachusetts Bay was seriously concerned with the possibility of an outbreak of Indian warfare with the Narragansetts. A base of operations like Pawtuxit, close to the Indians' homelands, might act as a deterrent. If that failed, it might serve as a useful base for operations against the Indians. Winthrop also reveals the colony's expansionist dreams: "and likewise [it would provide] for an outlet into Narragansett Bay." Finally, Winthrop displayed his own pragmatism when he concluded, "and seeing it come without our seeking and would be no charge to us, we thought it not wisdom to let it slip." [12]

Having taken these four men under its jurisdiction, the Massachusetts General Court proceeded to appoint them officers for the maintenance of peace in Pawtuxit and issued a warrant to the residents of Providence defending the minority position in the land dispute (which had already been settled by Williams).[13]

The vast majority of the Providence settlers, including those who had originally petitioned Massachusetts Bay for assistance and who had not been willing to submit themselves to Massachusetts jurisdiction, were very angry with the Arnolds, Coal, and Carpenter. They felt that these four had seriously jeopardized their independence. While Gorton and his friends probably had already made up their minds to leave Providence, this Massachusetts claim to jurisdiction certainly sped them on their way. If they could not live in peace in Plymouth, Rhode Island, or Providence, then surely they would have no peace under the jurisdiction of the saints of the Bay. Gorton and his followers had found a spot south of Providence, south of the Arnolds in Pawtuxit, and beyond the boundaries of the lands Massachusetts was claiming as hers. Before leaving, however, the Gortonists—now twelve in number— put their names to a letter to Massachusetts Bay attacking the Massachusetts claims on Providence. This tract was the beginning of Gorton's troubles with the magistrates of the Bay Colony, and it was the beginning of a long journey which would lead to Boston and then to London. It was also the first step in his career as a petitioner of parliaments—a career which would eventually lead to the interference in American affairs by the Parliament of England.*

Gorton was the author of the letter which was dated November 20, 1642, and whose tone can only be described as arrogant and insulting. He made his points well, but could not resist the temptation to throw in extra remarks which were usually heretical (in the eyes of his intended readers) and calculated to enrage his opponents.

Gorton began by acknowledging receipt of the Massachusetts warrant, adding that they had doubted its authenticity because the men who brought it to them—namely, the Arnolds, and so on—were men "whose constant and professed acts are worse than the counterfittings of men's hands," and because they thought the leaders of Massachu-

---

* The twelve were John Weeks, Randall Holden, John Warner, Robert Potter, Richard Waterman, William Waddle, Samuel Gorton, Richard Carder, John Greene, Nicholas Power, Francis Weston, and Sampson Shotton.

setts were wise enough to avoid such actions. Gorton's main argument was that they were beyond the borders of Massachusetts jurisdiction and so were those who had submitted to it. The arguments of the people of Providence were no business of the magistrates of Massachusetts Bay. No one had the power "to enlarge the bounds, by King Charles limited unto you." Gorton rejected also the offer of mediation in the Massachusetts courts:

> You are become one with our adversaries . . . Now if we have our opponent to prefer his action against us, and not so only, but to be our counsel, our jury and our judge, (for so it must be, if you are one with them, as you affirm,) we know, before hand, how our cause will be ended, and see the scales of your equal justice turned already, before wee have laid our cause therein.[14]

Gorton had made his point and had made it well. Massachusetts had no legal right to extend her jurisdiction beyond her borders as established in her charter, and the disputants in Providence would be foolish to submit their arguments to a mediation where the mediator had already committed itself to one party in the dispute. But having made his point, Gorton could not resist the temptation to say more and assault Massachusetts Bay with a host of charges and insults. He insisted that the Bay Colony was filled with hypocrites. He attacked the institution of the ministry in Massachusetts, since the ministers professed to be under the mediate call of Christ, where before they had been under the immediate call of Christ. Gorton claims that the Massachusetts clergy found twenty-six particulars of blasphemy in his letter of November 1642. He insists, however, that they had to twist his words and supply their own fanciful meanings to his thoughts in order to do it. He also claims that the ministers were so angry with the charges he leveled against them that they began a verbal attack on the Gortonists which they hoped would result in their seizure and execution.[15]

Despite the bravado of their response, Samuel Gorton and his friends had been frightened by Massachusetts' intervention in Providence affairs. Ten of the twelve signers of the letter of November 1642 moved to the new lands south of Pawtuxit. This land, called Shawomet by the Indians, was claimed by no Englishmen. In January 1643 Gorton, after meeting with the chief sachem of the Narragansetts, Miantonomo, offered to purchase Shawomet. The local sachem of the region, Pumham, was unhappy with the sale, but Miantonomo overawed him and he was forced to agree. The deed of sale was in Miantonomo's name, since he claimed sovereignty over Pumham, but Pumham acknowledged his approval by acting as a witness to the sale.[16] Miantonomo insisted that the land belonged to him as chief of the Narragansetts and that Putnam of Shawomet and Socononoco of Pawtuxit were subchiefs who owed him allegiance and paid him tribute. Gorton was in no position to challenge this view even if he had a mind to. Miantonomo was friendly and strong, and Gorton wanted the land.

Massachusetts Bay took an entirely different position. The magistrates were suspicious of the powerful and fiercely independent Narragansetts. They were powerful enough to challenge Miantonomo's assertion about the lands of Shawomet, and the sale of this land to the Gortonists was not at all in the interests of Massachusetts Bay.

The Arnolds and their friends in Pawtuxit, now loyal subjects of Massachusetts, were also outraged by Gorton's escape and feared that the Indians with whom they traded —the bands of Pumham and Socononoco—would be overwhelmed by the Narragansetts and that Gorton's connections with Miantonomo would destroy their trade with the local chieftains. In the spring of 1643 Benedict Arnold persuaded Pumham and Socononoco to come with him to

Boston and complain of the theft of their lands by Miantonomo and Gorton, as well as to request protection from
the Bay Colony by placing themselves, their peoples, and
their lands under Massachusetts jurisdiction. If Pumham's
submission were accepted by Massachusetts, then Shawomet too would be under Massachusetts jurisdiction and
Gorton would not have escaped the clutches of his enemies.

The whole matter of the validity of sale to Gorton and
the requested protection and submission was referred to
the May 1643 session of the General Court. Letters were
sent to Gorton and Miantonomo requesting their presence
at the Court. If Pumham were a vassal of the Narragansetts, then certainly the sale of his lands to Gorton could
not be challenged and Massachusetts would have little
right to place him under her jurisdiction. Miantonomo,
perhaps because of his planned war with the Mohegans
and his desire for Massachusetts neutrality in that war,
presented himself, while Gorton ignored the request. The
chief was asked if he could prove that Pumham was his
vassal. Winthrop states that he could not, although he did
cite the tribute that Pumham was accustomed to send him.
Cutshamekin, one of the sachems of the Massachusetts—
now a thoroughly English-dominated tribe—testified that
Pumham and Socononoco were free sachems like himself,
but that because Miantonomo was a great chief, the
weaker chiefs frequently sent him presents and had aided
him in his earlier war with the Pequots. This was a fine
distinction, but a significant one for Massachusetts Bay.[17]

The General Court appointed a committee to treat with
the sachems Pumham and Socononoco concerning their
submissions to Massachusetts Bay and their coming under
its jurisdiction.[18] And the magistrates and elders proceeded
to question the Indians concerning their desire to subject
themselves to the English. There was also a brief probe
into their understanding of the Ten Commandments

which gives a fine insight into the wonderful mixture of shrewdness and simplicity which comprised the Indian view of ethics. Finally, the two sachems were allowed to subject themselves, their lands, and their peoples to Massachusetts law and justice.[19] Massachusetts now had extra eyes watching the actions of the Narragansetts, and she had the weapons which she could use to continue her assault upon the "vile heretics" now living at Shawomet.

In order to ensure the legality of their position, the Massachusetts leaders turned to the United Colonies for further support. The commissioners were to meet in Boston on the seventh day of September 1643. At this meeting they agreed to leave the matter of Gorton in the hands of the Massachusetts magistrates, who were in effect to be the agents of the United Colonies as long as they did not call into question any legitimate claims to Pawtuxit and Shawomet which Plymouth Colony might have.[20]

On September 12 the General Court delivered a second warrant to the settlers of Providence, but this one was specifically addressed to the squatters at Shawomet. As if to emphasize the growing seriousness and urgency of the case, two of the deputies to the General Court, Humfrey Atherton and Edward Tomlins, carried the warrant personally to Gorton.[21] The second warrant informed Gorton and his friends that Massachusetts had found good reason to take the sachems Pumham and Socononoco under her jurisdiction. These chieftains had complained of injustices at the hands of the Gortonists, and for equal justice to be served, the Shawomet settlers were invited to come to answer these complaints before the General Court. Since some of the Gortonists had been banished for life from Massachusetts Bay at an earlier date, the General Court now promised a safe conduct to enter and to leave to all men of Shawomet who would come to the Court.[22]

Atherton and Tomlins found Gorton not at all disposed to accept Massachusetts' claim to jurisdiction over Shawomet. He insisted that he had purchased the lands legitimately, and the only foreign domination that he would accept was that of "the State and Government of Old England," implying in this that he and his followers were awaiting the disposition of their case in England, probably referring to the application that Rhode Island and Providence leaders were making for a charter from Parliament. In the meantime the Gortonists intended to live in peace and would be willing to accept impartial mediation of their disputes with the Indians. This is at least Gorton's report of his oral response to the Massachusetts deputies, if not the tone of the conversation as Atherton and Tomlins reported it to Winthrop, nor is it anything like the tone of the written response which was sent by the Shawomet settlers to the General Court. The deputies described a very belligerent group at Shawomet who boasted of their ability to defend themselves and their homes should Massachusetts attempt to attack them.[23] The formal answer, in all fairness to Gorton, was not composed by him. It was the work of his chief confederate, Randall Holden, and is clearly the most insulting and outrageous correspondence ever received by the magistrates of Massachusetts Bay.

Holden's answer is dated September 15, 1643, and is addressed to

> the great and honored Idol General, now set up in the Massachusetts, whose pretended equity in distribution of justice unto the souls and bodies of men, is nothing else but a mere device of man, according to the ancient custom and sleights of Satan, transforming himself into an angel of light, to subject and make slaves of that species or kind that God hath honored with his own image.[24]

Holden seldom stuck to the issue, but when he touched upon it, his comments were blunt. He refused to acknowl-

edge any justice in Pumham's complaints against the settlers of Shawomet, saying if he had any he should have
come to them first. He did not recognize any claims by
Massachusetts Bay to the lands of Shawomet as a result of
Pumham's submission. Holden accused that sachem of
breaking his covenant with the settlers at Shawomet and
classified him persona non grata in the future.

Holden warned the Massachusetts leaders that they
would find the Gortonists mirroring the attitudes of Massachusetts men. If they extended the hand of friendship,
it would be met in kind. If they continued to send letters,
they would receive letters in return. But if they should
come to them bearing arms, they had better be prepared
to fight, "for we are come to put fire upon the earth; and
it is our desire to have it speedily kindled." [25]

If the magistrates still wished them to travel to Boston,
God must have blinded their eyes to Gorton's first response. Holden insisted that he and his friends had better
things to do than to go trotting off to Massachusetts every
time some "heathen, thieving Indians" (or heathen English, for that matter) told lies about them. If the leaders
of Massachusetts wished to speak with the settlers of
Shawomet, let them come to Shawomet. Finally, Holden
said they were not going to Massachusetts, since they
doubted very much that they could obtain justice there.[26]

Holden, like Gorton, could seldom set his hand to pen
without expounding his own beliefs and attacking the beliefs of those opposed to him. He was a master of the insult. After his opening reference to the General Court as
"the great and honored Idol General," he went on to com-
pare Massachusetts Bay to Sodom and to call the voices
of the magistrates "the high wind instruments set up to
have dominion and rules as though there were not God in
heaven or in earth." He referred to the Pawtuxit settlers,
who had subjected themselves to Massachusetts, as "low
strength instruments who subjected themselves to their

fellow men as if God had ever intended man to be a vassal of his own kind." He compared the Massachusetts principle of magistracy to principles of the Kingdom of Darkness and of Satan, claiming that such a state would have more profitably proven itself Christian before consorting with "Heathen Indians": "We are not a cup fitted for your so eager appetite, no otherwise than if you take it down, it shall prove unto you a cup of trembling, either making you vomit out your own eternal shame, or else to burst in sunder, like your fellow confessor for hire, Judas Iscariot." [27]

In this letter Holden also expressed the familiar Gortonist view on the ministry and the magistracy:

> In that you say our freedom granted to come unto you takes away all excuse from us, we freely retort it upon yourselves to make excuses, whose laws and proceedings with the souls and bodies of men, is nothing else but a continued act, like the horse in the mill, of accusing and excusing; which you do by circumstances and conjectures, as all your fathers have done before you, the diviners and necromancers of the world, who are gone to their own place and have their reward.

Holden had a few choice words about the Lord's Supper as well:

> . . . when you are about dished-up dainties, haveing turned the juice of a poor, silly grape, that perisheth in the use of it, into the blood of our Lord Jesus, by the cunning skill of your magicians, which doth mad and drunk so many in the world.[28]

From the letters of Holden and Gorton, it should have been abundantly clear to the magistrates of Massachusetts Bay that they were dealing with men with highly "dangerous" religious and political opinions. They rejected the institution of the civil magistracy—at least as it was established in Massachusetts; they opposed the ministry, referring to clergymen as "necromancers"or dealers in black magic; in addition, Gorton and his friends rejected the sacraments and oath taking. Many of these same "heresies" later would drive the orthodox leadership of Massachusetts to persecution of the Quakers; and in 1643 they were prepared for drastic actions to silence Gorton's heresies. The Massachusetts response was short and to the point. A commission headed by George Cooke and including Humfrey Atherton and Edward Johnson, escorted by forty armed men, were to be sent to Shawomet to force the Gortonists to repent and retract all their writings or to return with the commissioners to face the justice of the Massachusetts courts. If they rejected these alternatives and resisted the armed might of the Bay Colony, they were to be destroyed.[29]

This small Massachusetts army crossed over the border into Rhode Island, and after a brief siege of the Gortonists at Shawomet in which no one was killed (no Gortonist ever fired a shot in anger), Gorton and his friends were marched back to Massachusetts.[30] Gorton was now at the mercy of his enemies.

On October 17, 1643, a lecture day in Boston, the trial of Samuel Gorton before the General Court began. The allegations against him were presented. He and his associates were blasphemous heretics who denied the nature of Christ since they professed belief that the atonement of Christ was effectual to the Old Testament fathers before the time of the incarnation. They were defamers of the churches of Christ. They denied all the ordinances of the churches. Finally, they were accused of denying the powers of the magistrates because they had refused to obey the ordinances and commands of the magistrates of Massachusetts Bay.

Gorton objected that the charges were inaccurate and unfair. He and his friends did honor the magistracy, but they denied the power of the Massachusetts magistracy to act some twenty-four miles beyond the boundaries granted to them by His Majesty, King Charles. He asserted that if they had been within the jurisdiction of the Bay Colony, they would most certainly have been as obedient and docile as they had been since they were brought to Boston and under the legitimate authority of the magistrates. Winthrop replied that if their settlement at Shawomat was not within the boundaries of Massachusetts Bay, it was certainly a part of one of the United Colonies, and Massachusetts Bay had been commissioned to act in this affair for the other confederated powers. If by some remote chance they lived outside the jurisdiction of all the colonies, then Massachusetts had no one to turn to for justice and had to settle her arguments by force of arms, as she had done. The Gortonists' claim to jurisdiction by right of purchase from the Indians was a matter for consideration, however. They should produce their deed and witnesses to prove that the Indians had legally sold the land to them and until they did Massachusetts would regard its agreement with the Indians as still in force.

Gorton responded to the charge of heresy by asserting that the charge constituted persecution for conscience. Winthrop rejected this countercharge. No one had questioned them about their religious opinions initially; Massachusetts had made inquiry on a strictly civil plane. It was the Gortonists who had thrust the religious question upon them by their blasphemous responses. Winthrop then ordered the letters of the Gortonists read before the Court,* and the prisoners were asked if these were their beliefs. Gorton, as spokesman for the group, answered that

* This is Winthrop's version. Gorton denies that his letters were read. He states that he requested a reading and was refused, with Thomas Dudley threatening him with chains if he opened his mouth again. His characterization of Dudley has a ring of truth to it, but I can see no reason why Winthrop should refuse to have the letters read, since they were quite damning.

they were, but only "in that sense wherein they wrote them." [31]

On the next day, October 18, the trial continued. During this session the magistrates allowed the Gortonists to answer particular passages from their writings which were being used against them. The elders of the colony were present in great numbers to witness and to interpret the answers of the accused. But when particular charges were leveled at Gorton and his friends, their answers gave some of the elders reason to pause. The oral interpretations they gave to the meanings of their writings were apparently quite different and contrary to the words of the letters. Their explanations made their opinions seem rather close to the orthodox views held by the elders. When this was pointed out to them, the Gortonists nevertheless refused to retract either their writings or their oral explanations.[32] The Court then proceeded to present a formal charge against the ten Shawomet men:

> The charge of the Prisoners, Samuel Gorton and his Companions
>
> Upon much examination and serious consideration of your writings, with your answers about them, wee do charge you to bee a blasphemos enemy of the true religion of or Lord Jesus Christ and his holy ordinances, and also of all civill authority among the people of God, and particularly in this jurisdiction.[33]

For the next three weeks or so, the General Court in private session questioned the individual prisoners on their beliefs. Finally, Gorton was called before the Court. When Winthrop warned him that he was about to be questioned and that his answers might very well determine whether he lived or died, Gorton quickly objected that if he was on trial for his life, he had to be allowed to appeal his case to England, asserting that it was from that state that his judges derived their powers as judges and that they could not rightfully deny his appeal. But deny it they did, with Endecott warning him not to dream of any such thing, for no appeal would be granted to him.[34]

The case had taken an entirely different turn. The original interest in Gorton on the part of Massachusetts Bay had been strictly political, as had been the basis for the intervention in his affairs. But his political "crimes" were minor, consisting basically of land dispute with some subjects of Massachusetts Bay and a rather half-hearted resistance to arrest. These, however, were hardly actions which could prompt thoughts of capital punishment in the minds of the elders, magistrates, and deputies. His heresies, though, were another matter and could lead to the severest penalties under Massachusetts law. Gorton testified that the elders were preaching against them all during the three weeks of individual questioning and that Pastor Wilson of Boston was calling for their execution.[35]

The writings of the Gortonists in answer to the Massachusetts warrants had first drawn the attention of the Massachusetts leadership to the heterodox thinking of Samuel Gorton. Now, in their possession, he seemed even more dangerous. Although Winthrop accused them of being ignorant men incapable of writing a good sentence in their native English, it is clear today and must have been clear to the elders and magistrates that Gorton had a sharp mind and was an extremely clever foe.[36]

After Winthrop's warning, Gorton was put to the test. The questions he was asked were strictly theological and were prompted by his earlier writings. The defendant was then given fifteen minutes to compose his answers to the questions in writing. Gorton objected that no man should be required to compose so profound a piece of work in so short a time, especially since his life depended upon how he answered. He was granted thirty minutes instead. The Court gave him pen, ink, and paper, placed him in a private room, and told him to work. Shortly after he began, he was interrupted and notified that he would not have to return his answer that day. It was late Saturday afternoon, the eve of the Sabbath. Elders, magistrates, and deputies, especially those who had far to travel to their homes, wanted to adjourn for the day and renew the work of the Court on Monday morning. One would like to think also that some in the Court recognized the incredible unfairness of the burden placed on Gorton and either objected to the proceedings or used the Sabbath eve excuse to obtain more time for him. Unfortunately, there is no record of any such action.[37]

It must have been a difficult time for Gorton. He was a brave man, but he was no fool. Certainly he must have been frightened when he was presented with the Court's questions and told his life depended upon his answers. On the other hand, it would probably have been easier in many ways to stand and defy the Court during those first fifteen minutes, leaving with his principles intact. But now granted extended periods of time for thinking, broken only by Sunday visits to the Boston meetinghouse to listen to Wilson preach sermons calling for his blood, Gorton must have been presented with grave temptations. He consulted with his companions, but clearly the burden rested with him, and the lives of his friends also depended on his answers.

On Monday morning when the Court reconvened, Gorton presented moderate answers to the four questions. He requested permission to read his answers aloud, and when he had completed the task, he was ordered to sign his answers and leave the meetinghouse while the Court debated his fate. In due time Gorton was recalled and again confronted his judges. Saltonstall complained to him of a change in the wording between the questions as presented to him by the Court and the answer to the questions returned by him, on which point Gorton apparently satisfied him. Since Winthrop stated that the members of the Court could find little to disagree with in the answers, they now proceeded to ask him if he was prepared to retract his earlier writings. Gorton said he would not—that there was no disagreement between his initial writings and the answers he had just read.

Gorton would not admit the changes or withdraw any of his writings, whereas Winthrop stated that he could agree with Gorton's most recent effort, but certainly not with his sentiments in the letters addressed to the General Court. At this point, Thomas Dudley interrupted the governor and in some agitation shouted that he would not consent to being associated with any of Gorton's writings "whilst he lived."

Winthrop attempted to question Gorton further, but finally stopped when Bradstreet objected to Gorton's being further interrogated on entirely new theological points unless "he was free to speak unto them"—presumably meaning unless he was given a guarantee of immunity from prosecution for anything he might say.[38]

While Gorton's moderate answers to the questions saved his life, his refusal to retract his earlier writings nearly cost him his life. The elders were called upon for advice, and their recommendation was that the crimes by the word of God demanded death. The voting on the sentencing of the Gortonists followed the party line of the day. All but three of the magistrates voted for the execution of Samuel Gorton. We are not told who the three dissenters were, but the temptation is strong to conclude that they were Saltonstall, Bellingham, and Bradstreet. By a large majority the deputies voted against the death sentence.[39] The reasons for the split were complex. For one thing, this hearing was occurring in the middle of the great debate on the negative voice. The very fact that the magisterial party desired Gorton's death was probably enough to prompt some deputies to vote to save him. They would not be undermining their own position by casting a veto, despite the magistrates' interpretation of it, since enough of them would be voting for clemency to constitute a clear majority of the whole Court—deputies and magistrates together. There may have been pressure from constituents sympathetic to Gorton's cause, but this does not seem really likely. Gorton consistently throughout his account cites examples of how the common people of Massachusetts Bay were really on his side. Yet most of his concrete evidence is of occurrences after his imprisonment, when his clearly visible sufferings rather than his ideas must have aroused sympathy for his plight. The deputies were agreed that Gorton's ideas were dangerous heresies, but they were determined not to support the position of the elders and the magistrates. The internal squabble between the great gentlemen and the lesser gentry was probably responsible for preserving the life of Samuel Gorton.

The elders, charged by divine decree with responsibility for the souls of the members of the churches, were naturally afraid of infection and probably panicked at the thought of "heretics" like Gorton being allowed to proclaim freely his "foul" ideas. There is little evidence of any serious divisions among the elders on this point.* Cotton may have called for reasonableness initially, but his final preachings before the sentencing had called for the most serious of punishments. In this, he was in full accord with his colleague in the Boston pulpit, John Wilson.[40]

The votes of the majority of the magistrates are explained by their fear of the influences of men like Gorton. Just as the elders were bound to expound orthodoxy, the magistrates were bound to defend it, and they seemed convinced that Gorton was a mortal foe who should be eliminated. His experience would serve as a useful warning to others who would disturb the peace of God's people. In addition, his religion, which at certain times seemed to re-

* See n. 40 on p. 250, below, for Gorton's account of one rather amusing episode of division within the ranks of the clergy.

ject the institutions of the magistracy, was a direct threat to them. Perhaps a fearful punishment for contempt of the magistrates for this heretic would deter others from launching further assaults on the dignity of their office. The deputies obviously did not feel as pressed by Gorton as the magistrates did. In fact, considering the bitter feelings between the two groups, they were probably secretly enjoying the magistrates' discomfort. But they could agree that Gorton's religious opinions were highly dangerous, and that he and his followers should be punished, but by means other than death. Finally, on November 3, the General Court came to an agreement:

It is ordered that Samuel Gorton shall be confined to Charlestown, there to be set on work, and to wear such bolts or irons, as may hinder his escape, and to continue during the pleasure of the court, provided that if he shall break his said confinement, or shall in the mean time, either by speech or writing, publish declare, or maintain any of the blasphemous or abominable heresies, wherewith he hath been charged by the general court, contained in either of the two books sent unto us by him, or Randall Houlden, or shall reproach or reprove the churches of our Lord Jesus Christ in these United Colonies, or the civil government or the public ordinance of God therein, (unless it be by answer to some question propounded to him or conference with any elder, or with any other licensed to speak with him privately under the hand of one of the assistants,) that immediately upon accusation of any such writings or speech he shall, by such assistant to whom such accusation shall be brought, be committed to prison till the next court of assistants, then and there to be tried by a jury, whether he hath so spoken or written, and upon his conviction thereof shall be condemned to death and executed.[41]

Weeks, Holden, Potter, Carder, Weston, and John Warner
were confined under the same terms in Ipswich, Salem,
Rowley, Roxbury, Dorchester, and Boston respectively.
William Waddle was confined to Watertown but was apparently considered less culpable and was not chained or
placed at labor. Richard Waterman was dismissed but
ordered to post a one-hundred-pound bond for his appearance at the next General Court and not to leave Massachusetts Bay without permission of the Court. Nicholas
Power was dismissed with an admonition.[42] The cost of
maintaining them in their imprisonment and the cost of
fetching them and trying them were to be paid for by the
sale of their confiscated livestock.[43] Bolts and chains were
brought into the Court and were fitted to the convicts.
They remained in Boston until lecture day, when Cotton
again preached. All then proceeded to the places of their
confinement. Gorton was fairly fortunate, for he had
merely to walk to the shore and board a boat for Charlestown, but others like Weeks, Holden, and Potter had to
make the long journeys to Ipswich, Salem, and Rowley
in chains.[44]

Gorton and his six followers spent the winter of 1643–
44 working for their keep and in chains. But there is clear
evidence that they were not deterred from communicating
with sympathizers. Gorton states that soldiers who served
under Cooke came to him secretly and told him that they
had been tricked into fighting against him.[45] Considering
its source, this assertion must be taken with some caution,
but others testify to the fact that Gorton was winning
friends in Massachusetts. Emanuel Downing of Salem,
writing to his brother-in-law, Governor Winthrop, in February of 1643/4, reported that Randall Holden was as
busy as usual:

> I feare the lord is offended for sparing the lives of
> Gorton and his Companions, for if they all be as

buisye as this at Salem, there wilbe much evill seed sowne in the countrye; I hope some of them wilbe brought to tryall next Court for breach of theire order, and if yet you shall spare them, I shall feare a Curse upon the land.[46]

In April, John Endecott gave further evidence of Holden's work:

We have here divers that are taken with Gortons opinions, which is a great griefe unto us, and Mr. Norrice [Edward Norris, a Salem minister] is verie much troubled. There is one of them that hath reviled Mr. Norrice and spoken evill of the Church. I thought good to advise with you whither it were not best to bynde the partie over to Boston Court, to make such a one exemplarie, that others might feare, For assuredly both with you and with us and in other places, that heresie doeth spread which at length may prove dangerous.[47]

Endecott had claimed that there were Gortonists in Boston as well as Salem, and Gorton himself supports this view:

Usually coming to us into the prison [before their sentencing and therefore meaning in Boston], many of them together. As also when we were put apart in the time of our examination, one of the members of the Church of Boston, telling some of us in his own house, that he was persuaded that he did not worship the true God, for, saith he, then he not have permitted you to be brought down from your own plantations amongst us; for, saith he, I am persuaded that our Churches shall not be overcome by any people that should come out against them; his wife standing by, being an ingenious woman, made answer to our content before we could speak; Husband (saith she)

pray do not boast before the victory be known, it
may be the battle is not yet ended.[48]

Between the Downing complaint and the Endecott complaint about the work of Holden in Salem, the source of
the difficulty was removed. Winthrop had a tough decision
to make. By the order of the General Court, Holden, at
least, had violated the terms of his sentence and should
have been brought to trial for his life. The governor was
a moderate man, however, and although he may have been
willing to go along with the death sentence the previous
November, he was not willing to initiate the proceedings
in February. Perhaps Holden's success in Salem had far
outweighed the successes of his colleagues. Salem men and
those of other Essex towns were enraged with Winthrop
and the Suffolk magistrates in the winter of 1643–44. They
believed they had been needlessly exposed to the possibility of war with the French in Acadia. In all probability,
they were willing to listen to any fellow victims of the injustices "of the greedy magistrates in Boston." The French
business probably influenced the case in another way. Winthrop's enemies were determined to bring about his defeat in 1644, and doubtlessly he had no desire to give them
any more ammunition to use against him. If, in all likelihood, he ordered a new trial before the Court of Assistants,
Holden and any others tried with him would be found
guilty. They could then appeal to the General Court,
which again would split. Winthrop knew he would not
be able to get enough deputies' votes to get a conviction
in the General Court, and he would again offer his enemies the opportunity to request decisions on the basis
of a majority of the total vote of the Court. To the governor the preferable alternative seemed to be to make the
best of a bad case—to release the Gortonists and banish
them from all Massachusetts territory including Shawomet. It probably had been the best move from the very

beginning. Winthrop mentions only that at the next Court the Gortonists were released because they were discovered corrupting the people with their heresies—"especially the women." [49]

> It is ordered that Samuel Gorton and the rest of that company, who now stand confined, shall be set at liberty, provided that if they, of any of them shall after fourteen days after such enlargement come within any part of our jurisdiction, either in the Massachusetts, or in, or near Providence, or any of the lands of Pumham or Sachonocho, or elsewhere within our jurisdiction, then such person or persons shall be apprehended, weresoever they may be taken, and shall suffer death by course of law, provided also that during all their continuence in our bounds inhabiting for the said time of fourteen days, they shall be still bound to the rest of the articles of their former confinement upon the penalty therein expressed. [50]

When the news of his release was presented to Gorton, he objected to the terms and claimed he would not have his irons struck off. The leading men of Charlestown ordered the town smith to strike them and then allowed Gorton to do whatever he wanted for the next fourteen days. The former prisoner than recrossed to Boston, apparently planning to await the arrival of his companions from the more distant towns. He asserts that he was greeted with great joy by the people of Boston, although this was not Winthrop's interpretation. On March 9 or 10 the governor issued a warrant "To the Marshal, or his Deputy":

> I am informed that Samuel Gorton and his company are now abiding in the town, and go divers houses, giving offence thereby, and cause suspicion, of attempting to seduce some of our people; you are

therefore to command them to depart out of the town, before noon this day, upon pain of being apprehended and further proceeded with, according to their deservings.[51]

Gorton determined to obey the order to leave Boston and in fact to leave Massachusetts as soon as possible. He and as many of his followers as had assembled in Boston set out together before the deadline established by Winthrop. They traveled quickly and spent their first night in Shawomet. They were all in a defiant mood and determined to continue the struggle. They decided to exploit what they considered to be a loophole in the Massachusetts banishment. The lands of Indians subject to Massachusetts jurisdiction were to be off limits for the Gortonists, but they had never agreed to the Massachusetts claim that Pumham was legally within the jurisdiction of Massachusetts. Besides, Shawomet was theirs, not Pumham's. On March 25, 1644, the Gortonists wrote another letter to Massachusetts Bay requesting further explanations.[52] Winthrop responded on the first of April.

This is to let you know, that the expression and intent of the order of our last General Court, concerning your coming within any part of our jurisdiction, doth comprehend all the lands of Pomham and Saccononoco; and in the same are included the lands which you pretended to have purchased, upon part whereof you had built some houses, (the place called Shawomet or otherwise;) so as you are not to come there, upon peril of your lives. This I testify to you. . . . You must know withal, that the Court did not intend their order should be a scarecrow (as you write,) for you will find it real, and effectual, if you shall transgress it.[53]

Winthrop's tone was clear. He meant to carry out his threats. Gorton and his friends had good reason to believe that the governor was not bluffing. To remain in Shawomet would be foolhardy. After receiving Winthrop's message, Gorton, Holden, and the others retreated to the island of Rhode Island and, they hoped, to safety.

Gorton, however, was not yet beaten. It must have been humiliating for him to return to the scene of his public punishment, but at least he was no longer molested there. He had already determined his next course of action: he would appeal to England. Massachusetts and Plymouth pressures on Providence had convinced Roger Williams that his only alternative was to seek a patent and protection from Parliament. Perhaps Gorton was influenced by this decision, for he determined on the same course.

Some time after June 1644, Samuel Gorton, Randall Holden, and John Greene left Rhode Island and traveled to the Dutch town of New Amsterdam, where they boarded a ship and set sail for England. They carried with them the submission of the Narragansett chieftains to the Crown of England which Gorton had arranged after his release from Massachusetts, along with a burning determination to rectify the great injustice done to them. They were determined to return to their homes in Shawomet even if they had to plague every member of Parliament to do so.[54]

At this point the story of Samuel Gorton takes on added significance for the history of Massachusetts Bay. Gorton's intention was to appeal to the Commission for Foreign Plantations—a Parliamentary committee headed by the Earl of Warwick, and including in its membership such men as George Fenwick (who was deeply involved in New England settlement) and Samuel Vassall (brother of William Vassall of Scituate in Plymouth Colony). The commissioners had instructions from Parliament to act in the same capacity toward the colonies as the king had formerly acted before the disturbances that separated him from his Parliament had begun.

We have very little information concerning Gorton's activities in England. We do know that he received a sympathetic hearing from the commissioners. Why he should have received this sympathy is difficult to explain. Winthrop accounted for it by English hostility toward Massachusetts intolerance and a growing lack of orthodoxy in England: "The petitioner being favored by some of the commissioners, partly for private respects, and partly for their adhering to some of their corrupt tenets, and generally out of their dislike for us for our late law for banishing anabaptists, they seemed to be much offended with us for our rigorous proceedings (as they called it) against them." [55]

The experience of Massachusetts residents giving support to heretics like Gorton prompted a crackdown on the native crop of heretics in the colony. Winthrop reports that in 1643

> The lady Moodye, a wise and anciently religious woman, being taken with the error denying baptism to infants, was dealt withal by many of the elders and others, and admonished by the church of Salem, (whereof she was a member,) but persisting still, and to avoid further trouble, etc., she removed to the Dutch against the advice of all her friends. Many others, infected with anabaptism, removed thither also.[56]

Baptists were not necessarily as radical as Gortonists, but neither could they be described as orthodox. In November 1644, after ridding themselves of Gorton, and before word of his activities in England could have arrived, Massachusetts Bay passed legislation banning from the colony all who opposed infant baptism and all who would seduce others in opposing it.[57]

One year after the ban on Baptists, when it became obvious that the Massachusetts law was quite unpopular in

England, a petition from "divers merchants and others" was presented to the General Court complaining about the law and stating it gave offense to many godly men in England and that Massachusetts church members were being denied communion in English churches because of the offense. The petition was signed by at least one man of prominence, Emanuel Downing of Salem, Winthrop's brother-in-law, who had been so vocal about the need to execute Randall Holden. Other signers included Nehemiah Bourne, Robert Sedgwick, and Thomas Fowle.*

Despite the prominence of the petitioners, the answer they received from the October 1644 session of the General Court was short and not particularly friendly:

> In answer to the peticon of Emanuel Douning, Nehemiah Bourne, Robert Seduike, Thomas Foule, with others, for the abrogacon or alteration of the lawes against the Anabaptists and that lawe that requires speciall allowance for new comers residing here, itt is ordered, that the lawes in their peticon menconed shall not be altered or explayned at all.[58]

It was the influence of the elders which brought about the rejection of Downing's petition so swiftly. They appealed to the deputies and magistrates about the danger of the growing Baptist heresy in England and in Massachusetts Bay. And their intervention was spectacularly successful.[59]

In May 1646, in time for the next General Court, a counterpetition, citing the great dangers of "Anabaptism" and signed by seventy-eight citizens of Dorchester and Roxbury, was presented and accepted by the General Court.[60] Orthodoxy was preserved at home, but with unfortunate consequences abroad.

* Bourne was a Boston shipbuilder who had either just returned or was about to return to England to serve under Cromwell. Sedgwick was a member of the General Court and major general of militia, and upon returning to England achieved high rank in the Parliamentary armies. Thomas Fowle will be introduced below, p. 236.

In England advocates of religious toleration—many of them Independents, and many of them good friends of Massachusetts Bay—were placed at a serious disadvantage by the Massachusetts policy of strictly enforced orthodoxy. They could not advocate religious toleration in England and then support Massachusetts against petitioners who asked for an extension of the policy to New England.

Gorton argued his case for almost two years before achieving a success which was totally unexpected by Massachusetts Bay. His case before the commissioners was strengthened by the policy of intolerance which the Massachusetts leadership had adopted. He could and did appear as the victim of an unpopular persecution. In addition, his case was strengthened by the element of surprise. Massachusetts Bay was not prepared to answer his charges before the commissioners. When Thomas Weld, the colony's agent in London, was called upon to represent Massachusetts in a hearing on Gorton's charges, he had absolutely no instructions and was apparently quite ignorant of the facts of the case.[61] Massachusetts leaders, it seems, also believed that there was no pressing need to defend themselves before the commissioners since they could not believe that a notorious heretic's word would be accepted over theirs. But the magistrates and deputies had underestimated the strength of Gorton's case and they had fallen out of touch with the realities of English politics. Also, Gorton's cause was immeasurably improved by a grant in 1644 of a charter to Roger Williams which included the territories of Shawomet, and under which local government would be established by the Gortonists who had moved back to their old homes in defiance of the Massachusetts General Court.[62]

In May 1646 the petitioners of Shawomet desired to return to New England and to their families. Since Massachusetts had still not furnished evidence countering their charges of unjust treatment, the commissioners agreed to issue them safe passage, allowing them to land in Massachusetts Bay and travel through its territory on their way to their homes on Narragansett Bay.[63] At the same time, the commissioners issued a warrant which in effect gave to Gorton, for the time being at least, everything he had been seeking in England for the past two years.

The commissioners addressed themselves to the leaders of Massachusetts Bay and stated that this warrant was not to be considered a sign of their acceptance of the veracity of Gorton's story. Massachusetts Bay was noted for its principles of justice. Yet, since it did not seem that Massachusetts Bay was in a position to answer the charges because of the great distances and difficulties of communication, and since any further delays would work undue hardships on the Shawomet petitioners, the commissioners had been forced to act. Nevertheless, although their safe conduct was temporary, they could not help but agree with Gorton that the Shawomet area was beyond the boundaries of the Royal Charter of Massachusetts Bay:

> And therefore upon the whole matter do hereby pray and require you to permit and suffer the petitioner and all the late inhabitants of Narragansett Bay, with their families and such as shall hereafter join with them, freely and quietly to live and plant upon Shawomet and such other parts of the said tract of land within the bounds mentioned in our said charter, on which they had formerly planted and lived, without extending your jurisdiction to any part thereof, or otherwise disquieting them in their consciences or civil peace, or interrupting them in their possession until such time as we shall have received your answer to their claim in point of title, and you shall thereupon have received our further order therein.[64]

In September 1646, when Randall Holden arrived in Boston aboard a London vessel, bearing the commissioners' safe conduct and warrant, he requested permission to land. Winthrop refused to grant it on the grounds that the governor could not lift a ban imposed by the whole General Court. The Standing Council had a meeting forthcoming, and Winthrop advised Holden to await its decision.

The governor met with the Council and requested the advice of the members. The advice he received was divided. The magistrates, attending the Council's meeting, then applied for assistance from the elders of the region. About ten of them were in Boston for the lecture. But they, too, were divided in their opinions. Finally, since a majority of the magistrates and elders consulted argued for honoring the safe conduct, Holden was allowed to land and pass through Massachusetts Bay to Shawomet.[65]

The Massachusetts leadership was surprised and deeply disturbed by the warrant from the Commission for Foreign Plantations. It is inconceivable to think that they did not know what Gorton and Holden were up to in London. Apparently they never took their adversaries very seriously. But now they would have to change their attitudes and change them quickly. Not only had Gorton succeeded in depriving Massachusetts Bay (at least temporarily) of her hoped-for window on Narragansett Bay, and had placed his infectious ideas once again within striking distance of Massachusetts Bay, but also Gorton had succeeded in establishing a most deadly precedent. He had managed to force a Parliamentary Commission to assert its authority in the New World. The much cherished independence of the Puritan colony was now clearly threatened. If Gorton could appeal to England from Massachusetts judicial decisions, then anyone could. Massachusetts was on the verge of losing the freedom of action she had gained by winning her charter and bringing it to the New World. The experiment in pure churches and godly society was in grave danger.

The November 1646 session of the General Court, now

pressed by another case with appeal potential—that of Dr. Robert Child—got to work in an attempt to rectify the damage to their independence which Gorton and their own indifference had managed to achieve. Edward Winslow of Plymouth Colony was persuaded to act as agent for Massachusetts Bay after Winthrop declined a request that he undertake the task. A petition to the Commissioners for Foreign Plantations was drawn up to be presented to them by Winslow, acknowledging their submission to the realm of England *under their charter,* but arguing that the intervention of the commissioners was prejudicial to their liberties as Englishmen:

> Our humble petition (in the first place) is, that our present and future conformity to your orders and directions may be accepted with a salvo jure, that when times may be changed, (for all things here below are subject to vanity,) and other princes or parliaments may arise, the generations succeeding may not have cause to lament, and say, England sent our fathers forth with happy liberties, which they enjoyed many years, not withstanding all the enmity and opposition of the prelacy, and other potent adversaries, how come we then to lose them, under the favor and protection of that state, in such a season, when England itself recovered its own? [66]

The petition then went on to disagree with the commissioners' contentions that Massachusetts had exceeded its legitimate authority in reaching down into Shawomet and seizing Gorton. He was their professed enemy and "attempted their ruin." The General Court offered documentary evidence, in the form of Gorton's and Holden's letters, to the General Court. Since they were professed enemies of Massachusetts and were living outside the jurisdiction of Massachusetts civil authority, the only course left to the Court was to seek justice by force of arms—an action permitted by the terms of the charter, and an action for which Massachusetts had the support of the United Colonies. As far as any error in banishing the Gortonist was concerned, if they erred in this, they erred on the side of leniency. Gorton deserved worse!

At this point the Massachusetts petition to the Commissioners for Foreign Plantations turned from the particulars of the Gorton case and raised the basic principle involved. There were in Massachusetts men of unquiet dispositions given over to scandalous and seditious petitions. Gorton's success and the possibility of further appeal was inspiring them to slander Massachusetts justice and seek redress from the commissioners. In hearing Gorton's case the commissioners had opened a Pandora's Box which could well mean the overthrow of order in society. If constant appeals were allowed, all judgments would become meaningless and the authority of the magistrates and the charter would be destroyed:

> And this in special, if you shall please to pass by any failings you may have observed in our course, to confirm our liberties, granted to us by charter, by leaving delinquents to our just proceedings, and discountenancing our enemies and disturbers of our peace, or such as molest our people there, upon pretence of injustice.[67]

Gorton did not return to Shawomet with Holden in 1646. He was aware that Massachusetts would respond quickly to his victory, and that he would have to remain on the scene to defend its fruits. Gorton revealed the scope of his activities from 1646 to 1648 in England when in 1669 he answered the charges made against him by Nathaniel Morton in his history of Plymouth. He apparently was in great demand as a preacher among radical groups and worked hard sowing his ideas in the fertile soil of civil war England. He was summoned before another Par-

liamentary Commission on charges of preaching blasphe-
mies, leveled against him by Independent ministers. The
commissioners dismissed the charges on the grounds that
he was "a preacher of the gospels." An England committed to religious toleration had no recourse but to free
him.[68]

Gorton, in an effort to offset any propaganda the Massachusetts agent might attempt to use against him, published in 1646 his major political writing—*Simplicity's
Defence against Seven-Headed Policy*. In this book he
faithfully reproduced almost all the documents in his
case—even those which damned his cause. Gorton would
proclaim in the text how moderate he had been in his
responses and other dealings with Massachusetts and then
quote some of his more radical statements as found in his
letters to the magistrates, thus undermining his claim of
moderation. The Massachusetts agent Edward Winslow,
when he arrived in London, answered Gorton with a
book, *Hyposcrisie Unmasked*. Winslow obviously based his
work on Winthrop's notes for his Journal and repeats
most of Winthrop's arguments, but Winslow was not
above embellishing the facts to make his case appear
stronger.

Winslow hoped to upset the favorable decision which
Gorton had obtained from the Commission for Foreign
Plantations, but he was more concerned with efforts to
block the consequences. He hoped to reverse the decision
of the commissioners to accept an appeal from Massachusetts courts. With Shawomet now safely within the boundaries of the newly united and chartered colony of Rhode
Island and Providence Plantations, there was little chance
that Massachusetts would again interfere with Gorton.
Knowing this, in 1648 Gorton could make his plans for
his return to New England. In May, armed with a safe
conduct from the Earl of Warwick, Chairman of the Commission, Gorton arrived in Boston. He was allowed to pro-

ceed to Shawomet, which he renamed Warwick in honor of his benefactor. He was not molested again.[69]

Samuel Gorton, religious enthusiast, tormentor of orthodoxy, beloved founder and leader of his own religious sect, was instrumental in initiating a major assault upon the independence of action of the Puritan experiment in Massachusetts Bay. In the eyes of the orthodox he had first appeared as a troublesome gnat, then as a danger to the moral health of New England, but in the end—in his success in bringing about the introduction of English power into the New World—he became the mortal threat to the very existence of freedom of action in reforming the churches and state without supervision.

The threat he offered was to the fundamentals for which Massachusetts was founded. Defeating him and those who followed his example had to take priority over the jurisdictional battles between magistrates and lesser gentry. The deputies, previously free to attack the magistrates before the general public, could no longer so indulge themselves. Cowed by their overwhelming defeat in the impeachment attempt, and frightened by English intervention, they would now have to rally to the support of their old foes—the magistrates. Unity would be even more imperative in the months ahead, since an even greater threat than Gorton's was at hand in the form of the Remonstrance of 1646.

5   William Vassall and the Remonstrance of 1646

The struggle between deputies and magistrates for political power within the settlement made in the first decade, culminating in the great debate over the Hingham militia, lent credence to the theory that Massachusetts Bay was fundamentally divided. To those who wished to promote change in the colony such a division had to be exploited. Moreover, Samuel Gorton's victory introduced a new concept to those who were plotting change. It was hoped that appeal to England would bring English power to bear on the leaders of Massachusetts Bay and force them to accept change if popular agitation from within could not. Certainly neither of these possible approaches escaped the notice of William Vassall. It was he who thought to exploit the disagreements of the General Court, and there is evidence that it was he who masterminded the Hingham demand for the impeachment of Winthrop. Nor could Vassall have overlooked Gorton's idea of appeal to the Commission for Foreign Plantations. If an "infamous heretic" could receive a hearing from so distinguished a body, how much better were the chances of an appeal against Massachusetts civil and church practice by William Vassall, considering that his brother, Samuel, was a member of the Commission.

Vassall was the major figure in the struggles within the General Court from 1645 on and the major figure in the attempted appeal to England in 1646. His motivation for entering this struggle was undoubtedly complex. He seems to have been dedicated to the overthrow of the rule of magistrates, whom he regarded as a direct threat to the

survival of the rights of Englishmen. He took strong exception to the view held by Massachusetts and Plymouth
magistrates, that their colonies were unique experiments;
and in the case of Massachusetts, that its charter set it
apart from England, exempted it from certain aspects of
English law, and allowed it to establish its own customs
and set its own precedents. He seems also to have been a
Presbyterian—opposed to Congregational polity—and to
have worked to establish a proper church reform. Since
his motivations mixed politics and theology, his program
would reflect the mixture. But from the beginning, the
political motives of necessity dominated the religious.

Vassall's effort took the form of petitions to the General
Courts of Massachusetts Bay and Plymouth. But obviously, considering the different histories of the two colonies, different approaches would have to be made in
each. Plymouth, with its small population, would not be
the major goal. Massachusetts was the great prize. In addition, since Plymouth had a long history of separatism
and of greater liberalism in church and state, its petition
would take the form of an appeal for religious toleration
of all Christians. But in Massachusetts Bay, with its ten
year insistence on unity within one church, and with its
history of a limited church membership controlling the
franchise, the petition would require greater subtlety.

The events in England in the decade of the 1640s had
upset the leadership in Plymouth Colony. Heresies of the
worst sort were spreading in England, and the moral tone
given in the colony by newcomers from the mother country was not desirable. William Bradford, in his history of
the colony under the date of 1642, expressed the anxiety
of the leadership: "But it may be demanded how came it
to pass that so many wicked persons and profane people
should so quickly come over into this land, and mixe them
selves amongst them? seeing it was religious men that be-
gane the work, that they come for religions sake." [1]

In 1645 the situation was not improved. The pressures of heresy were leading Massachusetts Bay to adopt legislation banishing the heterodox from the colony. Apparently Bradford and his closest supporters in Plymouth government—Edward Winslow and Thomas Prence—were of the opinion that Plymouth should follow the Massachusetts lead and initiate similar legislation. At a meeting of the Plymouth Court of Assistants, just prior to the 1645 Plymouth Court of Elections with the governor and three of the six assistants present, a ruling was given which was meant to lead to a banning of heretics from Plymouth. In the next days William Vassall led an attack upon it and called for a program of general toleration in Plymouth. Only a high-handed ruling from the chair by Governor Bradford prevented a victory for Vassall and for the principle of toleration.[2]

In September 1645 Edward Winslow wrote Winthrop a panicky and almost despairing account of the proceedings of the Plymouth Court of Elections which served as a warning to Winthrop. In particular, Winslow wished to warn his friend of the dangers to orthodoxy and civil order presented to all New England by the ideas and actions of William Vassall.

Winthrop would have been wise to consider Winslow's letter carefully, because the struggle was about to move from Plymouth to his own colony. Vassall would have to approach Massachusetts Bay very differently, however. An assault based upon the principle of total religious toleration met with opposition in Plymouth and would stand no chance of victory in intolerant Massachusetts.

Most historians have assumed that the approach Vassall used in Massachusetts Bay was one which expected defeat and was ultimately aimed at appeal to England, using his rejection by the Massachusetts courts as an excuse for such an appeal. But one should not assume that Vassall had no hope of receiving support from within Massachusetts Bay.

From his vantage point just across the border in Scituate, he must have known of pockets of discontent within the neighboring colony. His connection with the town of Hingham made obvious the discontent there. His handling of that town's petition against Winthrop brought to his attention the discontent of the deputies and the representatives of Essex County, while the prominence of the Presbyterian Hobarts in Hingham probably led him to believe that the Presbyterians were a force in other parts of Massachusetts as well.

William Vassall based part of his attack on the status quo in Massachusetts on an appeal for Presbyterian support. Obviously, he was inspired by a conviction that if he were rejected, he could turn to Presbyterians in England, but he was also seeking the support of Massachusetts Presbyterians. He must have been encouraged in his efforts by the events of the ministerial convocation which met in Cambridge in September of 1643, and which attempted to win over New England Presbyterians to the Congregational way.

Thomas Lechford in his *Plain Dealing,* discussing the Massachusetts churches in 1642, stated: "Of late some Churches are of opinion, that any may be admitted to Church fellowship, that are not extremely ignorant or scandalous: but this they are not very forward to practice, except at Newberry." [3] In fact, it was the Newbury church and its admissions policy, as well as the opinions of its pastor, Thomas Parker, and its teacher, James Noyes, concerning the relationship of the ministers toward the congregation which had prompted the meeting of the convocation. Together with Hobart of Hingham, Parker and Noyes constituted the leadership of the Presbyterian movement in Massachusetts Bay.[4]

The meeting ended in a rejection of some aspects of the Presbyterian system and the support of certain aspects of

Congregationalism, but without the approval of the Presbyterian faction.

> We have had a Synod lately, in our College, wherein sundry things were agreed on gravely; as 1. That the votes of the People are needful in all admissions and excommunications, at least in the way of consent; all yielding to act with their consent – 2. That those that are fit matter for a church, though they are not always able to make large and particular relations of the work and doctrine of Faith, yet must not live in the commission of any known sin, or the neglect of any known duty. – 3. That Consociation of Churches, in way of more general meetings yearly; and more privately, monthly, or quarterly; as Consultiative Synods; are very comfortable, and necessary for the peace and good of the Churches. – 4. It was generally desired that the *exercitium* of the churches power might only be in the Eldership in each Particular Church unless their sins be apparent in their work. – 5. That Parish Churches in Old England could not be right without a renewed Covenant at least, and the refusers excluded.[5]

The convocation had taken a mixed stand on Presbyterianism—not supporting it but not outlawing Presbyterian ideas and practices either. The position advocating the necessity of the votes of the congregation was opposed by Parker and Noyes, who would have limited the votes of the people to the calling of the ministers to their offices.[6] Yet the second resolution seems to be backing away from the insistence of proof of the work of saving faith in the soul of the proposed member of the church— a unique feature of the New England Way. The church of the visible saints was not the practice of the Newbury and Hingham churches, although it had become widespread in the others.[7] The convocation, however, seemed to attempt a compromise with the Presbyterian minority.

The point is clear, nevertheless, that Massachusetts Bay had a Presbyterian minority which worried the leaders of the colony, to the extent that they called the convocation together and attempted to bring the Presbyterians into the fold by compromise. William Vassall was aware of these developments. There was a Presbyterian minority to whom he could appeal for support if he based his appeal on grounds which Presbyterians were likely to find agreeable. If his appeal to the local Presbyterians failed, he could then appeal to the English Parliament, now clearly in the Presbyterian fold, and appear to be the agent of New England Presbyterianism.

But Vassall's approach to Massachusetts Bay was not wholly theological. He knew of the large group of adult males who were legally denied the vote, and hoped to find support from them by advocating a broadening of the franchise. He was encouraged in this approach by the attitudes of the leaders of Massachusetts Bay, who were also aware of the problem of the unenfranchised. In March 1644 a bill was introduced in the General Court "for yielding some more of the freeman's privileges to such as were no church members that should join in the government." The matter was postponed and another bill introduced in 1645 which would have had the effect of granting freemanship to certain nonchurch members who possessed considerable wealth. This bill was pending when Vassall presented his petition.* The usual interpretation

* Vassall failed to receive his expected support from the nonvoting masses of Massachusetts Bay. Perhaps they were afraid to act. Certainly protesters in the past had not been gently treated. But perhaps they were indifferent to his appeal. It might be that Vassall (and the later historians) were taken in by the bills of 1644 and 1645, thinking that the worries of the leadership were based on discontent among the voteless. The proposed franchise bill might have had very different origins and purposes. Considering what has been shown already about probably wide-

is that the leaders of Massachusetts, rather than appear to be pressured by the petition, postponed action on the bill until 1647.[8]

Closely connected with the approach of an appeal for a broader franchise was Vassall's call for support from the deputies to the General Court. The years of struggle— deputy against magistrate—and the attempted impeachment of Winthrop had probably convinced Vassall that if he had any support within the government of Massachusetts, it would come from the deputies. He may have misunderstood the conflicts of the preceding years, seeing fundamental differences between the factions concerning the nature of the government, while only a fierce struggle for power within the existing framework of the government was occurring. Perhaps he correctly understood the disagreements within the General Court, but thought to play on angry tempers and cajole the deputies into supporting his movement. It is clear, however, that he hoped for support from political groupings within Massachusetts. If they failed him, then he could appeal to England and appear as the champion of English law against arbitrary government.

Vassall would appeal, therefore, to three groups within Massachusetts—the Presbyterians, the unenfranchised, and the deputies. His petition would have both religious and political overtones. Although Vassall apparently was a Presbyterian,[9] the objective which tied him and his associates together was more likely the political goal of upsetting the domination of the magistrates in Massachusetts.

---

spread illegal voting in the remoter areas, these laws granting the franchise to some of those already voting illegally may have been an attempt to check illegal voting. By establishing uniform standards for the whole colony and enforcing them, and allowing wealthy nonchurch members to vote, it may have been possible to prevent the mass of illegal voters from voting in the future. The franchise bills of 1644 and 1645, rather than being a contemplated extension of the franchise, may have been restrictive in purpose.

The petitioners were of too broad a religious spectrum to be held together by Vassall's religious goals:

> The persons were of a Linsiewolsie disposition, some for Prelacy, some for Presbytery, and some for Plebsbytery, but all joined together in the thing they would, which was to stir up the people to dislike of the present Government . . . the matter they petitioned for, was a bottom to build their quarrel upon, under the name of a Presbyterian Government, and this they supposed would suit well with their Bill of complaint, which they intended for England, not that they cared for a Presbyterian Church, for had they so done, they might have found out one in the country before they petitioned.[10]

In May 1646, near the end of the General Court session, the Remonstrance and Humble Petition was presented to the Court. While Willian Vassall was not a signatory of it, being a nonresident of Massachusetts Bay, there was no doubt in the mind of John Winthrop who was behind it:

> One Mr. Vassall, sometimes one of the Assistants of the Massachusetts, but now of Scituate in Plymouth jurisdiction, a man of a busy and factious spirit, and always opposite to the civil governments of this country and the way of our churches, had practised with such as were not members of our churches to take some course, first by petitioning the courts of the Massachusetts and of Plimouth, and (if that succeeded not) then to the parliament of England, that the distinctions which were maintained here, both in civil and church estate, might be taken away, and that we might be wholly governed by the laws of England.[11]

Those who did sign the petition were Dr. Robert Child, Thomas Fowle, Samuel Maverick, Thomas Burton, John Smith, David Yale, and John Dand.[12]

The Remonstrance was a strong document. Indeed, the tone it assumed on many issues was so antagonistic to the established order that it seemed to invite rejection. This has led historians ever since to assume that it was composed purposely in this tone so that the petitioners could be rejected speedily and then proceed to appeal to Parliament. Yet, for the reasons outlined above, one must not conclude that the petitioners were not seeking help from dissident elements within Massachusetts, and that they had given up hope of internal revolutions, altering the established order. There are sections of the document which appeal directly to the Massachusetts Presbyterians; others which appeal to the disfranchised; and many more which appeal for the support of the deputies to the General Court.

The Remonstrance began with an invocation which alone allowed it to be entitled "Humble Petition":

> The Remonstrance and humble Petition of us whose names are underwritten, in behalfe of ourselves and divers others within this jurisdiction, humble sheweth, That we cannot but withall thankfulness acknowledge your indefatigable paines, continuall care and constant vigilancy, which, by the blessing of the Almighty, hath procured unto this wilderness the much desired fruits of peace and plenty: While our native land, yea the Christian world is sharply afflicted with the devouring sword and the sad consequents of intestine wars. And further, that you whom the Lord hath placed at the helme of these plantations and endowed with eminent gifts fitt for such honourable callings, are best able to forsee the clouds which hang over our heads, the storms and tempests which threaten this poor handfull here planted and timoresly to amend them.[13]

These were the first and last kind words found in the Remonstrance. The Lord who had carried the settlers to the new land, asserted the petitioners, had now deserted them and had turned against them, "blasting all our designs." "Many good estates are brought to the brink of extreame poverty." [14] This last was a reference to the economic depression gripping the colony, and apparently the result of the end of the great migrations and the halting of the chief trade of Massachusetts—the sale of livestock to newcomers. The document then continued to list the signs of God's recent disfavor. The petitioners reminded the General Court of the outbreak of shameful diseases.* Poverty and disease—the fruits of sinfulness—abounded in the colony. Those in positions of responsibility had failed.[15]

The Remonstrance then listed, more specifically, those grievous faults of the colony which had caused the Almighty to turn his face from them. Despite the existence of the charter granting them many rights and immunities, incorporating them, and allowing them to choose rulers and make laws not repugnant to those of England, "We cannot, according to our judgments, discerne a settled forme of government according to the lawes of England, which may seeme strange to our countrymen, yea to the whole world, especially considering we are all English." [16]

The petitioners followed their complaints of a lack of their traditional rights as Englishmen by asserting that there was no body of laws for the colony. They criticized strongly the failure of the government to collect and publish the colony's laws, claiming that many in the colony viewed "the procrastination of such settled lawes to proceed from a overgreedy spirit of arbitrary power (which it may be is their weakness) such proceedings being de-

---

* The petitioners, in speaking of "shameful diseases," were referring to an outbreak of syphilis. See n. 15 on p. 253, below, for Winthrop's account of one of these outbreaks.

testable to our English nation, and to all good men." The Remonstrance continued:

> Further, it gives cause to many to thinke themselves hardly dealt with, others too much favored, and the scale of justice too much bowed and unequally balanced: From whence also proceedeth feares and jealousies of illegal committments, unjust imprisonments, taxes, rates, customes, levyes of ungrounded and undoing assessments, unjustifiable presses, undue fynes, unmeasurable expences and charges, of unconceyvable dangers through a negative or distructive vote unduly placed, and not well regulated.[17]

A more blatant appeal for the support of the deputies could not have been made. A major dispute between them and the magistrates had been over the negative voice, and here the petitioners echoed the deputies, calling the negative voice a dangerous tendency toward arbitrary government. Another desire of the deputies was a book of laws prescribing fixed penalties for specific crimes—an effort to limit the discretionary power of the magistrates. The petition gave both programs—the elimination of the negative voice and the compilation of a book of general laws—its wholehearted support, hoping to receive the endorsement of the deputies in return.

Child and his fellow petitioners made another appeal to the nonfreemen protesting their political disabilities and claiming to speak for "many thousands in these plantations." They were "debarred" from office-holding of any kind and had no "vote in choosing magistrates, captains or other civill and military officers." This disability was based on no valid grounds, since these nonfreemen were born Englishmen, paid equal taxes with the freemen, and should therefore have enjoyed the same rights.[18]

There was only one remedy for such abuses—that civil liberty and freedom had to be granted to all those who were truly English and that the nonfree must be granted the same rights as the freemen. Massachusetts Bay, they asserted, was not a free state but a corporation of England and English law, and the rights of Englishmen must prevail over the privileges of a corporation.[19]

The petitioners, after making their appeal to the deputies and their appeal to the nonfree, then turned their attention to the third minority—the Presbyterians:

> Whereas there are divers sober, rightious and godly men, eminent for knowledge and other gracious gifts of the holy spirit, no wayes scandalous in their lives and conversations, members of the Church of Endland [sic] (in all ages famous for piety and learning) not dissenting from the latest and best reformation of England, Scotland, etc. yet they and their posterity are deteined from the seales of the covenant of free grace, because, as it is supposed, they will not take these church covenants.[20]

They would not own these covenants because they could see no scriptural proof of their necessity; moreover, the covenants differed from church to church, further confusing the potential signers and casting further doubt upon the whole process.

The Remonstrance cited additional evidence against New England Congregationalism. Not only were those who were not covenanted barred from the sacraments and therefore victims of a great injustice, but the offense was further compounded by laws forcing the nonchurch members under penalty of heavy fines to attend church services and on many occasions to pay for the support of a minister who rendered them no service in return.

The solution to these church grievances offered by the petitioners had little chance of a favorable hearing. They requested that the General Court open all the churches of the colony to all members of the Church of England "not scandalous in their lives and conversations." And, if this proved impossible, the Court should at least grant to those denied membership the right to organize themselves into churches "according to the best reformations of England and Scotland." [21] In short, Massachusetts Bay, to satisfy the petitioners, must drop the concept of the church of the visible saints and replace it with the Presbyterian concept of membership for all except public sinners—either this, or allow the establishment and toleration of Presbyterian churches in the colony. This last point was weak, since at least two of the Massachusetts churches were Presbyterian in sympathy and were tolerated. Later Edward Winslow, while agent of Massachusetts Bay, would hit out at this point. If they merely desired Presbyterian churches, they could have them. "This I know to be false for I heard them demand in Court the Presbyterian government and it was granted to them." [22] What in fact was demanded was a change in the church structure of Massachusetts Bay.

Finally, should all these things be done and the Remonstrance receive a favorable hearing, the blessings of the Lord would descend upon Massachusetts; religion would thrive; the economy would boom; the fear of arbitrary government would be banished; and Englishmen, secure in their rights, would bask in the warmth and light of God's peace! [23]

It is clear from the content of the document that the petitioners were hoping for support. They had not written it with the assumption that it would be rejected by the General Court. They expected nothing but condemnation from the magistrates, but they hoped for support from the deputies. Either the petitioners thought that the deputies could be duped into supporting a call for fundamental changes in the political and religious structure of the colony by appeals to their deepest political desires or else the petitioners themselves were duped into thinking the

deputies desired an overhaul of the frame of government.
If the deputies failed them, however, the petitioners could
always turn to the nonfreemen, whom they claimed to represent, and could seek the support of those outside the
narrow confines of Congregationalist orthodoxy. Finally,
if all failed, they could follow the example of Samuel Gorton and appeal to the power of Parliament.

The Remonstrance was presented to the General Court
near the end of the May session of 1646, and since the content of the document was so serious, the Court decided
not to take it into consideration until the next session,
which was scheduled for the fall.[24] The delay was necessary in order to give the magistrates and ministers a
chance to prepare an adequate answer to the Remonstrance and to test the reaction to it both among the
deputies and nonfreemen. Would the deputies use the Remonstrance, with its call for the adoption of their policies,
to enhance their position against the magistrates at the
risk of undermining the settlements reached in the first
decade, or even more dangerous, at the risk of undermining the basic independence of action which the colony enjoyed? Allowing a call for English intervention would undermine their position in the framework as well as the
magistrates'. Or would they seek revenge for the defeat
in the Hingham case despite the consequences? Would the
Presbyterian minority in the colony willingly sacrifice their
tolerated position and their political independence under
the charter to achieve the overthrow of Congregational polity? Would the nonvoting minority in the colony willingly
answer to a call for greater political voice even though
most agreed with the government policies and many were
voting illegally anyway? These were the questions that
would have to be answered in the months that followed—
the crucial questions whose answers would determine not
only the outcome of the debate between the lesser and

greater gentry but the future of the colony in the decades to come.

Both magistrates and ministers began a campaign to discredit the Remonstrance, while the petitioners busily distributed copies of their petition throughout the colony, and in Plymouth, Connecticut, and New Haven as well. Copies apparently reached the Dutch at New Amsterdam and the English in Virginia. Even far-off Bermuda knew of the troubles in Massachusetts Bay.[25]

The ministers—"not all, some few being silent"—used their pulpits to attack the ideas contained in the petition and to attack the petitioners as well. According to Major John Child's account, the ministers preached that the petition was sedition "full of malignancie, and subvertive both to Church and Commonwealth." Some ministers compared the petitioners to the sons of Belial, to Judases, and to the sons of Corah. The sermons preached during the summer of 1646, according to John Child, usually included a clarion call for the arrest and punishment of these disturbers of the Lord's people.[26] Apparently some of the magistrates, too, took advantage of their "pulpits"—the judges bench—to lecture their "congregations" concerning the evils of the Remonstrance.

The reaction of the common folk of Massachusetts Bay to the Remonstrance during the summer seems not to have been very vigorous, thus dooming Vassall's attempt at internal pressure for reform. There is a letter from Samuel Symonds, the Ipswich magistrate, to John Winthrop dated at a much later moment in the controversy (January 6, 1646–47) which indicates some sympathy existing in Ipswich:

> I am informed that coppies of the petition are spreading here, and divers (spetially yonge men and women) are taken with it, and are apt to wonder why such

men should be troubled that speake as they doe, not
being able suddenly to discerne the poyson in the
sweet wine, nor the fire wrapt up in the straw. and
albeit I doe conceive that this Towne affourds very
few malignants yet withall I doubt not but here are
some active spirits for any such projects once sett on
foote. I am informed of the suspitious expression
here and there of some, but I shall attend full matter
and the fittest season, before I thinke to meddle with
them. I perceive that our people here when through
the cunying of some and mistake of others any doubts
concerning the publique proceedings are in minds,
they are soone satisfyed when they are rightly informed. Upon these and such like considerations I
do desire you would be pleased to hasten the sending
of a Coppy of the Courts answere to the peticion and
remonstrance, alsoe of the Charge: of there answere
thereunto: and also of a reply (if any be made unto
it) if none be made, then a coppy of the reply to their
answere in the first particular, which I suppose is
with the rest in Mr. Secretaries hands. If it be not too
much trouble to you, I should desire now and then, a
few lines from you how matters proceed at the Bay.
Its none of the least poynts of the pet. policy to beare
people in hand of multitudes to be of their mind,
but its conceived that its a meere empty vant, for
except a few (not affected to religion, and others erroneous in opinions) the people are firme. . . . If
you think it meete, I pray send alsoe a Coppy of their
peticion found in Dandds studdy.[27]

This sympathy for Child and the others may have been
present from the beginning. The fact that younger men
and women sympathized with the petitioners may indicate
discontent among the second generation, who desired
greater political power. It is also significant that sympathy

for the petitioners should be found in the remote parts of Essex County. A call for greater participation in the franchise could hardly seem seditious in a community where evidence indicates that the majority of the adult males—freemen and nonfreemen alike—were already casting their ballots. Calling for the universal adoption of an already common practice in Ipswich and other remote towns hardly seemed worthy of all the commotion going on in Boston. It is also significant that the worried Ipswich magistrate wanted copies of the most damning evidence against the petitioners. The Remonstrance itself was not exciting anyone in Ipswich to the dangers implicit within it. Symonds wanted people to read the damning explanations of the petitioners' ambitions, and most importantly, he wanted copies of their later petitioners calling for the overthrow of the Massachusetts Bay government. It was Symond's belief that these documents would alert Essex men to the seditious nature of the Remonstrance and put an end to any sympathy for the petitioners. Essex men wanted more power for Essex. They did not wish to surrender sovereignty to Parliament.

Throughout all of Massachusetts Bay the threat of Parliamentary intervention was probably the most useful tool of those who worked against the Remonstrance, and it reveals the deep dilemma that Vassall and those who drew up the Remonstrance faced. If they appealed solely to the people of Massachusetts Bay, they lost the advantages of their most powerful possible support—the Commissioners for Foreign Plantations. If they appealed solely to Parliamentary power, they aroused the entire population of the colony and lost the support of dissident groups within Massachusetts. The petitioners tried to appeal to both with greater emphasis in the humble petition on an appeal to the dissatisfied groups within Massachusetts, but with the threat of Parliamentary appeal quite explicitly presented. And it was this threat which allowed the magistrates to rally support against the petitioners or to silence potential support for their ideas. Magistrates, deputies, ministers, and freemen, who together constituted a majority of the adult male population, valued their freedom of action without English supervision above all else. In all likelihood, those who did not become freemen and who might have, had they wished to (the body of adult male church members who never took the oath), and those who did not qualify for freemanship but who voted illegally in their own towns were also in sympathy with the majority. They might not see sedition in the Remonstrance, but they would not be sympathetic to fundamental changes which would subordinate Massachusetts Bay to the Parliament of England. They would gain nothing by such a change and might possibly lose everything. The success of the magistrates and ministers was achieved by hammering home this point.

Immediate steps to counter the Remonstrance were planned by the General Court before adjourning in May 1646. A first step concerned the draft proposal for extending the franchise which had been held over from 1645: "And whereas a law was drawn up, and ready to pass, for allowing non-freemen equal powers with the freemen in all town affairs,—and to some freemen of such estate, etc., their votes in elections of magistrates, it was thought fit to defer this also to the next session." [28] This action has been interpreted as reluctance on the part of the General Court to seem to be acquiescing in the wishes of the petitioners: rather than seem to be pressured into broadening the franchise, they deferred action until a more favorable season. But there are other possible interpretations. Since there was considerable atention given to a similar bill in 1644, before the agitation aroused by Vassall, the franchise bill of 1645 was more than just an effort to steal the thunder from any possible agitators by removing one of their main arguments. It is possible that both the bills of

1644 and 1645, rather than liberalizing moves, were intended as crackdowns on illegal voting.

The 1645 bill allowing nonfreemen to vote in local affairs would grant legality to voting already going on (although illegally) in remote areas of the colony, especially in Essex and Norfolk counties. It is true that this bill would have a liberalizing effect in Suffolk and Middlesex by allowing nonfree to vote in local elections, but this would be more than compensated for by guaranteeing that illegal voting would not be extended to colony elections. The nonfreemen who were not church members would be given freemanship on the basis of property holdings, thus preventing the masses of nonfreemen from casting ballots for governor and magistrates—if it were properly enforced, and the provisions of the bill indicate that it would be. The postponing of any action in 1646 on this bill could then be understood as an effort not to antagonize the nonfreemen illegal voters and avoid making ready converts for Vassall and Child. Since the petitioners complained about too limited a franchise, it would not be wise to pick that exact moment to crack down on illegal voting. No matter what the reasoning, however, the General Court decided to drop the franchise bill for the present.

A second action that the General Court took in May of 1646 was to call for a synod of the New England churches. There is no doubt that this move was under serious consideration before the Remonstrance was presented to the General Court, but agitation such as that in the Hingham church and the political agitation on religious toleration in Plymouth, combined with Presbyterian triumphs in England and Presbyterian sympathies at home, made the more orthodox ministers desirous of a statement of orthodoxy. The presentation of the Child-Vassall protest made the meeting all the more imperative.[29]

The synod sessions of 1646 accomplished nothing of
importance. For its first meetings the most prominent
theologian of the colony, John Cotton, was not an official
member, and little could be attempted without him. Even
had he been present, the absence of Hooker of Connecticut and Davenport of New Haven, as well as that of
messengers from the other United Colonies' churches,
combined with the small likelihood of their arrival in
Cambridge before winter set in, made it imperative to
postpone any action to a later session. After meeting for
only fourteen days, the synod adjourned until the following June.[30]

The third step taken by the General Court to counter
the Remonstrance was to appoint a committee to continue
in an effort to codify the existing laws and to publish a
book of laws.[31] This was a project dear to the hearts of the
deputies, and the magistrates probably were willing to go
along with them now that the lack of such a compilation
had become a matter of public debate and was being used
by opponents of the status quo. Failure to support the
deputies on this issue at this time woud leave the magistrates open to the charge of a tendency to arbitrary government hurled at them in the Remonstrance. Appointing committees, of course, was not the same thing as passing bills establishing a book of laws. If such a committee
helped win the support of the deputies against the Remonstrance, it was a small price to pay.

The fourth action taken by the Court was more directly
to the point. Several answers to the Remonstrance had
been drawn up by interested persons, and in October
1646, during a brief session of the General Court, Winthrop, Bellingham, Dudley, and Nathaniel Duncan were
ordered to constitute themselves as a committee "to peruse
and examine all the answers that are brought into this
Corte to the petition of Doctor Child and Mr. Fowle, etc.,
and out of all to draw up such an answer thereto as they

thinke most meete; and present the same to this Corte." [32]

The committee drafted an answer to the Remonstrance which was ready for publication before the end of the November session of the General Court, and entitled *A Declaration of the General Court Holden at Boston 4 (9) 1646, concerning a Remonstrance and Petition Exhibited at Last Session of This Court by Doctor Child, Thomas Fowle, Samuel Maverick, Thomas Burton, John Smith, David Yale and John Dand.*[33] It began by casting suspicions on the expressed goal of the petitioners. The authors of the *Declaration* observed that the authors of the Remonstrance had undermined their position by acknowledging that the "indefatigable paines, continuall care and constant vigilancy" of the magistrates had brought peace and plenty to the wilderness, while England and the whole Christian world suffered. To the magistrates this was a clear indication that they were doing their job and that their opponents had no grounds for complaint. The whole petition was so self-contradictory that the General Court would be within its rights to throw it out without considering it.[34]

The *Declaration,* however, rather than merely discussing the innate weaknesses of the Remonstrance, proceeded to answer the complaints of the latter document one by one. The basic law of the Massachusetts Bay Colony was as compatible with that of England as the differences between a prosperous and ancient kingdom and an infant colony would allow. The *Declaration* listed the fundamentals of England beginning with Magna Charta and proceeding to the common law, and contrasted the fundamental laws of Massachusetts Bay in parallel columns.[35]

The comparison was skillfully done to stress the similarities between English law and Massachusetts law and to ignore the discrepancies. The *Declaration* depends heavily on the charter and the Body of Liberties of 1641 in expounding the fundamental law of Massachusetts Bay. The use of the Body of Liberties would require, however, that that document be given an entirely different tone. Originally, the Body of Liberties justified each of its specific capital provisions with a citation from Scripture, rather than by any reference to Magna Charta or common law. In the *Declaration* Scripture references are deleted. Moreover, the *Declaration*'s authors were forced to attempt to cover obvious differences between common law and the Body of Liberties. In the area of capital crimes the *Declaration* states the principles of England as: "Notorous and greate felonies, as treason, murther, witchcraft, sodomie, etc., are punished capitally, but simple theft and some other felonies are not punished with death, if the offender can reade in scripture." [36] The Massachusetts principle, cited as an example of similarity, had some important differences even if the choice of words is similar: "Treason, murther, witchcraft, Sodomie, and other notorous crimes, are punished with death: But theft etc. is not so punished, because we reade otherwise in the scripture." An even more obvious discrepancy can be found in the *Declaration*'s statement on adultery. It cites the common law on adultery as: "Adultery is referred to the canon or spiritual lawe." The corresponding Massachusetts fundamental is cited as: "Adultery is punished according to the canon of the spirituall lawe, viz. the Scripture." [37] In other words, and in words of far greater clarity, adultery was punishable by death in Massachusetts Bay. This point is quite clear in the Body of Liberties, which in this particular instance was not quoted: "If any person committeth Adultery with a married or espoused wife, the Adulterer and Adulteresse shall surely be put to death. (Lev. 20: 19 and 18: 20 and Deut. 22: 23–24.)" [38]

The authors of the *Declaration* could not have hoped to fool anyone in Massachusetts Bay by such deceit. In particular, the deception on adultery must have been obvious to the residents of the colony. Almost everyone remembered the trial and executions of James Britton and Mary Latham for adultery in 1644, and must have recalled a more recent trial of an anonymous young man and woman of Boston who were tried for their lives and were acquitted of adultery but found guilty of adulterous behavior and condemned to stand upon the gallows for a specified period of time. Only their insistence that they had not attempted anything adulterous and the lack of witnesses to anything but highly suspicious behavior saved them.[39]

Everyone in Massachusetts Bay knew that one could be executed for adultery. The attempted deception in the *Declaration,* therefore, must have been intended for less knowledgeable readers. This and similar examples in the *Declaration* show quite clearly that it was prepared not to satisfy any of the discontented within the colony but rather to mollify any English critics of Massachusetts Bay. Winthrop, Dudley, Bellingham, and Duncan had already anticipated that the internal threat posed by the Remonstrance was negligible, and that its appeal to the deputies would not succeed. Whatever appeal the movement might have had for the deputies was canceled by the clear call to England for assistance. This was as much a threat to the status of the deputies as it was to the magistrates. Vassall and Child could not have both the support of the deputies and the appeal to Parliament. By the end of summer 1646 it must have also been clear that the petitioners would get little popular support within Massachusetts. The real fight would occur in London.

The *Declaration* then continued with a point by point refutation of the various charges in the Remonstrance. The magistrates' spokesmen asserted that arbitrary government did not exist in Massachusetts Bay, and cited her courts as ones based on common law, while at the same time reminding the petitioners that the chancery courts of equity in England were courts which "doe judge arbitrarily (secundum aequum et bonum)." The *Declaration* admitted to the negative voice, but confessed that the leaders of Massachusetts did not know how to rid themselves of it without turning their government into a "democracy."*

The *Declaration* denied forcing any extra oaths on any man outside of the oaths required under the charter. No civil covenant had been drawn up and forced on any person. But there were church covenants. And if the petitioners were as godly as they claimed to be, and wished to join the church, why did they refuse covenants which would require nothing of them that godly men would not be happy to promise? In addition, such covenants were used by other Christian peoples like the Dutch, and were advocated by English Presbyterians.[40] The taking of these covenants would also open to them the rights of freemanship.

On this question the *Declaration* specifically stated that lack of freemanship did not deprive a man of his rights. The right to vote was nowhere considered one of the basic rights of all Englishmen. Furthermore, there were no illegal taxes in Massachusetts, since they were voted by the elected representatives of the people, and expenditures were kept to an absolute minimum, with the magistrates serving without pay. Nor were there any illegal commitments to prison.†

The arguments of the four committeemen-authors effectively proceeded to discredit the petitioners' claim to be representatives of the nonfreemen of the colony. That only the seven petitioners had come forward to support

* By this they meant that without the negative voice for the magistrates—the people (i.e. the freemen) would rule without any check from the aristocracy (i.e. the magistrates). The magistrates still refused to regard the deputies as anything but the voice of the freemen. It is of course the deputies who would dominate if the negative voice were abolished.

† The Remonstrance probably referred to the Hingham militia case in this charge. To the magistrates that case had ended with the guilty fined and the innocent exonerated.

their position was noted by the authors of the *Declaration*. In the four months since the Remonstrance was first presented, no one else had come to its defense. Moreover, in order to make up the seven petitioners, they had been forced to gather a most unlikely and unimpressive group:

The first [Child] (and he that must (ducem agere in hujus militiae) be the leader in this designe) is a Paduan Doctor (as he is reputed) lately come into the country, who hath not so much as tasted of their grievances, nor like to doe, being a batchelour and only a sojournor, who never payd penny to any publick charge, though (of his owne good-will) he hath done something for publick use. A second [Fowle] is a church member, but will be no freeman; he likes better to be eased of that trouble and charge. A third [Maverick], is a freeman, but no member of any church, and the reason hath beene his professed affection to the hierarchie. A fourth [Burton], is a clarke of the prothonotaries office, a sojourner also, and of no visible estate in the country, one who hath never appeared formerly in such designe, however he hath been drawne into this; it is like to be as those who were called by Absolom to accompany him to Hebron.* A fifth [Yale], is a young merchant, little acquainted with commonwealth affairs. We are willing to suppose he might also be one of them, who were invited by Absolom to Hebron, but sure we are, it is no small griefe to his honored godly friends to find him there, when they prayed and waited dayly to heare of him in Jerusalem. A sixth [Smith], was taken up by accident, being none of this jurisdiction, but himselfe and familie inhabiting at Rhode Island. The seventh [Dand], is an ould grocer of London, whose forgetful-

---

* The prothonotary in England was the chief clerk or register in the Courts of Chancery, of Common Pleas, and of the King's Bench.

ness of the laws and customs of that citty, and un-
mindfulness of his dutie to the government under
which he now lives and prospers, we may impute to
his age and some other infirmities. And these are the
champions who must represent the bodie of nonfreemen. If this be their head, sure they have (in-
sulsum caput et non multo sale defaecondum) an unsavory head, not be seasoned with much salt.⁴¹

When the *Declaration* was completed, before the General
Court of November 1646 met, the Court referred it to a
group of elders who were meeting to advise the magistrates concerning the sending of an agent to answer the
charges of Samuel Gorton. As a result, it was not ready for
publication until later in the session. The elders gave
their approval of the contents, although they did not advise the magistrates on suitable further actions.⁴²

The General Court's last session for 1646 opened on
November 4. Early in the session it was learned that one
of the signers of the Remonstrance, Thomas Fowle, was
planning to leave Massachusetts Bay for England and that
another, John Smith of Rhode Island, was in Boston
temporarily, perhaps not to appear again. William Vassall,
encouraged by Gorton's success in England, which had
been demonstrated so resoundingly by Holden's arrival in
September bearing the safe conduct of the Earl of Warwick, and aware that his appeal to dissident elements in
Massachusetts Bay had fallen on deaf ears, determined to
take his case to England immediately. Fowle had already
decided to resettle in England, and the fact that the two
planned to leave together took the magistrates by surprise.
Apparently they had not known of Fowle's plans, or
knowing of them, did not regard his presence as essential.
Their case against the Remonstrance was not prepared,
nor did they wish to rush into a hearing. Nevertheless,
the propaganda effort of the magistrates and ministers had

been so effective that the deputies took matters into their own hands. The magistrates and elders had convinced the deputies that the Remonstrance, with its threat of appeal to England, was as great a threat to politicians striving for magisterial dignity as it was for those who had already achieved that dignity. The petitioners' appeal to the deputies was a complete failure. Winthrop, in a letter to his son, indicated that it was the deputies who forced a premature hearing: "I had thought we should only have declared our apprehensions concerning the Petition, without questioning the Petitioners but the deputies called upon it, whereupon Mr. Fowle was forced to put in bond to Answer etc." [43]

When Fowle and Smith, under the custody of the marshal, were brought before the General Court, Winthrop asked them whether they would admit to signing the petition, whether they saw any evil in it, and if they did, whether they wished to retract any portions of the Remonstrance. Fowle and Smith admitted that they had signed the petition, but refused to admit to any evil in the document or to retract anything. Moreover, they complained that they should be singled out and called into court while the others were not summoned. Winthrop could not say that the magistrates had not planned to have this hearing, and that the deputies had forced it on him; he merely had to make the best of it. Fowle and Smith were required to post a bond of one hundred pounds each as security for their appearance in court to answer any charges, since they might not be available when the Court might want to press charges: "Mr. Smith spake, and said he would not give in security, but did appeale to the gentlemen commissioners for plantations, and would engage himself to prosecute it. and so said Mr. Foule, in the same expressions." [44] When Winthrop asked if they made their appeal to England with deliberation, they answered yes!

Perhaps the magistrates realized that there was some

justice to the objection of Fowle and Smith that the others
were not called to court. This questioning had come un-
expectedly against their better judgment, and rather than
leave themselves open to any future charge of irregularity,
they may have thought it wise to call in the other petitioners. On the other hand, they may have called in the
others because the questioning was going so well. Winthrop's reaction to their appeal to England was important.
He wanted it perfectly understood that they had appealed
to England before any decisions were rendered by the
General Court and that they had made that appeal after
careful consideration. Thus their appeal would be interpreted as a clear contempt of the General Court. He may
have called in the others to allow them the same amount
of rope. All the other petitioners—with the exception of
Maverick, who apparently was not in Boston at the time—
were brought to the General Court.

When all had assembled, Robert Child, in the name of
the others, demanded to know what the charges against
them were and asserted that it could not be for merely
petitioning, which certainly could be no offense. The
Court responded that they were not questioned for the
act of petitioning but rather because of the petition's
contents. Again Child demanded charges, and again the
Court evaded this request until the magistrates were
forced to admit that they could not present charges against
him since they were not as yet prepared. The Court had
not planned to call them, but with several of them leaving the colony—perhaps never to return—it was determined that they should be questioned. Still, Child demanded charges and finally forced the Court to cite a
specific clause in the Remonstrance which it regarded as
offensive.

With this, Child moved to a different approach. He
claimed he had erred in petitioning the General Court in
the first place. He should have appealed to the Commission

for Foreign Plantations from the very beginning. This was just what Winthrop had been waiting for. He jumped in quickly. There would be no appeal to England. The charter did not allow appeals, and if the Court did allow them, they would render themselves slaves to petitioners. Furthermore, Winthrop let it be known that he and the Court regarded the statement of Child as contemptuous and that Child and the others would be called to account for it.[45]

The Court then turned again to Smith and Fowle, and called upon them to post bond. They refused, with Fowle asserting that he would not do so unless he received a presentment of charges against him, and if he received the charges, he would appeal to England, since the General Court was then a party to the dispute and not a competent judge. The Court turned Fowle and Smith over to the marshal with instructions to hold them in custody until bond was paid. The other petitioners were warned to remain available until called by the Court.[46]

According to Edward Winslow, the two prisoners consulted with William Vassall, who was in Boston making ready to sail for England with a copy of the Remonstrance and a petition to Parliament calling for its intervention in New England. Apparently Vassall was deeply disturbed by this turn of events. He could not without embarrassment present the Remonstrance to Parliament since he had never signed it. He could not complain of the injustices of the government of Massachusetts Bay because he did not live there. He wanted Fowle—a signer of the Remonstrance and a resident of Massachusetts Bay—to accompany him to England even if it cost one hundred pounds. After the consultation, Fowle and Smith each posted that sum and were released.[47]

Thomas Fowle, one hundred pounds poorer, made preparations to sail with Vassall aboard the *Supply*. The day after the court hearing, November 5, was a Thursday, and many of the passengers of the *Supply,* which was scheduled to sail on Friday, attended the lecture in the Boston church. Edward Winslow of Plymouth who was being called upon to serve as agent for Massachussetts Bay was in Boston on that same day and attended the lecture also. He has left an account of what occurred.[48]

John Cotton preached a sermon to his congregation from the Song of Solomon, second chapter, fifteenth verse: "Take us the foxes, the little foxes, that spoil the vines: for our vines have tender grapes." The Boston teacher then applied his text to the existing situation, and turning to those in the congregation who were about to leave for England, he wished them a safe passage, but added ominously:

> But if there bee any amongst you my brethren, as 'tis reported there are, that have a petition to prefer to the high court of Parliament (which the Lord in mercy goe on blessing to blesse as heehath begun) that may conduce to the distraction, annoyance and disturbance of the peace of our churches and weakening the government of the land where wee live, let such know, the Lord will never suffer them to prosper in their subtill, malicious and disparate undertakings against this peiple, who are as tender unto him as the apple of his eye. But of there be any such amongst you that are to goe, I doe exhort and advise such in the feare of God when the terrors of the Almightie shall beset the the vessell herein they are, the heavens shll frowne upon them, the billowes of the sea shall swell above them, and dangers shall threaten them (as I perswade my selfe they will) I would have them then to consider these things for the time of adversitie is a time for Gods people to consider their wayes. I will not give counsell as was taken concerning Jonah to take such a person and cast him into the sea; God

forbid: but I would advise such to come to a resolution in themselves to desist from such enterprises, never further to engage in them and to cast such a petition into the sea that may occasion so much trouble and disturbance.[49]

One can imagine the strained glances and uneasiness that filled the Boston meetinghouse at Cotton's words. One listener, Thomas Peter, brother of the Reverend Hugh Peter and himself a minister, was so frightened that he canceled his plans to sail on the *Supply* and booked passage on a later ship for England via Spain.[50]

The *Supply* had difficulty getting out of Boston harbor. Contrary winds and storms delayed departure for some time. If Mr. Cotton's study had a view of the harbor, he might well have had a smug expression on his face every time he looked out his window. He proved a good prophet, although many, including Cotton himself, have pointed out that predicting a rough passage for a November sailing on the North Atlantic was fairly safe.

Nevertheless, the *Supply* had one of the worst crossings ever recorded. Winslow states that for over seven hundred leagues the navigators could not make a sighting on either sun or stars. In one storm the master of the vessel thought he was about two hundred leagues from Land's End, although he did not know for sure. During the last watch one of the quartermasters sighted rocks dead ahead—the rocks of Scilly.* For one quarter hour, in stark terror, the master and crew guided the ship using the sound of the breakers and white water as aids. Finally, the ship ran aground between two islets and was firmly wedged on the reefs as the tide ebbed. By dawn the passengers and crew marveled at their escape, for straight ahead and on both sides of them were killer rocks. Finally, a pilot was hailed

---

* A group of islands (140 in number, yet totaling only 6 square miles) off Land's End famed for their dangerous reefs.

from shore, the ship was floated free with the high tide, and the journey continued.

Some two weeks before this worst of storms, however, during the height of another tempest, Jonah was cast overboard. The two sources of the story, while agreeing on details, disagree in tone. Winslow insists that the removal of Jonah in mid-ocean took place with the greatest sobriety and calmness, while John Child says it was done in a panic. Considering that the action stemmed from a dire prediction of a minister, and that it was accomplished because of fear of the wrath of God and during a great storm at sea, the Child version seems much more plausible.

Not long after the *Supply* finally sailed, she was struck by a series of vicious North Atlantic storms. At the height of one of these gales, at about midnight, the passengers below decks panicked. They requested the offending documents from Vassall and Fowle, and after they were provided with copies of the Remonstrance, they tore them into pieces and threw them into the angry sea. No doubt the terrified passengers were psychologically prepared to accept even the slightest abatement of wind and rain as a sign of God's acceptance of their offering. During the night and on the following day the storm died down, and all agreed that they had been saved by a miracle.

The continued storms of the next two weeks were attributed to the continued presence of an even more offensive document aboard ship. The seemingly miraculous escape from the Scilly reefs convinced all, however, that they had been destined for doom and that only their following of Mr. Cotton's advice had saved their lives. Surely Vassall and Fowle's petition was the work of the devil. When they reached England, the story of Jonah and the miracle at sea, embellished with each telling, spread far and wide—no doubt assisted by the friends of Massachusetts Bay.[51]

Vassall and Fowle, once in England, began to plot their

campaign and appeal to the Commission for Foreign Plantations, but so destructive to their efforts was the propaganda of the passengers of the *Supply* that Robert Child's brother collaborated with Vassall in publishing a pamphlet attacking the popular account of the voyage and explaining their version of the debate raging in Massachusetts Bay.*

Shortly after Vassall and Fowle had sailed, a committee of the General Court busily worked on charges to be presented against the petitioners. Before the November session of the Court was over, the committee was ready to act. The five signers of the Remonstrance still in Boston (Fowle was of course on his way to England, and Smith had apparently returned to Rhode Island, while Maverick had returned to Boston) were called back into the Court to answer a charge of signing a petition tending to sedition.

Specifically, the Court found objectionable and tending to sedition the calling of the government of Massachusetts "an ill-compacted vessel." It also found offensive the fact that the afflictions recently suffered by Massachusetts were displayed in their worst possible light—as punishments from God for which the magistrates were responsible. The Court was angered by the assertion of the Remonstrance that the charter granted to all Englishmen the rights of free-born Englishmen. This was merely an attempt to de-

---

* The pamphlet—*New England's Jonas Cast Up at London*—bears only the name of John Child, but Winslow in his answering pamphlet insisted that Child was not the real author, and that not only did the information it contained but even its style betray the true authorship—that of his old neighbor from Plymouth, William Vassall. Winslow is probably correct. One slip of the pen lends some support to his contentions. At one point in *Jonas* the pamphlet reads: "but the storm did not leave *us* [italics mine] upon the throwing of this paper overboard" (p. 115). The use of the first person indicates actual participation. Yet John Child was not a passenger aboard the *Supply*.

ceive the people. The General Court asserted that in reality the charter granted rights only to the freemen of the colony and company. Also objectionable was the petitioners' assertion that those in authority were working to establish arbitrary government. Moreover, the petitioners weakened the authority of Massachusetts law by stating they were repugnant to English laws and that no one's life or liberty was safe under the laws of Massachusetts Bay. They falsely stated the facts on some issues—such as the claim that Massachusetts denied the vote to the militia in the selection of their captains. Their speeches claiming thousands of discontented men in the colony tended to sedition by inflaming to actions those few who actually were discontented. They slandered the churches by stating that godly, sober, peaceable men could not live in the colony like Christians. They slandered the Massachusetts government with charges of tyranny when it imprisoned them, and so on, "unjustly." They slandered the people of God by contending that Christian vigilance was not exercised toward nonchurch members. They further slandered the people of God by asserting that their brethren in England were indignant with them for their practices. And finally the charge stated:

> Lastly, that it may yet more clearly appear, that these evils and obliquities, which they charge upon our government, are not the mere jealousies of others, but their own apprehensions, (or pretences rather,) they have publicly declared their disaffection thereto, in that, being called by the court to render account of their misapprehensions and evil expressions in the premises, they refused to answer; but, by appealing from this government, they disclaimed the jurisdiction thereof, before they knew whether the court would give any sentence against them, or not.[52]

The objective observer must conclude that evidence of sedition is not abundantly found in the charges. The last

—that of attempt to appeal to England before the Court had reached a verdict—may have been contempt of the General Court, but it was not seditious action. In fact, the other charges were also more indicative of contempt of court than of sedition.

The charges were read to the petitioners before a capacity audience in the Boston meetinghouse. After hearing them, the accused requested time to prepare an answer, and the request was granted. The petitioners, after consulting on a reply, wrote an answer and returned to Court, where it was read aloud to the entire body, although the reading was frequently interrupted by the Court to respond to various parts of the petitioners' answer.[53]

After hearing the charges and the response to them, the Court went into deliberation. It must have been clear from the beginning that the overwhelming majority of the Court were in favor of conviction, although on what specific charge was unclear. Rather than press the charge of tending toward sedition, the Court seems to have decided to punish them for contempt—both in petitioning the Court, since it was an obnoxious petition, as well as in their actions during the hearing, and especially for appealing to English justice before any sentence was passed by the Massachusetts' courts.

By heavy majorities in both houses of the General Court, the petitioners were found guilty of "blameworthy actions." There were thirty-six deputies to the General Court in November 1646, from twenty-four towns. Thirty-one of the thirty-six voted to convict the petitioners. Of the thirteen magistrates of 1646, ten voted for a conviction.[54]

Those who voted to acquit the petitioners are an interesting group. The magistrates were the same three who had voted together on most of the issues of the past when the magistrates were split—Saltonstall, Bellingham, and Bradstreet. The opposition was quite explicit; they voiced their disapproval of everything that had occurred in the proceedings. We are not given the reasons why. In the past Bellingham and Saltonstall usually were courting the favor of the deputies by their opposition to the magistrates, but in this case the deputies were in favor of a strong action against Child. Palfrey attempts to explain the opposition of Bellingham by citing his constant opposition to Winthrop. If Winthrop was on one side of an issue, Bellingham was sure to be found on the other, and he states that Bradstreet was much under Bellingham's influence, while Saltonstall, considering his father's stand for toleration among English Independents, could do little else but call for greater toleration in New England.[55]

Although Palfrey may have been right on all counts, more must have been involved. Bradstreet may have been influenced by Bellingham, but he was also influenced by his father-in-law, Thomas Dudley, who was voting with the majority. Bradstreet had sided against Winthrop in the La Tour-d'Aulnay issue because he was deeply concerned about a possible attack upon his own section of the colony—Essex County. Bradstreet would oppose if the interests of his section were involved. Saltonstall would not have been the first son to take a stand in opposition to his father's principles. It may well be that the votes of the three, rather than stemming from innate perversity of nature, were rather the result of concern in Essex County about the procedures of the General Court. Bradstreet of Andover, Saltonstall of Ipswich, and Bellingham, who had many connections with Essex, may have been reflecting the conviction of many Essex voters that what Child and the other petitioners were asking for was really not so farfetched and certainly not worthy of harsh punishments. Calling for a broader franchise may have seemed rather a mild request in a section of the colony where widespread illegal voting had made the franchise very broad indeed. Calling for a check on the powers of the magistrates was a request which would meet with the approval of many

Essex men. They would not approve of English intervention in Massachusetts affairs. However, the negative votes
of Bellingham, Saltonstall, and Bradstreet may have
meant that they were convinced that the surest way to
bring about that intervention was to convict the petitioners and deny their harmless requests.

Samuel Symonds of Ipswich, in his letter to Winthrop
written a few months later, supports the contention that
the Remonstrance had supporters in Essex or at least in
Ipswich (cf. above, pp. 171–72). The Presbyterian overtones of the Remonstrance in its call for a reformation of
the New England churches on the model of England and
Scotland probably won additional support for the petitioners among the Presbyterians of the church of Newbury. The town of Rowley in Essex contained some who
felt the petitioners were being harshly treated. One of the
deputies from the town, Edward Carleton, refused to go
along with the vote of the Court and refused to find
Child and the others guilty of contempt. The following
June, in 1647, at the opening of the second session of
the Cambridge synod, the Reverend Ezekiel Rogers of
Rowley preached to the assembled magistrates and deputies: "Mr. Rogers in his sermon took occasion to speak of
the petitioners, (then in question before the Court), and
exhorted the court to do justice upon them, yet with desire of favor to such as had been drawn in, etc." [56] Rogers
was influential in Rowley and a man of some prestige in
the colony. In the past he had taken an anti-Winthrop position concerning the reelection of the same man as governor two years in succession. In this case, he was hardly
taking a pro-Remonstrance position, but in calling for
their punishment, he was calling for punishment tem-
pered with mercy. Although this was not the majority
opinion on the case in the whole colony, it seems to have
been the position of many in Essex,* whose support was

---

* Another one of the deputies who voted against the conviction of the
petitioners was Henry Bartholomew of Salem in Essex.

194   MASSACHUSETTS BAY: THE CRUCIAL DECADE

really more sympathy than support. These Essex men did not agree with Vassall and Child, but neither did they agree with the rest of the General Court that they should be harshly punished.

In addition to the Essex sympathizers, the petitioners received support from the town of Hingham. The feeling there against the magistrates in general, and against Winthrop in particular, must have been very strong. Thomas Burton, one of the petitioners, was from Hingham, and the two deputies from Hingham in November 1646, Joshua Hobart and Bozoan Allen, voted against the conviction of Child and others.

During the discussions on the Remonstrance and on Gorton's appeal later in the session, the Court called for a meeting of the elders to seek their advice. One of those who attended was Peter Hobart of Hingham:

> Mr. Hubbard of Hingham came with the rest, but the court being informed that he had a hand in a petition, which Mr. Vassall carried into England against the country in general, the governour propounded, that if any elder present had any such hand, etc., he would withdraw himself. Mr. Hubbard sitting still a good space, and no man speaking, one of the deputies informed the court, that Mr. Hubbard was the man suspected, whereupon he arose and said, that he knew nothing of any such petition.[57]

Winthrop then rose to speak. He asserted that since Hobart's name was now out in the open, he would express his opinion. He did not think that Hobart should presume to give advice to authority, considering his history of contempt for that same authority, and since he had just recently been bound to good behavior. At this, Hobart stood and left the meeting. After his departure Winthrop continued by stating his disturbance over the fact that too often the most secret business of the General Court was being published abroad, which he regarded as a matter of great unfaithfulness. Hobart, Winthrop was sure, was a spy for the petitioners and was a close supporter and follower of William Vassall. He was also implying that there were other spies within the General Court,* and probably had in mind when he uttered these words the deputies from Hingham, Joshua Hobart and Bozoan Allen.[58]

The Court found the petitioners blamable for the contents of their petition and for their contempt in appealing before the Court reached a decision—but in varying degrees. Dr. Robert Child was found the most culpable of all, "as being guilty not only of his offence in the matter of appeal and remonstrance, but also in charging the courte with breaches of privileges of Parliament and contemptuous speeches and behavior towards them." [59] He was fined fifty pounds. John Smith received the next highest fine on the basis that he was as guilty as the others but that since he was not a resident, he had even less reason for signing a contemptuous petition. He was fined forty pounds. The others, with the exception of Maverick, were fined thirty pounds each. Maverick, since he had never appealed to the jurisdiction of England, was considered less guilty than the others and was fined only ten pounds.[60]

When the petitioners were given an opportunity to repent their offenses and have their fines returned, all refused and the sentence of the Court stood. Child and the others once again announced their intention of appealing the case to England and submitted a written paper to that effect, which the Court received but refused to read or in any way signify an acceptance of the principle.

The deputies, with the exception of the few from Essex and the representatives of the town of Hingham, refused to exploit Vassall's charges against the magistrates. In fact,

* See n. 58 on p. 255, below, for another indication of pro-Remonstrance feeling in Hingham, the case of Thomas Joy.

as a group, they were sterner than the magistrates in dealing with the Remonstrance. The arguments of the years of bickering had been set aside in the face of the dangerous threat of English intervention.

The leaders of Massachusetts cherished their independence and freedom to pursue the reforms they so ardently advocated. There were to be ties to the Crown only through the charter, and if the king threatened the charter, he was to be resisted. As early as 1640, Winthrop had rejected any ties with Parliament:

> Upon the great liberty which the King had left the parliament to in England, some of our friends there wrote to us advice to send over some to solicit for us in the parliament, giving us hope that we might obtain much, etc. But consulting about it, we declined the motion for this consideration, that if we should put ourselves under the protection of the parliament, we must then be subject to all such laws as they should make, or at least such as they might impose upon us; in which course though they should intend our good, yet it might prove very prejudicial to us.[61]

In 1648, however, the matter was becoming more pressing. There existed a parliamentary commission, charged to fulfill whatever role the king and privy council formerly filled toward the colonies, and those who were dissatisfied with conditions in the colonies were taking advantage of its existence. Gorton had appealed successfully from Massachusetts justice, and now a far more influential group was about to appeal their cause before the same commissioners. The magistrates were convinced that no longer could Massachusetts simply ignore developments in England. They would need representation before the commissioners—an agent who would work to restore the old independence and undo the efforts of Gorton and Vassall.

The magistrates called together the elders to confer with them on how they stood in relation to England and who might be sent there.* Now altogether in charge, the magistrates began the meeting by asserting that the charter was the foundation of government. But some (we are not told whom) thought that, nevertheless, they were so subordinate to Parliament that that body might veto acts of the colony. This latter group thought that Massachusetts ought to seek another charter from Parliament granting her exclusive control over her own affairs. Most of the magistrates, who completely disagreed, asserted that the present charter was more than sufficient. Their relationship with Parliament was one of allegiance but not subordination. They were still independent "in respect of government." Searching the past for examples, these magistrates cited the relationship of Gascony and Normandy to the Crown of France when ruled by the King of England, as well as the relationship of the towns of the Hanseatic League to the Holy Roman Empire—independent but paying homage.

A majority of the meeting—both of the magistrates and the elders—supported the view that Massachusetts was dependent upon England as the source of the charter, and therefore indirectly the source of all authority in the colony. But in practice, Massachusetts was free. She needed no further extensions of power. Those she already had were sufficient. What was necessary, however, was the sending of an agent to England to obtain a clarification of the question of appeal so that the colony would not be constantly plagued by every malcontent who wished to bring charges against Massachusetts before the Commission for Foreign Plantations.[62] The search for an agent

---

* This was the meeting which began with a request to the Reverend Peter Hobart of Hingham to leave because of his connections with Vassall and the Remonstrance.

had already begun and a man was already selected by the time of this conference.

The arrival of Randall Holden in Boston in September 1646, bearing a safe conduct from the Commission for Foreign Plantations and a warning to keep out of Shawomet affairs, made it urgent for Massachusetts Bay to be represented in London. So dangerous was the situation that some of the elders, when they were called together in September before the Child case had even come into court, suggested that Winthrop himself and John Norton, teacher of the church of Ipswich, be sent as agents to argue the colony's case in England. Winthrop, who was fifty-nine-years-old and weary, did not wish to go. Although he said he would agree to if that was the will of God and the colony, he was greatly relieved when others in the colony raised objections. Winthrop was a man of some prominence in the Puritan world. Hugh Peter, since returning to England and in a position of great influence, was calling Winthrop to return also and to serve the Parliamentary cause. Many Winthrop supporters in New England feared he would never return to Massachusetts Bay if he left. Many were returning to England in 1646, and if the governor returned, there might be a mass exodus out of the colony. Its leaders therefore decided to turn elsewhere.[63]

In October the General Court in its brief session appointed Winthrop, Dudley, Bellingham, and Duncan to consider the Remonstrance with a view to answering it and also to approach Edward Winslow of Plymouth Colony as a possible agent for Massachusetts Bay.[64] Winslow was a friend of Winthrop's, and the Massachusetts governor had probably suggested his name. While he was not a resident of Massachusetts Bay and therefore not directly involved in the Child case, it was not too great an obstacle, since he would spend most of his time attacking William Vassall, who was no resident of Massachusetts either. Winslow would also be working on the Gorton case, and his colony was deeply involved with the Gortonists, since Plymouth claimed that Shawomet was within its boundaries. Winslow accepted the mission, and both the elders in their November meeting and the General Court in its November session approved the choice, even though there was apparently some resentment in Plymouth Colony circles. Obtaining his services solved only half of the problem. The colony treasury was in debt to the amount of one thousand pounds.[65] Yet Winslow would have to be paid and given expense money. The General Court ordered "that one hundred pounds should be suddainly raised for the furnishing of Mr. Edward Winslowe, whom this Courte hath chosen and appointed to negotiate with them in England." [66] It was one thing to vote the money and another to find it. Finally, the colony was forced to borrow the money from private individuals promising to repay by means of the next tax levy. In an effort to lighten the burden Massachusetts Bay wrote to Plymouth and New Haven suggesting that they might want to make use of Winslow's services, while "bearing such proportion of the charges with us as they shall thinke meete." [67] The shortage of funds in Massachusetts Bay probably had much influence on the size of the fines levied on petitioners. The £220 in fines would repay the loan for Winslow's expenses and help toward clearing up the large colony debt.

As Winslow prepared to depart immediately for England, the General Court proceeded to draw up instructions for him. He was told to answer the "divers false and scandalous matters against us" uttered by Gorton and his friends. And anticipating Vassall's action, he was to combat "any other complaints, in any kind, made against us before the said commissioners, or before the high court of parliament." [68]

Anticipating the type of questions which the Commission might present to Winslow, the General Court gave

him secret instructions on how to answer each. These are
an extraordinary exposition of Massachusetts' belief in her
own independence. To those who objected that Massachusetts carried on the business of government without
use of the king's name, he was to reply that carrying on
the business of government in the king's name would be
to renounce the power of government granted to them by
the charter. They did not govern Massachusetts as if by
commission, "but by a free donation of absolute government." Massachusetts Bay was subject to England in that
they paid one-fifth of all their gold and silver, they were
"faithful and firm to the state of England endeavoring to
walk with God in upholding his truth etc. and praying
for it," and they framed their government according to
the charter. Their relationship with England consisted of
these ties and no others. Winslow was to reject any plan
which would undermine the Massachusetts charter or sub-
stitute a general governor for the present system. The
charter of Massachusetts Bay gave absolute authority to
the governor and company. They had transplanted themselves to the New World on those terms and not on any
others:

> Other plantations have been undertaken at the
> charge of others in England, and the planters have
> their dependence upon the companies there, and
> those planters go and come chiefly for matter of
> profit; but we came to abide here, and to plant the
> gospel, and the people of the country, and herein
> God hath marvellously blessed us.[69]

In short, Winslow was to reassert the independence of action of Massachusets, while recognizing a special relationship between the colony and England *under the charter.*

After his fining by the General Court, Robert Child
decided that he had had enough of Massachusetts and

made haste to depart for England. He booked passage on a vessel scheduled to leave Boston about one week after the General Court hearing on his petition was concluded.[70] The first of the further petitions he was to carry to Parliament was one complaining of much the same things as the original Remonstrance to the Massachusetts General Court and probably differed very little from the petition to Parliament which Vassall had taken with him when he sailed earlier in the month. It called for the establishment of English laws and the banishing of arbitrary power; it requested the establishment of reformed churches and the guarantee of all the liberties of English freeholders. The difference between this new petition and Vassall's was that this one took the form of an appeal from the ruling of the General Court. The appeal, like Vassall's petition, went beyond the Remonstrance and called for the establishment by Parliament of a general governor for the colony.[71]

Child had also prepared a series of questions he hoped to have Parliament or the Commission for Foreign Plantations answer. They concerned the validity of the Massachusetts Bay charter and how it might be revoked if still valid. Moreover, they quoted speeches and sermons in Massachusetts and requested a ruling on whether or not they were high treason. These questions were an effort to give the Parliament—particularly its Presbyterian majority—the impression that Massachusetts was a hotbed of anti-Parliament sedition and that the charter should be revoked and government placed under the direct supervision of the motherland.[72]

The third document which Child prepared should have been his most important effort. This was a petition by the nonfreemen of Massachusetts Bay in which they showed how they had fled England because of the tyranny of the bishops only to find themselves suffering under a new tyranny. The petition called for liberty of conscience and a general governor.[73]

Winthrop states that the agents of the petitioners traveled up and down the colony looking for discontented nonfreemen.* He does not tell us how long these agents were working. They could have been attempting to gather signatures since May. But certainly they had been working since Vassall's departure. In any case, they were not overly successful. The petition speaks of many thousands of discontented nonfreemen and pretends to speak for them. Yet it contains the names of twenty-five men only. We do not know their names, although Winthrop, who must be regarded as prejudiced against them, refers to them as "profane persons," Marblehead fishermen just recently arrived from Newfoundland to fish for a season and planning to return to Newfoundland again. Others who signed, according to the governor, were youngsters and servants who "never had any show of religion in them." Or they "were men of no reason." Winthrop cites, as a typical reason for signing the petition, that of a Boston barber who, when questioned by Winthrop (perhaps while receiving a trim), stated that he signed the petition because the petitioners were good customers and he hoped to please them.[74]

The small number of signers of the nonfreemen's petition can be explained several ways. First, it might have been the result of the lack of time to gather signatures and seek out supporters. This, however, does not seem an adequate explanation. The petitioners and their agents had at least a week. Maverick, who was in charge of the work, was not in Boston for the opening of the November session of the General Court. How long he had been out of town is uncertain. If Winthrop is correct that several of the petitioners were Marblehead fishermen from Essex County, then the petitioners had been able to reach their

* One of these agents was Thomas Joy, mentioned below, p. 255. Another was a Mr. Clarke—an innkeeper at Salem. Maverick apparently was in charge of gathering forms.

Salem agent (Clarke) and get him started on collecting names. If they had time to reach Salem, then they had time to reach the rest of the Essex County towns, where the most likely potential signers could be found.

Another explanation is that most of the nonfreemen were afraid to put their names on a document advocating "sedition" no matter how much they might have agreed with its contents. But even more plausible is the argument that few people signed the nonfreemen's petition because very few agreed with it. It was one thing to advocate a broader franchise. Nonfreemen in towns such as Ipswich, where they voted anyway, could approve of this, and would be puzzled or angered by the treatment Child and the others were receiving from the General Court. But it was quite another thing to call upon the power of Parliament to overthrow the charter. What could be gained from such a move? It might well deprive them of what they already had. Why jeopardize the colony's freedom? For the most part, Essex men wanted to thwart the power of Suffolk-Middlesex magistrates and gain some of that power for themselves. They did not wish to become dependent upon English magistrates. It is significant that the Ipswich magistrate Samuel Symonds, in warning Winthrop that the Remonstrance had much support in Ipswich, asked for copies of the petition to Parliament, the questions to Parliament, and the nonfreemen's petition. He stated that they would be most useful in combating the existing support in the town. In short, Essex men could support a call for domestic reform, but they would not support a call for English intervention against the charter (see above, pp. 171–72). Primarily, the nonfreemen's petition received so little support in Massachusetts Bay probably because there was very little support for its contents.

Robert Child, however, was going to England with his petitions no matter what kind of support he received. The magistrates knew this and would have been derelict in their duty if they had not known what Child and the others had been up to. The contents of the petition of nonfreemen must have been known to them, since it had to be shown publicly in order to obtain signatures. Now the problem was what was to be done about it. If they seized Child with this petition on his person, they clearly had sufficient evidence to try him again on a more serious charge. Perhaps they feared Child's presence in England and thought he might provide the extra support Vassall would need in Parliament, posing as a victim of Massachusetts intolerance—a living reminder of what all could expect from the New England Way. Perhaps the magistrates feared his nonfreemen's petition, not knowing how many people had signed it. Whatever the reason, however, the magistrates determined not to let Child sail.

A meeting of the Court of Assistants was scheduled for Boston the day before Child was due to leave the colony. We do not know who assembled for the meeting—probably only the magistrates from Suffolk-Middlesex. Only one of the dissenters among the magistrates in the November hearing on the Remonstrance was present for the Court of Assistants—Richard Bellingham of Boston. Winthrop pressed the magistrates for a decision to stop Child, and to search his baggage and Mr. Dand's study for copies of the suspected petitions. The governor must have been in possession of specific information concerning the whereabouts of the incriminating evidence: he knew exactly where to look for it. The magistrates agreed to halt Child's departure because of his failure to pay his previous fines and to carry out the search for further evidence.

The magistrates made no effort to communicate with those of their body who were not present for this Court session. Apparently Bellingham, swayed by the dangers to Massachusetts's independence presented by these new petitions, voted with the others and agreed to the search. On the next day, however—the day of Child's scheduled departure—the magistrates had another meeting, at which Bellingham changed his mind and refused to go along with the others. He was voted down, but was then seen speaking with someone who, according to Winthrop, would surely relay the magistrates' decision to the petitioners. Although the magistrates wished to seize the petitions in Child's possession aboard the ship, they decided they could no longer wait and would have to act immediately if they wished to regain the element of surprise. The officers of the Court were sent out to fetch Robert Child, to search his lodgings and his baggage, and to repeat these actions at Mr. Dand's home.[75]

The officers arrested Child and then seized his trunk, but found nothing damaging in his possession. They had better luck at Dand's. Although they did not find him at home, they found, as they entered his study, another of the petitioners, John Smith of Rhode Island. Smith, perhaps realizing that a search was on and also realizing how incriminating were the documents in Dand's study, caught up the evidence in an attempt to either hide it or destroy it (it was probably a little too bulky for swallowing). Perhaps he had had no time to think and, surprised and alarmed, had picked up the evidence in a reflex reaction not really knowing what to do with the documents—the appeal to Parliament, the questions to Parliament, and the nonfreemen's petition. He was arrested and the three documents were seized with him.

Smith, as soon as he recovered from shock, fell into a rage and made statements against the government which would be used against him later. When told that the officers of the Court were searching and seizing by order of the magistrates, he replied that he had hopes that before long he would have orders to search the governor's closet and do as much for him as they did for them. Child,

Dand, and Smith were all placed under arrest—Child and Dand because the petitions were in their known handwritings, and Smith because of his words and his efforts to thwart the order of the Court of Assistants.[76]

When the three petitioners were brought before the magistrates, Child, who was also in a rage over his arrest, grew abusive and loud until Winthrop called him up short. He told the doctor that the Court regarded him as a person of quality and that he would be given the respect due to a gentleman and scholar, "but if he would behave himself no better, he should be committed to the common prison and clapped in irons." [77]

Smith and Dand refused to be questioned and were ordered confined without bail, although they were not sent to the common jail but were placed in a local inn with free access to their friends. Child, too, was committed to the marshal's care for two or three days until his ship sailed. Although he was extremely upset over the delay, he offered to pay his fifty-pound fine but was informed that now the charges were much more serious and he would have to await a new trial before the Court of Assistants. After his ship left, the Court allowed him to post bond (eight hundred pounds), but the Court confined him to his home.[78]

The Court of Assistants met again in December 1646. Its decision was to ignore those whose names appeared on the nonfreemen's petition, since they had been drawn into the movement unwittingly; they were few in number and obviously not a serious threat. The magistrates decided to punish instead those who had obtained the signatures, especially Clarke of Salem and Samuel Maverick—"these having taken an oath of fidelity to the government, and enjoying all the liberties of freemen, their offence was far greater." [79] They were bound over to the next General Court for trial. Smith and Dand now agreed to give security to pay their fines of forty and thirty pounds respectively, and were allowed to post bail and remain at liberty until the next General Court.

Robert Child was offered the opportunity to post bond and his freedom if he would agree to remain confined to Boston Neck. The magistrates were determined to keep Child out of England. They postponed the new trial until the next General Court, which would not meet until May 1647.[80] It was imperative to keep an eye on Child so that he might not escape to another seaport town or to another colony and find a ship for England. He was to be kept in Boston and his bail was to be set extremely high (eight hundred pounds) to discourage any attempt at flight. Child refused to post bail, selecting prison instead. He was allowed to remain in a local inn under confinement.[81]

When the new General Court assembled on May 27, 1647, many of the members were repeaters from the Court of November 1646. Winthrop states that a concerted effort was made by friends of the Remonstrance to overturn Winthrop and to elect new magistrates. But once again the petitioners rallied little support. Winthrop won by two or three hundred votes over his nearest competitor. Dudley was reelected deputy governor, while all eleven assistants of 1646 were reelected in 1647. One new magistrate was added, however, raising the total of assistants to twelve. He was Robert Bridges of Lynn in Essex County and it seems doubtful that he was a Child supporter. He was a former speaker of the lower house and had been speaker in November when the Remonstrance was condemned. He had not expressed opposition to the majority position, although the deputies followed the procedure of allowing the Speaker a vote only in case of a tie. If the election of Bridges was a victory for anyone, it was a further victory for the deputies. They had elected their Speaker to the magistracy and presumably had added a new vote in the upper house for programs advocated by them.[82] Bridges's election was also a victory for Essex

County men, for he was known to be sympathetic to their point of view. Since his residence was in Lynn, the Essex town closest to Boston, he would presumably be able to attend many more meetings of the assistants than magistrates from remote Essex towns.

In the lower house the changeover was greater. Sixteen of the thirty-five deputies of November 1646 were reelected in May 1647. Richard Dummer, a representative of Salisbury in 1646, was representing his own town of Newbury in 1647, while Joseph Hills, the new Speaker in 1647, represented the new town of Malden, whereas in 1646 he had served for the parent town of Charlestown. Another six of the May 1647 deputies had served in the General Court since the deputies had begun their struggle with the magistrates. Nineteen of the thirty-five members of November 1646 were not reelected in 1647. Yet there does not seem to be any direct connection between pro- or anti-Child feeling in these failures to be reelected. Two of the nineteen were men who had voted against the censure of Child and the others—Richard Russell of Charlestown and Henry Bartholomew of Salem. Since only five men voted against the censure, the failure of two of the five to be returned to the General Court would normally seem significant, except that Charlestown apparently sent no deputies at all to the May session, and in Salem, Henry Bartholomew was replaced by Jacob Barney, the only man in the May session to refuse to condemn the petitioners. It does not seem, therefore, that Russell and Bartholomew failed to return because of their votes in the Child case. Of the new men elected in May 1647, ten were from Essex-Norfolk and nine were from Suffolk-Middlesex. In May eight deputies disagreed either totally or partially with the final verdict of the General Court. Of the eight, six were Essex-Norfolk men (four of them new men) and one, Brian Pendleton, deputy for Watertown in 1647, had extensive interests in Essex-Norfolk and later moved his residence there. If any pattern can be discerned in the new composition of the lower house in May 1647, it is that the Essex-Norfolk viewpoint on the Child case was a few votes stronger. They could not condemn the petitioners' efforts to broaden the franchise, but they would not support their attempts to call on England for intervention. They would agree to punishing the petitioners, but they wanted a milder punishment than their colleagues from the Boston area.

The Court began its session on May 27, but did not get around to the discussion of the case of Dr. Child and the others until early June, and did not reach a verdict until June 8, finding the petitioners guilty, with only Jacob Barney of Salem refusing to agree to the verdict. If there was any opposition among the magistrates, there is no record of it. Child was fined £200 and ordered to prison until he either paid it or gave security for payment. John Dand was given the same punishment; John Smith and Thomas Burton were each fined £100, while Samuel Maverick was fined £100 for being party to the conspiracy, and an additional £50 for appealing to England in violation of his freeman's oath. When this £750 in fines was combined with the £220 in fines assessed earlier, it made a healthy dent in the colony's £1,000 debt.[83]

Several members of the lower house rejected the findings of the Court in varying degrees. As mentioned above, Jacob Barney of Salem rejected the verdict totally. Pendleton of Watertown, Robert Payne of Ipswich, and Edward Carleton of Rowley would have reduced the fines of all those charged and would not have punished Child at all over and above his recent imprisonment. William Pelham of Sudbury would have reduced the fines of all and would have fined Child the lowest amount—£40. Thomas Lothrop of Salem and Robert Clements of Haverhill would have ordered lower fines for all.[84]

The Court reached its decision: Child would have to

pay his fine, which for the day was an enormous sum of money; if he did not, he would have to remain in prison. Sometime during the summer he arranged payment, and in September he sailed for England—ten months after his original sailing date. During those months Edward Winslow had been busily at work against him in England. John Dand apparently did not have the money to pay his fine, nor was he willing to acknowledge his offense. He remained in prison until May 1648, when he made a humble submission, and his fine—not likely to be paid anyway—was forgiven him.[85] The others paid and remained in Massachusetts.

6   The Remonstrance Rejected

With William Vassall, Thomas Fowle, Robert Child, and Edward Winslow now in England, the next battles over the Remonstrance of 1646 and the attempt to force Parliament to intervene would be fought before the Parliamentary Commission for Foreign Plantations sitting at Westminster. Edward Winslow had two tasks to perform in England. The first was to reverse the thus far successful efforts of Samuel Gorton, and the second was to check the schemes of William Vassall. In effect, however, they could both be reduced to the same point—to force the commissioners to halt their intervention into the affairs of New England and to establish the principle of no appeals from the colony to England.

Winslow's efforts against Gorton were not successful. In the first place, the commissioners had already rendered a decision in the matter in 1646 (despite the opening they had left for Massachusetts Bay to answer) when they declared Shawomet beyond the jurisdiction of Massachusetts. In addition, Gorton proved a more than competent polemicist. His book *Simplicity's Defence against Seven-Headed Policy,* an able piece of propadanda communicating to its readers a sense of outrage against the intolerance and aggression of Massachusetts Bay, aroused a good deal of sympathy for the humble Christian Samuel Gorton.

At the same time, the Independents of England were courting the English counterparts of enthusiasts like the Shawomet settlers; and Gorton during his stay in England had become a man of great prominence among the English enthusiasts.[1] While the modern reader may not be attracted by the mysticism of Gorton's book, to his audience it made him all the more admirable.

Winslow published an atttack on Gorton in his *Hypoc-risie Unmasked,* which he dedicated to the Earl of War-wick. Although it was as devastating a piece of propaganda as Gorton's, Gorton won the day. On July 22, 1647, the commissioners addressed a letter to the colonies of Massa-chusetts and Plymouth, in which they stated the impossi-bility of determining within whose boundaries Shawomet stood:

> if it shall appear, that the said tract is within the limits of any of the New England patents, we shall leave the same, and the inhabitants thereof to the proper jurisdiction of that government under which they shall fall. Nevertheless, for that the petitioners have transplanted their families thither and there settled their residences at a great charge, we com-mend it to the government within whose jurisdiction they shall appear to be, (as our only desire at present in the matter) not only not to remove them from their plantations, but also to encourage them, with protection and assistance in all fit ways; provided that they demean themselves peaceably, and not endanger any of the English colonies by a prejudicial correspon-dency with the Indians, or otherwise, wherein if they shall be found faulty, we leave them to be proceeded with according to justice.[2]

With this letter the commissioners killed the issue. The community of Warwick (Shawomet) now regarded itself as firmly within the jurisdiction of Rhode Island.

Samuel Gorton, intrinsically interesting as he may be, is important to this study only because of the influence he exerted on William Vassall and Robert Child. Indeed, despite his notorious reputation, Gorton had managed to thwart the expansionism of Massachusetts and to threaten the independence of action of the Bay Colony. Indirectly, he also helped to call a halt to the feud between magistrates and deputies. William Vassall would now attempt to do the same.

Almost from the very beginning of their campaign in England, Vassall and his friends were on the defensive. The fact that Child was not present to argue his cause, while perhaps useful in the beginning to indicate the injustices of Massachusetts, in the long run hurt the cause. His presence in England would have made the issue more immediate. As it was, to most men in England it was a little understood political dispute occurring some three thousand miles away. Thomas Fowle was apparently of little use to Vassall and dropped out of the debate shortly after arriving in England. The story of the miraculous landfall of the *Supply,* and the stories of the Jonah cast overboard, prejudiced the minds of many before the issues were even debated in England. John Child and William Vassall tried to offset this initial bad impression by publishing a propaganda pamphlet, *New England's Jonas Cast Up,* in which they attempted to state the issues in a light calculated to display Massachusetts in its worst possible manner. They stressed the persecution of Robert Child for his opposition to arbitrary government. They claimed that the elders of Massachusetts were as autocratic as the Lord Bishops of the Anglican Church. The magistrates of Massachusetts Bay were said to subvert English law. To Englishmen attempting to upset Charles Stuart's subversion of the laws of England, Child and Vassall implied that there was little to choose between tyrannical kings and tyrannical magistrates. Robert Child was presented as the champion of the cause of Presbyterianism, indicating that the reformed Church of England was being persecuted in Massachusetts Bay.

New England's Jonas attempted to disassociate the Gorton case from its own and attacked what was thought to be an effort by Winslow to connect the two cases in his book

Hypocrisie Unmasked. It would be natural for men attempting to appeal to Presbyterian feeling in England to want to stay as far away from Gorton as possible. Yet Massachusetts was linking the two cases together by handling them as two examples of attempts to appeal to England in violation of the Massachusetts Bay charter.

In addition to the initial bad impression and bad publicity, Vassall's friends would simply have more trouble with the Commission for Foreign Plantations than Gorton ever did. The enthusiasts of Shawomet had taken Massachusetts by surprise. The Bay Colony leaders were totally unprepared to defend their actions in London. With only one side of the issue adequately presented, there was not much the conscientious commissioners could do other than delay and then finally offer the Gortonists protection. But as Vassall and Fowle left for England, Massachusetts Bay was contacting its influential friends in London, attempting to bring to bear all the influence at its disposal. Many friends of Massachusetts were disturbed by the unyielding stance taken by the magistrates and deputies, but were still friends of the colony. One of the commissioners, George Fenwick, gives a good insight into the Massachusetts tactics in his letter to Winthrop of April 1647:

> I am very sorrye that the people begin to rise amongst yow and labor to ingage in a partie against your settled way. I hope they shall gett noe great incouragement from hence. What friendes I have interest in I will procure to appeare for yow in your Just cause, or they only I doubt will seeme strante heare that yow confine all civill fredome within the lynes of your church: but how or when yow may take it into consideration amongst your selves or how dangerous it may be or convenient to mak alteration in that particular I leave to your owne wisdom: The

best service I conceave for yow heare wilbe to keep
of what we can, the Committees intermedling with
your affaires ther: but if the lord raise troubles
amongst yow, your condition is but as your brothers
heare have bene and for ought I can see are like to
continue . . . I hope yow will be carefull to keep
noe other lawes amongst yow then such which if they
should fall into the worst handes they could not
therby offend the harts of any that were conscientious. yow had need to be carefull of your practise
ther, for what ever yow doe that may have the least
shaddow of severitie is hightened hear, and cast in
your brethrens teath by those who in other things
wilbe as much against yow as them.[3]

There had occurred changes in the composition of the
Parliamentary Commission which would also aid Massachusetts and hurt Vassall's plans. In 1646, when the commissioners wrote letters to Massachusetts Bay favoring the
Gortonists' return to Shawomet, the members of the Commission numbered at least fifteen: Robert Rich, second
Earl of Warwick, chaired the Commission and was mildly
Presbyterian in his sympathies. He withdrew from government after Pride's Purge and the abolition of the House
of Lords, although he remained personally friendly with
Cromwell. Algernon Percy, tenth Earl of Northumberland, was also described as mildly Presbyterian. Philip
Herbert, fourth Earl of Pembroke, was firmly in the Independent camp and after the dissolution of the Lords returned to Parliament as an M.P. for Berkshire. The sympathies of Charles Howard, third Earl of Notthingham,
are not clearly ascertainable. Edward Montague, second
Earl of Manchester, was Warwick's son-in-law, a Presbyterian and a bitter enemy of Cromwell's. The opinions of
Francis Lennard, fourteenth Baron Darce, are also un-

known. These were the nobles who sat on the Commission for Foreign Plantations in 1646. The commoners were: Samuel Vassall, brother of William Vassall and a Presbyterian who was later purged from the House by the army; William Waller and Benjamin Rudyard, both Presbyterians; and Cornelius Holland, William Purefoy, Dennis Bond, George Snelling, Francis Allin, and George Fenwick, all Independents.* If Notthingham, Darce, and Rigby are excluded from the calculation, the Commission was evenly divided between Presbyterians and Independents—six of each persuasion.

In 1647 subtle changes had taken place. Three of the six Presbyterian members of 1646 were peers, and the House of Lords was under serious public attack. Its prestige had declined considerably. As this decline occurred, more and more of the Parliamentary peers took a moderate position, seeking accommodation with the defeated king. Moreover, several of the Presbyterians who had served on the Commission in 1646 do not seem to have served on the Commission in 1647, and there were several Independent additions both among the peers and the commoners. The peers of 1647 included: Warwick, Manchester, and Baron Darce, who were still in attendance; Basil Fielding, second Earl of Denbigh, who sided with the army in its disputes with Parliament; and William Fiennes, Viscount Saye, and Sele, an ardent Independent. The Presbyterian Northumberland, and the Independent Pembroke seem not to have served. Among the commoners who served in 1647 there was only one Presbyterian, William Waller. All the others—Sir Arthur Haselring, Miles Corbet, Francis Allin, William Purefoy, George Fenwick, and Cornelius Holland—were Independents. Among those

* Another person signing the letter to Massachusetts Bay in 1646 was a certain Fer. Rigby. The only Rigby serving in Parliament during the Long Parliament was Alexander Rigby, member for Wigan and an Independent.

whose sympathies are known, the balance switched to eight to three in favor of the Independents, and among the increasingly prestigious commoners the total was six to one.[4]

The change in the composition of the Commission could only hurt William Vassall's plans, especially since one of the missing Presbyterians was his brother, Samuel. Furthermore, although an Independent Commission might be sympathetic to the Congregationalists in Massachusetts Bay, it was not likely to overturn the earlier ruling on Gorton, considering how the English Independents were courting English enthusiasts. But under no circumstances were the Independent commissioners likely to sympathize with an appeal partially based on a call for Presbyterian reformations. The changing political realities of England were to have marked effects on the continued independence of action of the Massachusetts Bay Colony.

Edward Winslow, after writing his answer to Gorton, took up his pen to respond to John Child. He wrote a pamphlet entitled *New England's Salamander Discovered,* which is basically a point by point refutation of *New England's Jonas,* with an additional assertion that it was not John Child, but rather William Vassall (the Salamander), who wrote the defense of the Remonstrance. Winslow denied any plot to tie Gorton and the petitioners of 1646 together. The Massachusetts agent insisted that Robert Child and his friends were punished not for petitioning to Parliament or petitioning the General Court of Massachusetts Bay, but rather for the sedition contained in their petitions and for actions tending to the creation of factions and possible insurrection. Winslow restated the points raised in the charges against the petitioners made by the General Court. They were fined and imprisoned, insisted Winslow, after the business of the Remonstrance was over, and this time for separate petitions "far more factious and seditious than the former." [5] Winslow continued by asserting that the government of Massachusetts was not arbitrary. Laws were made by elected officials chosen by the freemen in annual elections:

> And however there are many that are not free amongst us, yet if understanding men and able to be helpful, it's more their own faults then otherwise ofttimes, who will not take up their freedome lest they should bee sent on these services (as our Salamander and most of his disciples who are too many I must confesse and yet it is the same with many thousands in this kingdome who have not libertie to choose.[6]

All men, be they freemen or not, had the right of trial by jury in civil and criminal cases, and even if they had no set code of penal laws and punishments for crimes, " 'tis true I confesse, neither can they finde any Commonwealth under heaven, or ever was, but some things were reserved to the discretion of the judges, and so it is with us and no otherwise." Neither were the authorities of Massachusetts Bay hostile to Presbyterianism. There were Presbyterians and Presbyterian churches in Massachusetts Bay.* Indeed, at the time of the hearing on the Remonstrance, Winthrop offered a Presbyterian church polity to the petitioners. He, Winslow, had been present and heard the offer with his own ears.[7]

Finally, Winslow stated in print, and he would argue the point orally before the Commission for Foreign Plantations later on, that Massachusetts Bay was not an independent state. She owed allegiance to the state of England. But should this colony, three thousand miles across the ocean, be forced to submit to a constant stream of appeals across the seas and have to respond to them and bear the expense of them? If so, then for all practical purposes governmental authority would have been transferred to England, and England was too far away to properly administer justice in Massachusetts. If Parliament upheld

---

* He had cited Noyes, Parker, and Hobart as Presbyterians earlier.

the right of appeal, then Englishmen who had fled arbitrary government in Anglican England would once again be living under arbitrary rule. Ironically, this rule without justice would be imposed upon the hitherto free men of Massachusets Bay by their friends in England at just the moment when these same friends had overturned arbitrary rule in the homeland.[8]

Before Robert Child set foot aboard ship for England, the issue had been settled. After listening to Vassall and to Winslow, the Commission, even though intending to make further and more detailed studies on the matter, came to an important decision which was revealed in a letter to Massachusetts Bay dated May 25, 1647:

> We have since received a petition and remonstrance from you by your commissioner, Mr. Winslow, and though we have not yet entered into a particular consideration of the matter, yet we do, in general, take notice of your respect, as well to the parliament's authority, as your own just privileges, and find cause to be further confirmed in our former opinion and knowledge of your prudence and faithfulness to God and his cause. And perceiving by your petition, that some persons do take advantage, from our said letter [that of May 1646, supporting Gorton] to decline and question your jurisdiction, and to pretend a general liberty to appeal hither, upon their being called in question before you for matters proper to your cognizance, we thought it necessary (for preventing of further inconveniences in this kind) hereby to declare, that we intended not thereby to encourage any appeals from your justice, nor to restrain the bounds of your jurisdiction to a narrower compass than is held forth by your letters patent.[9]

The Commission was making an important distinction which even the more Presbyterian Commission of the previous year would probably have agreed with. The commissioners would uphold their ban on Massachusetts intervention in Gorton's affairs. In this case they allowed an appeal from Massachusetts courts precisely because Massachusetts courts were incompetent to judge; and the government of Massachusetts itself had admitted that Shawomet was beyond its jurisdiction according to its patent. But the case of Robert Child and the Remonstrance of 1646 was quite different. This was an internal matter, decided with full competence by the courts of Massachusetts Bay, and therefore the commissioners would allow no appeal.

The concept of appeal to Parliament first employed by Samuel Gorton and successfully used by him had failed for William Vassall. Further hearings would be held before the commissioners, with Edward Winslow more than fulfilling the hopes that the magistrates of Massachusetts Bay held for him.[10] Robert Child arrived in England in the fall of 1647, but his presence added little to Vassall's cause. The unity of action which had typified the petitioners in the past also began to crumble. Child presented his own petition to the Commission and included in it the name of Thomas Fowle. When Fowle heard of this, he protested and disassociated himself from the movement. John Dand, still in Boston and in prison, begged the pardon of the General Court and was forgiven. William Vassall, seeing that all was lost, gave up on New England and sailed for Barbados.

For Robert Child there was to be one further humiliation. While still in London, he met Francis Willoughby of Charlestown (later deputy governor of Massachusetts Bay). When in the course of the conversation the bitter Child began to rail against Massachusetts as a land of rogues and knaves, Willoughby grew angry and said anyone so saying was himself a knave, whereupon Child gave him a box on the ear. They were separated by friends before more blows could be exchanged. It is not certain what happened next. Willoughby either had Child arrested for assault or called him out for a duel. Whatever the result, Child was determined to extricate himself. He agreed to terms calling for him to apologize to Willoughby and to promise never again to speak ill of New England in the future.[11]

Robert Child, despite his harsh words had not totally given up on New England. In a letter to the younger Winthrop written in May 1648, he stated his willingness to invest one hundred or two hundred pounds in Winthrop's graphite mine if his fines were restored to him by Massachusetts Bay. But the magistrates and deputies of the Bay Colony did not take up his offer. Child may not have totally given up on Massachusetts, but it is quite clear that Massachusetts had had its fill of Dr. Robert Child.[12]

When the decade of the 1640s began, the old issue of liberty versus order in society was resolved. What remained of it was merely rhetoric. But no sooner were the differences between freemen and magistrates resolved when they were replaced by new problems. Instead of involving the basic political structure of the Puritan society, they involved the distribution of powers within that basic structure.

The rise of a new social and economic elite at the local level constituted of men of relatively greater wealth and prestige than the freemen was an accomplished development by 1640. In the towns this elite had been accumulating political power with the evolution of the post of selectman. They had themselves elected selectmen and then were consistently reelected in the years that followed. During that time the selectmen grew accustomed to making decision without reference to the town voters, until the annual elections, when the English tradition of deference to betters and the Puritan deification of the ruler combined to ensure their reelection. The most prominent of this local elite usually came to fill the post of deputy to the General Court also.

By the beginning of the colony's second decade, the local leaders, through their spokesmen, the deputies, were strong enough in their political base to begin to challenge the exclusive authority of the magistrates. They would strike at what they considered the basic sources of magisterial power—the Standing Council, the negative voice, and the discretionary judicial powers of the magistrates. But it must be remembered that in attacking the magistrates and the sources of their power, the deputies were not attempting to undermine the balance between democracy and authority achieved in the first decade; nor were they attempting to thwart the holy experiment in purifying the churches; nor were they at all interested in weakening the independence of action which Massachusetts Bay had achieved through its charter. What they desired was a share of the magistrates' powers for themselves. They wished to reduce the prestige of the magistrates and thus enhance their own. They wanted power. The politics of the second decade in the General Court differ very little from the traditional struggles between the upper and lower houses of a legislative body.

In the course of their dispute with the magistrates, the local politicians could count on allies on some issues. If they wished to put a different candidate into the office of governor, they could count on the support of a large number of the elders who seemed to have formed the opinion that it was dangerous for one man to be continually reelected governor (although they seemed not to have the same qualms at all about annual reelection to the remaining posts). And on almost every issue, the local politicians could count on a large amount of support on all levels in Essex and Norfolk Counties. In these remote areas nonfreemen, freemen, selectmen, deputies, even some magistrates, farmers, merchants, and clergymen—all were jealous of the more populous, wealthy, and dominant Suffolk-Middlesex region. Any reduction in the power of

Boston and of the magistrates of Suffolk-Middlesex would meet with the approval of Essex-Norfolk men.

From 1642 to 1645 the issue was debated in the General Court, reaching a climax with the attempted impeachment of Deputy Governor Winthrop on the issues raised in the Hingham militia case. The deputies lost not only this case but whatever chance they had to reduce the magistrates to their own level.

While the politicians argued in the General Court over the distribution of power, a threat to the fundamental on which that power was based—Massachusetts independence —was developing in New England. The debate in the General Court itself encouraged the enemies of Massachusetts independence to feel that there was serious disagreement of a fundamental nature in the colony. William Vassall of Plymouth Colony, who emerges as the leading enemy of Massachusetts Bay and who had close connections with the leadership of Hingham, was influenced to believe that he had strong support in Massachusetts for an attempt to bring Massachusetts Bay under closer English supervision.

At the same time, the world outside Massachusetts was changing. In England old friends, the Independents, having helped overthrow the king and desperately needing the support of the splinter enthusiastic groups in England for a new struggle with the Presbyterians, both English and Scot, turned their backs on the old virtue of orthodoxy and proclaimed the new vice of intolerance. Massachusetts Bay, lacking the same compulsions, continued on her former path and demanded orthodoxy. When horror for enthusiasm combined with aggressive expansionism to lead Massachusetts to sieze and prosecute Samuel Gorton of Rhode Island, the colony was quite unprepared for Gorton's retaliatory appeal to England and even more unprepared to face his drawing of Parliamentary attention to his plight. When he succeeded in winning support for his cause from the Parliamentary Commission for Foreign

Plantations, the magistrates and deputies of Massachusetts were stunned.

Gorton's victory further encouraged those who wished to alter the fundamental structure of Massachusetts Bay. If the heretic, Gorton, could appeal successfully to Parliament and obtain a command for Massachusetts to desist in its persecution, then certainly more orthodox men— with more important connections in England—could hope for Parliamentary intervention into the affairs of New England. The Remonstrance of 1646 was the result of this combination of factors.

The supporters of the Remonstrance failed for several reasons. Vassall had either misunderstood the nature of the deputies' discontent or miscalculated in thinking he could dupe the deputies into actions contrary to their own interests. The deputies were, in fact, his staunchest foes. The nonfreemen failed to support him, because he really had nothing to offer them. The petitioners also failed because, while Gorton had taken Massachusetts by surprise with his appeal, they could not. The Bay Colony marshaled all its resources and friends in England to preserve its independence of action under the charter. With the efforts of Vassall, however, came a complete halt of the lesser gentry's efforts to achieve equal power with the magistrates. They were not willing to sacrifice Massachusetts independence or to encourage other malcontents in order to achieve that power for themselves.

Epilogue: The Victory of Reaction

There are those who would see the glimmer of ultimate victory in the defeat of the Remonstrance, attributing to the pressures applied in 1646 the responsibility for later "liberalizing" steps.[1] Yet a better case can be made for the opposite view.

The Remonstrance of 1646, although not necessarily directly responsible, gave added impetus to a movement toward consolidation of institutions in the colony of Massachusetts Bay. For some years before 1646 there had been a movement afoot for enumeration and consolidation of church principles and practice. Discrepancy of practices in various bodies had led to concern among the elders and politicians. Peter Hobart in Hingham preached sermons during the strictly civil wedding ceremonies of Massachusetts Bay and, more seriously, baptized the infants of nonchurch members in his community.[2]

Others were questioning the necessity of the test for saving faith for admission to membership, and at Newbury under Mr. Noyes and Mr. Parker the broader admission policy was in effect.[3] At the same time, a growing diversification of sects in England warned the orthodox of Massachusetts of what could happen to them if they failed to present a united front. Signs of the beast—enthusiasm—were already present with a growing population of "anabaptists" within the colony.

The ministerial convocation called in 1643 was an effort to resolve differences, particularly with Noyes and Parker of Newbury, but it had failed. In 1646 the matter was even more pressing. As the magistrates and deputies waited for the presentation of the Remonstrance or some such effort by William Vassall, they were presented with a

request by leading members of the clergy for a synod to
which the churches of New England might send messengers and in which the discussions could center on
church polity. There was a debate over the propriety of
the civil arm calling for church synods, and the synods'
accomplishments were rather frugal in 1646. Under the
pressure of increased heterodoxy in England and America,
however, and in the face of the Congregational—Presbyterian, Parliament—Army struggle in England, and now
with the threat of possible Parliamentary intervention in
the Child case, the synod was called back into session in
June 1647. Shortly after the session began, many of the
messengers were taken ill and another adjournment was ordered.[4] But all the reasons for holding a synod intensified
with the passage of time, and finally, in late summer 1648,
the synod reconvened at Cambridge.

The General Court in October 1647 had appointed a
committee of elders to consider a confession of faith along
with a declaration of polity. However, when the synod
considered the work of the committee, it was agreed that
the confession of faith developed by the Westminster
Assembly was perfectly acceptable to the New England
churches. On matters of doctrinal faith Presbyterianism
and Congregationalism were not far apart.[5] But this was
the only "concession" to Presbyterianism that the synod
would make. In the platform of church polity the elders
would present a thoroughly Congregational point of view:
"The state of the members of the Militant visible church
walking in order, was either before the law, Oeconomical,
that is in families; or under the law, National or since the
coming of Christ, only congregational." [6] In 1643 the ministerial convocation seemed to be willing to attempt to
placate Presbyterians on the question of church membership, but in 1648 the ministers were no longer so flexible:

The matter of a visible church are Saints by calling.
By saints we understand,

1. Such, as have not only attained the knowledge of the principles of Religion, and are free from gros and open scandals, but also do together with the profession of their faith and Repentance, walk in blameless obedience to the word, so as that in charitable descretion they may be accounted Saints by calling,

The *doors* of the Churches of Christ upon earth, doe not by Gods appointment stand so wide open, that all sorts of people good or bad, may freely enter therein at their pleasure; but such as are admitted therto, as members ought to be *examined* and *tryed* first, whether they be fit and meet to be received into Church society, or not.[7]

The synod was equally firm in describing the rights of the congregations in selecting and removing their elders:

Ordinary church powr, is either power of office, that is such as is proper to the eldership: or, power of previledge, such as belongs unto the brotherhood. The latter is in the brethren formally, and immediately from Christ, that is, so as it may accordingly to order be acted or exercised immediately by themselves: the former, is not in them formally or immediately, and therefore cannot be acted or exercised immediately by them, but is said to be in them, in that they design the persons unto office, who only are to act, or to exercise this power. . . .

And if the church have powr to *chuse* their officers and ministers, then in case of manifest unworthyness, and delinquency they have powr also to depose them.[8]

The final assertion of the Congregationalism of the Cambridge Platform concerned the independence of the individual churches, which, although allowing for synods (which were to be consultative and could not bind) and the common bond of Christ's mystical body, nevertheless still argued for essential uniqueness and equality of congregations: "Although Churches be distinct, and therefore may not be confounded one with another: and equall, and therefore have not dominion one over another: yet all the churches ought to preserve *church–communion* one with another, because they are all united unto Christ." [9]

The synod of 1648 had carefully defined a Congregational church polity—one that withstood the assaults of the next few decades. Rather than adjust to the realities of religious change both in old England and New England, the churches of Massachusetts Bay had instead stood firm and embraced the status quo. In all likelihood, the definitions of the synod were the views of the vast majority of Massachusetts residents, but in their inflexible definitions of their Congregationalism and in their continued demand for unalterable orthodoxy, the clergy and the churches of the Bay established reactionary religious views that would not bend before change. The inflexibility of the churches—in many ways a reaction to the assaults of the 1640s—was greatly responsible for the inability of the churches to meet the challenge of the future decades.

The failure of the efforts of the petitioners in 1646 had a similar effect on the political scene. In 1644 and 1645 bills for broadening the franchise on the local level and introducing nonchurch members into freemanship (substituting a property qualification for the religious qualification) were pending in the General Court. In May 1647, in the same session in which Child was fined for the second time, the General Court finally passed a new franchise law:

> This Courte, taking into consideration the useful partes and abillityes of divers inhabitants amongst us, which are not freemen, which, if improved to publicke use, the affayres of this country maybe easyer

carryed an end in the severall tounes of this jurisdic-
con, doth hereby declare, that henceforth it shall and
maybe lawfull for the freemen within any of the said
tounes to make choyce of such inhabitants, though
nonfreemen, who have taken, or shall take, the oath
of fidelity to this government, to be jury men, and to
have their vote in the choyce of the select men for
toune affaires, assessment of rates, and other pru-
dentialls proper to the select men of the severall
tounes, provided still, that the major parte of all
companyes and of select men be freemen, from time
to time, that shall make any valid act, as also where
no select men are to have their vote in ordering of
schooles, hearding, laying out of highwayes, and dis-
tributing of lands, any lawe, usage, or customs notwithstanding to the contrary; provided also, that no
nonfreemen shall have his vote untill he hath at-
tayned the age of twenty fower yeeres; provided also,
that none that are or shallbe detected and convicted
in any Courte of any evill carriage against the government or churches, it being intended to be immediately
donn, shallbe capable to vote until the Courte where
he was convicted or sentenced hath restored him to
his former liberty.[10]

Most historians have noted in this law a broadening
of the franchise on the local level and have cited it as a
liberalizing effect of the Remonstrance and an indirect
victory for Vassall and Child. Seldom is anything said of
the fact that the 1647 law makes no mention of creating
nonchurch-member freemen such as was contemplated in
the bills of 1644 and 1645. The government of Massachusetts was to remain in the hands of the saints. There
would be no broadening of the franchise on the colony-
wide level for almost twenty years, and by then it would
be too late.

The failure of the General Court to proceed on this

point and to broaden meaningfully the colony-wide franchise raises some question about the intent and effect of the 1647 law. The most crucial words in the text of the law are: "it shall and maybe lawfull for the *freemen* within any of the said tounes to make choyce of such inhabitants etc." [11] The law leaves voting privileges on the local level in the hands of the freemen of the towns. They would determine who would vote and who would not. If the earlier analyses are correct and the majority of the adult males in the Suffolk-Middlesex areas were freemen, and if illegal voting on the local level was not very extensive, then no changes would occur in these towns without the approval of the freemen—the majority group. But in the remote areas where the freemen were the minority of the adult males, and where there was widespread illegal voting on the local level, the nonfreemen's voting "rights" were suddenly placed at the mercy of a small minority.

The General Court seems also to have intended enforcement of the law. By establishing standards such as the twenty-four-year age limit, an oath of fidelity to the government, freedom from conviction for "evill carriage" against the government, an insistence that the majority of voters in certain instances be freemen and all under the jurisdiction of each town's freemen, the General Court was, in effect, cutting down on the number of illegal voters. By legalizing the few, they could eliminate the many. By establishing standards, the remote areas of the colony could be brought more in line with the practices of Suffolk-Middlesex.

It is not certain that the law had the desired effect. That would necessarily be the subject matter for another study. What is important here is the intent of the leadership and the fact that various factions—deputies and Essex men— went along with them. The threat of English intervention produced a reaction of defensiveness in the leadership and acquiescence in their followers. The leaders dropped any consideration of nonchurch members becoming freemen and attempted to establish the firm control of the freemen-elect on all levels of politics. The independence of Massachusetts, so necessary for the reform of church and state, would be best protected by the church-member freemen, and no others were trustworthy. In addition, indiscriminate illegal voting in the remote counties had produced a situation in which the enemies of Massachusetts independence had received their greatest support in the remote areas. This, too, would be corrected by the standardization established by the franchise law of 1647. Instead of compromise, the Massachusetts leaders chose inflexibility.

If the Remonstrance of 1646 had any appeal to the deputies, it was in its call for a book of laws. This was a program dear to the hearts of the membership of the lower house. In each struggle with the magistrates—over the negative voice and the Standing Council—they had been forced to compromise or were defeated. But on this issue the deputies were to taste victory. In November 1647 the Court announced that general agreement had been reached on a book of laws and appointed a committee to prepare the book for publication. The Court ordered the publication on March 14, 1647/48.[12]

The compilation and publication of the laws with set penalties for specific crimes, despite all the delays, was a victory for the deputies. After six years of trying, they had finally managed to bring about a reduction in the discretionary judicial powers of the magistrates. But considering that the negative voice was still in effect, the deputies could not have had their victory without the concurrence of the magistrates. For some reason the magistrates had decided to approve a measure which, even though only in a small way, nevertheless limited their freedom of action. The answer to why they agreed is found also in the reaction to the Remonstrance and its threat to Massachusetts independence.

The Remonstrance had made specific reference to the lack of a book of laws as a tendency toward arbitary government. Magisterial acquiescence in the establishment of such a book would silence this charge forever and would be a small price to pay for peace on the issue of arbitrary rule. At the same time, Vassall and John Child, in their propaganda efforts in England, made much of this lack as proof of the existence of "arbitrary rule" in Massachusetts Bay. Winslow found it enough of an embarrassment to make a concerted effort to refute the charge, and his answer was not very satisfactory.[13] The agreement of the magistrates on the establishment of a book of laws was an effort to bolster a more important cause—Massachusetts independence.

In the long run, it was not much of a victory for the deputies. The lengthy struggle between the deputies and the magistrates was over, and with the exception of the *Book of General Laws,* it had been settled on the magistrates' terms. Further agitation considering the possible threats from abroad would not develop. After all, both deputy and magistrate were committed to the basic political structure of the Bay Colony. Their struggle for power had misled others into thinking they might attack the basic structure with impunity; therefore the power struggle had to be set aside, and the deputies, chastened by their defeats, fell in line behind the magistrates. Massachusetts Bay would not again experience the divisions of the early forties for several decades.

The period of the second decade of Massachusetts history was a crucial one for the colony. It was a period when the colony was forced to come face to face with the outside world—to leave off momentarily internal considerations of religious and political orthodoxy and confront a definite threat to its freedom of action in the form of English intervention. Massachusetts took a firm stand in defense of its rights and preserved its independence. In accomplishing this, instead of realizing that it was but the first incidence of a constantly recurring problem and trying to adjust its institutions, accommodating and compromising to meet anticipated demands, the leadership of Massachusetts responded to threat by retrenching—by consolidating religious and political institutions—to present a more united front to all future assaults. The spirit which guided the actions of Massachusetts until the effective revocation of the charter in 1686 was molded in the second decade. The leaders never seemed to realize that the struggle—no matter how consolidated their institutions—was one-sided and that in the end they must lose. For the next few decades at least, orthodoxy was to hold sway, and after Winthrop died in 1649, it was to be uncompromising and harsh. The Remonstrance of 1646 and the reaction to it by orthodox Puritans would force upon Massachusetts the major tragedies of the next decade and the frustrating failures of the decades beyond.

Appendix

The biographies of the Remonstrants are given here in descending order of importance, just as they are listed in in answering *Declaration*.

Robert Child was a doctor of medicine with degrees from Cambridge and the University of Padua in Italy. He visited Massachusetts for the first time between 1638 and 1641, making the acquaintance of many of the leaders and becoming the firm friend and business partner of John Winthrop, Jr. He returned to Europe after 1641 to study vineyards in France and to develop ideas on scientific agriculture. He hoped to carry out experiments in wine production and scientific farming in his adopted home in the New World. He returned to Massachusetts Bay in 1645, but before he could perfect any of his schemes, he became involved in the political disputes of 1646. As a result of his treatment at the hands of the magistrates, he gave up any plans he had for Massachusetts and returned to England to live. He seems to have been Presbyterian in his sympathies, despite Winslow's attempts to associate him with Catholicism: "As for Doctor Childe hee is a gentleman that hath travelled other parts before hee came to us, namely Italy; confessth hee was twice at Rome, speaketh sometimes highly as I have heard reported in favour of the Jesuits." [1] These words were written after the troubles of 1646 and are clearly an attempt at character assassination, but there is evidence that Child was under some suspicion before 1646. In June 1645 Hugh Peter, writing to the younger Winthrop, rather elliptically states, "Dr. Child is come that honest man who will bee of exceeding great use if the country know how to improve him, indeed he is very, very useful. I pray let us not play tricks with such men by our jelousyes." [2] In the seventeenth century the word *jealousy* meant suspicion. Peter is therefore urging men to forget their suspicions of Child. Winslow adds more understanding to Peter's letter:

"yea that the very yeare hee [Child] came over, a gentleman in
the country (Mr. Peters by name) was advised by letters from
a forraign part that the Jesuits had an agent that sommer in
New England. And that the countrey comparing his practices
with the intelligence were more jealous of him than any." It
was apparently his scientific activities that made Child seem
peculiar and therefore suspicious: "[he] fals upon a dilligent
survey of the whole countrey and painfully travells on foot
from plantation to plantation; takes notes of havens, situation, strength, churches, townes, number of inhabitants, and
when he had finished this toylesome taske, returns againe to
England, being able to give better account than any of the
countrey in that respect." Another suspicious grievance was
listed by Winslow: "he tooke the degree of Doctor in Physick
at Padua, yet doth not at all practise, though hee hath been
twice in the countrey where many times is need enough." [3]

Thomas Fowle, a merchant, came to Massachusetts Bay
prior to 1635. He was admitted to membership in the Boston
church on March 26, 1643. There is no record that he ever
became a freeman. He nevertheless served as a Boston selectman after his admission to the church. He was one of the
Boston merchants who became involved in the La Tour–
d'Aulnay controversy, although unlike the other merchants,
he seems to have been associated with d'Aulnay's side. He was
satisfied with Congregational church polity and was probably
the petitioner whom Winslow calls satisfied with the government of the churches in New England. But unlike the majority of Massachusetts Congregationalists, Fowle advocated the
adoption of the principle of toleration. In 1645 he joined with
Emanual Downing and others to protest the law banishing
Baptists from the colony. Apparently he supported the adoption of religious toleration as a pragmatic necessity. Falling
in line with his Congregational brethren in England, and not
antagonizing the Presbyterian majority of Parliament, was
good for business. It was probably this same feeling which in
1646 prompted him to petition for greater political freedom
and conformity with English law. According to his critics, how-

ever, he signed the Remonstrance only after having made his decision to leave Massachusetts and live in England.[4]

Samuel Maverick was discovered living on the shores of Boston harbor by Winthrop and his companions when they arrived in 1630. Apparently he arrived there in 1628. Maverick applied for admission as a freeman in October 1630 and was admitted in May 1631, before the church membership qualification was imposed. He never became a church member and was a lifelong Anglican. His normal position in Massachusetts was that of opposition to the government. He was fined heavily for taking into his household suspected adulterers who had escaped from prison. After his troubles with the petition of 1646, he stayed out of trouble until the restoration in England and was appointed by the king as a commissioner for the conquest of New Netherlands and the investigation of the political and religious situation in New England in 1664. He died the same year.[5]

Thomas Burton, a lawyer, came to Massachusetts Bay in about 1639 [6] and settled in the town of Hingham. There is no record of his admission to freemanship. His children were baptized in the Hingham church,[7] but Mr. Hobart baptized the children of church members and nonchurch members alike. Burton's motives for signing the 1646 Remonstrance were probably very mixed. His residence in Hingham during the dispute with the General Court over the town militia, the influence of Hobart's Presbyterianism, and his own concern as a lawyer for the preservation of the rights of Englishmen— all combined to prompt him to tempt the ire of the magistrates. They tried to dismiss him as one "to be as those called by Absolom to accompany him to Hebron," alluding to Absolom's revolt against his father, King David, in which unsuspecting and not very shrewd persons were drawn into the plot without much realization of what they were getting into.[8]

Not very much is known about *John Smith.* He had lived in Boston several years prior to signing the Remonstrance, but sometime before 1646 he moved to Rhode Island. Technically, therefore, he was not a resident of the Bay Colony and had no business petitioning the General Court. He did return to Boston during the height of the controversy.[9]

David Yale was a man of some prominence in New England. He was born in Wales and came to the New World in 1637 with the New Haven settlers led by John Davenport and Theophilus Eaton. Yale's mother, Ann Morton, daughter of Thomas Morton, Bishop of Chester, after the death of her first husband had remarried and was now the wife of the New Haven governor, Eaton. Yale's sister was married to Edward Hopkins, frequently the governor of the colony of Connecticut.[10] Yale left New Haven for Boston in 1641 and became a fairly wealthy Boston merchant. He was neither freeman of the colony nor member of the Boston church. His mother fell into serious religious troubles in New Haven despite her high position. She apparently fell under Baptist influence and doubted the validity of her own infant baptism. She suffered a humiliation at the hands of the New Haven church in 1644, which probably did nothing to endear her son to Congregational intolerance. His mercantile pursuits also seem to have convinced him of the need for closer ties with England and for an increased conformity with English civil and religious practices to counteract the poor image Massachusetts orthodoxy was creating in England. Yale's signature on the Remonstrance was highly disturbing to the magistrates as is testified to by their reaction:

> A fifth, is a young merchant, little acquainted with commonwealth affairs. We are willing to suppose he might also be one of them, who were invited by Absolom to Hebron, but sure we are, it is no small griefe to his honoured godly friends to find him there, when they prayed and wanted dayly to heare of him in Jerusalem.[11]

John Dand came to New England with the outbreak of the wars in England, and rented lodgings in Boston. He was apparently quite old and had been a London grocer before coming to New England. He was not a freeman nor was he a member of the Boston church. Yet by a process of elimination, and given the fact that he had lived in London, he seems to have been the petitioner who, when questioned concerning what form of church government he preferred, answered that he desired that particular government which Mr. John Goodwin in Coleman Street, London, was exercised in [12] (Goodwin was a Congregationalist or Independent of some renown). This answer of Dand's apparently led the magistrates to claim that his mind was failing him: "The seventh, is an ould grocer of London, whose forgetfulness . . . of his dutie to the government under which he now lives and prospers, we may impute to his age and some other infirmaties." [13] Of all the petitioners Dand alone recanted and had his fines returned.[14]

Notes

PROLOGUE

1 William Perkins, *The Works of That Famous and Worthy Minister of Christ in the Universitie of Cambridge, Mr. William Perkins*, 3 vols. (London, 1626–31), 2 : 155.

2 Wallace Notestein, *The English People on the Eve of Colonization* (New York, 1954), provides a brief summary of the local scene in 17th-century England.

3 Darrett Rutman, *Winthrop's Boston* (Chapel Hill, N.C., 1965), pp. 25–28, 280–83.

4 *The Winthrop Papers*, ed. Allyn Forbes, 5 vols. (Boston, 1929–47), 4 : 468.

5 *Records of the Governor and Company of the Massachusetts Bay in New England*, ed. Nathaniel B. Shurtleff, 5 vols. (Boston, 1853–54), 1 : 79 (hereafter cited as *Mass. Col. Rec.*). See also Edmund S. Morgan, *The Puritan Dilemma* (Boston, 1958), p. 90.

6 *Mass. Col. Rec.*, 1 : 80, 87, 366.

7 John Winthrop, *The History of New England from 1630 to 1649*, ed. James Savage, 2d ed., 2 vols. (Boston, 1853), 1 : 84 (hereafter cited as Winthrop's Journal).

8 *Mass. Col. Rec.*, 1 : 95.

9 Ibid.

10 Winthrop's Journal, 1 : 86–88, 91, 98–99, 99–103.

11 Ibid., p. 152.

12 Ibid., p. 153.

13 Ibid., pp. 157–58; *Mass. Col. Rec.*, 1 : 117–18.

14 Winthrop's Journal, 1 : 157.

15 *Mass. Col. Rec.*, 1 : 117–18, 145, 174, 195.

16 Winthrop's Journal, 1 : 167–68.

17 Ibid., p. 168.

18 Ibid., pp. 168–69.

19 *Mass. Col. Rec.*, 1 : 161.

20 Ibid., pp. 135, 136, 175.

21 Ibid., p. 161.

22 Ibid., pp. 167, 174, 195; Winthrop's Journal, 1 : 219–20.

23 Winthrop's Journal, 1 : 360–61.

24 Ibid., p. 361.

25 A petition to the General Court by the freemen of Roxbury presented the next day prompted the General Court to set down in writing the reasons for the limiting of the number of deputies and to submit this paper to the freemen. Ibid., p. 362.

26 Ibid., pp. 363–64.
27 *Mass. Col. Rec.*, 1 : 264.
28 Winthrop's Journal, 1 : 364; *Mass. Col. Rec.*, 1 : 264.
29 Winthrop's Journal, 1 : 360–61, 363–64, 2 : 3.
30 Ibid., 1 : 191.
31 Ibid., pp. 240–41; John Cotton, "A Model of Moses, His Judicials,"
    Collections of the Massachusetts Historical Society, 1st ser., vol. 5 (1816),
32 Winthrop's Journal, 1 : 388–89.
33 Winthrop states that Ward's frame was the real basis for the final
    product. Ibid., 2 : 66.
34 Ibid., 1 : 389.
35 *The Colonial Laws of Massachusetts*, ed. William H. Whitmore
    (Boston, 1889), pp. 35, 47, 49.
36 *The Laws and Liberties of Massachusetts*, ed. Max Farrand (Cam-
    bridge, Mass., 1929).

CHAPTER 1

1 Kenneth A. Lockridge and Alan Kreider, "The Evolution of Massachusetts Town Government, 1640 to 1740," *William and Mary Quarterly* 23 (1966): 549–74.
2 Those towns of Suffolk County and Middlesex County which have
   extant lists of selectmen are Boston, Dedham, Dorchester, Braintree,
   Watertown, Charlestown, Cambridge, and Sudbury. These eight towns
   elected a total of 219 selectmen from the time when the first elections
   were recorded up to and including 1646. Of those 219 men, 192 were
   freemen. Of the remaining 27, 2 were elected selectmen before 1637,
   when such elections would have been legal; 9 became freemen almost
   immediately after their election. Only 16 out of the 219 served as
   selectmen without ever becoming freemen of the colony. Yet in those
   areas of the colony which were some distance from the capital in
   Boston and therefore some distance from the seat of the Court of
   Assistants, where all freemen had to be enrolled before 1642, the
   figures were quite different. The Essex towns of Salem, Ipswich, and
   Gloucester, as well as the Norfolk town of Salisbury and the town of
   Springfield (in what would later become Hampshire County), have
   extant lists of selectmen for the pre-1647 period. They elected a total
   of 70 selectmen. Fifty of the 70 were freemen. Of the remaining 20,
   8 became freemen immediately after their elections; the other 12
   served as selectmen without ever becoming freemen. In short, 16 percent of the selectmen from towns distant from the capital were nonfreemen, while only 7 percent of the Suffolk-Middlesex selectmen were
   nonfreemen. This last figure may also be inaccurate. In 1642 the
   General Court of Massachusetts provided for the enrolling of freemen
   at the county courts. The court records for Essex and Norfolk are
   extant and almost complete. They list some 250 names of freemen
   admitted between 1643 and 1664. The records of the court at Springfield list another fifty names. If Essex, Norfolk, or Springfield men

were admitted freemen at their county seats and failed to have their admissions recorded in the colony records in Boston, we are still able to discover the fact of their freemanship in the county records. The same cannot be said for any Suffolk or Middlesex enrollments. The early records of both these counties are missing. Normally this would present no serious problems, since one could turn to the colony records for their names, but unfortunately, it appears certain that the freemanship records of the colony were carelessly kept, particularly after 1650. (Lists of freemen can be found appendixed to the end of each of the volumes of the colony records except vol. 3. See also Essex Institute, *Records and Files of the Quarterly Courts of Essex County, Massachusetts*, 8 vols. [Salem, Mass., 1911–21]. Hereafter cited as *Essex Court Records*. See also *Colonial Justice in Western Massachusetts, 1639–1702* [The Pynchon Court Records], ed. Joseph Smith [Cambridge, Mass., 1961], and Stephen Foster, "The Franchise in Seventeenth Century Massachusetts," *William and Mary Quarterly* 24 [1967].) The 16 percent figure for the remote towns is an accurate reflection of the number of nonfreemen serving in important elective posts in the local communities. The 7 percent figure for Suffolk-Middlesex should be lower.

In addition to revealing differences concerning the elections of selectmen in various parts of the colony, these statistics suggest clear distinctions concerning voting rights in different parts of the colony. If nonfreemen could be selectmen in the remote towns, then surely they were not barred from voting in local elections. This kind of voting by nonfreemen before 1647 was illegal—in violation of the direct rulings of the General Court—yet it went on in the remote towns of the northeastern counties and in the distant Connecticut valley.

3 In 1648 in the town of Dedham the average tax for the common citizen was 5s. 1d.; the freemen who were never selectmen paid 5s. 6d. and the nonfreemen 4s. 8d. The total for pre-1647 selectmen was 11s. 7d. The selectmen of Dedham (at least in 1648) had twice the amount of taxable property held by the other citizens (*Early Records of the Town of Dedham*, ed. Don Hill, 5 vols. [Dedham, Mass., 1888–94], 3 : 152–53; hereafter cited as *Dedham Town Records*). In the Watertown inventory of real property made from 1644 to 1646, the pre-1647 selectmen had 124 acres on the average, while the average for the rest of the citizens was 51 acres; 73 acres for freemen who were not selectmen; and 49 acres for nonfreemen (*Watertown Records*, 5 vols. [Watertown, Mass., 1894–19], vol. I, sec. 2 [Lands], pp. 15–146; hereafter cited as *Watertown Records*). In Charlestown in 1638 the selectmen averaged 135 acres, while the freemen who never served as selectmen before 1647 had 55 acres, and the nonfreemen 53 acres (*Third Report of the Records Commissioners of the City of Boston* [Charlestown Land Records], eds. William Whitmore and William Appleton, 2d. ed. [Boston, 1883]; hereafter cited as the Charlestown

Land Records). A land grant was made in the town of Cambridge in the year 1652, with the largest acreage going to those with the largest existing estates. The pre-1647 selectmen received an average grant of 219 acres of land, while the common citizens received 56 acres, 125 acres for those who were freemen but never selectmen, and 51 acres for nonfreemen (*The Records of the Town and Selectmen of Cambridge, 1630–1703* [Cambridge, Mass., 1901], pp. 97–98; hereafter cited as *Cambridge Town Records*).

The contention that the selectmen were richer than the common citizens is also supported by estate inventories made at the time of death by order of the county courts.

Town	Pre-1647 selectmen's inventory average	Freemen's average	Nonfree average
Boston	£926	£565	£424
Salem	362	505	203
Ipswich	933	594	310
Watertown	373	339	137
Charlestown	813	768	299
Dedham	484	410	185
Dorchester	947	527	492
Salisbury	344	334	200

These figures are averages of estate inventories for the towns. For a list of available probate records, see the Bibliography under the various counties.

4   *Mass. Col. Rec.,* 1 : 188.
5   Robert Emmet Wall, Jr., "The Membership of the Massachusetts General Court, 1634–1686" (Ph.D. diss., Yale University, 1965).
6   Ibid.
7   Ibid.
8   For a list of the available probate records, see the Bibliography under the various counties.
9   See *Cambridge Town Records,* pp. 97–98. The magistrates did not always pay the highest taxes since freedom from colony taxation for the first £500 of their holdings was frequently part of the magistrates' compensation.
10 This point is stressed by Larzer Ziff in *The Career of John Cotton: Puritanism and the American Experience* (Princeton, 1962), p. 206.

CHAPTER 2

1   Winthrop's Journal, 2 : 107ff.
2   Ibid.
3   Ibid., pp. 77–78; *Mass. Col. Rec.,* 2 : 5.

4   *Mass. Col. Rec.*, 2 : 21.
5   "John Winthrop to Anonymous Rev[erend] and Dear Sir—no date," in Forbes, *Winthrop Papers*, 4 : 347.
6   See above, pp. 43–44.
7   Winthrop's Journal, 2 : 107–09.
8   Perry Miller, *Orthodoxy in Massachusetts, 1630–1650* (Cambridge, Mass., 1933), p. 246.
9   *Mass. Col. Rec.*, 2 : 21, 31.
10 Winthrop's Journal, 2 : 119.
11 Later the nominating process passed to the freeman of the towns, yet no changes were made in the makeup of the magistracy. *Mass Col. Rec.*, 2 : 21, 31, 37, 87, 175, 210, 286–87.
12 Winthrop's Journal, 2 : 119.
13 Ibid.
14 Cf. Keayne's peculiar and lengthy last will and testament in *The Apologia of Robert Keayne*, ed. Bernard Bailyn (New York, 1965).
15 Winthrop's Journal, 2 : 83–84.
16 Ibid., p. 84.
17 Both men later are found in opposition to the magistrates on the sow case and the negative voice. Ibid., pp. 139–40.
18 Forbes, *Winthrop Papers*, 4 : 352; Winthrop's Journal, 2 : 84.
19 Winthrop's Journal, 2 : 85.
20 Ibid., p. 86; Forbes, *Winthrop Papers*, 4 : 359–60.
21 Forbes, *Winthrop Papers*, 4 : 352.
22 This account of the "Sow Case" is taken from Winthrop's Journal, 2 : 83–86; *Mass. Col. Rec.*, 2 : 12; and Forbes, *Winthrop Papers*, 4 : 349–52.
23 Forbes, *Winthrop Papers*, 4 : 359–60.
24 Ibid.
25 Ibid., p. 360.
26 Winthrop's Journal, 2 : 139.
27 Ibid.
28 Ibid., pp. 139–40.
29 *Mass. Col. Rec.*, 1 : 170.
30 Winthrop's Journal, 2 : 142–43.
31 Ibid., p. 143.
32 Ibid.
33 Forbes, *Winthrop Papers*, 4 : 383.
34 Winthrop's entire second treatise on the negative voice can be found in ibid., pp. 380–91.
35 Richard Mather, *Reply to Mr. Rutherford* (London, 1647), pp. 87, 88, as quoted in Williston Walker, *The Creeds and Platforms of Congregationalism* (New York, 1893), pp. 137, 137n., 138, 139.
36 Ibid.; Thomas Lechford, *Plain Dealing or Newes from New England* (London, 1642), in *Collections of the Massachusetts Historical Society*, 3d ser. (1833), 3 : 80 (hereafter cited as *Plain Dealing, MHSC*).
37 *Mass. Col. Rec.*, 2 : 46.

38 Ibid., pp. 58–59.
39 Winthrop's Journal, 1 : 139, 184.
40 Ibid., 2 : 51.
41 Ibid., pp. 106–07.
42 Ibid., p. 109.
43 Ibid., pp. 152–54.
44 "John Endecott to John Winthrop, 19 June 1643," in Forbes, *Winthrop Papers*, 4 : 394–95.
45 Ibid.
46 Winthrop's Journal, 2 : 153, 162–63.
47 Winthrop received a similar complaint from Thomas Gorges at Piscataqua, dated June 28, 1643. See Thomas Hutchinson, *Collections of Original Papers* (London, 1769), p. 114.
48 "Richard Saltonstall, et al. to John Winthrop, 14 July 1643," in *Winthrop Papers*, 4 : 397–401.
49 "John Winthrop to Richard Saltonstall et al., ca. 21 July 1643," ibid., p. 404.
50 Winthrop's Journal, 2 : 154.
51 Ibid., pp. 154, 162.
52 "John Endecott to John Winthrop, 26 July 1643," in Forbes, *Winthrop Papers*, 4 : 411–12.
53 "Simon Bradstreet to John Winthrop, 21 August 1643," ibid., pp. 412–13.
54 *Mass. Col. Rec.*, 2 : 47–48.
55 Ibid., p. 46.
56 Ibid., pp. 47–48; Winthrop's Journal, 2 : 204.
57 Winthrop's Journal, 2 : 210, 211.
58 Ibid., p. 204.
59 *Mass. Col. Rec.*, 3 : 2, 4.
60 Ibid., p. 5.
61 Winthrop's Journal, 2 : 204.
62 Ibid., pp. 204–05.
63 Ibid., pp. 205–06.
64 Ibid.
65 Ibid.
66 Ibid., p. 206.
67 This is exactly what they did do. See ibid., p. 228.
68 Ibid., p. 208.
69 Ibid., p. 283, for example.
70 Ibid., p. 208.
71 Ibid., p. 228.
72 Forbes, *Winthrop Papers*, 4 : 468.
73 Ibid., p. 472. The complete text of Winthrop's discourse on arbitrary government can be found in ibid., pp. 468–88.
74 Winthrop's Journal, 2 : 283.
75 Forbes, *Winthrop Papers*, 4 : 483.

76 Winthrop's Journal, 2 : 283.
77 Ibid., p. 251.
78 Ibid.
79 Ibid., pp. 250-57.

CHAPTER 3

1 Winthrop's Journal, 2 : 288.
2 "Manuscript Journal of Peter Hobart, entry of September 14, 1652," Town Clerk's Office, Hingham, Mass.
3 These conclusions concerning the nature of Hingham politics are confirmed by the recent studies of John J. Waters—especially his article "Hingham, Massachusetts, 1631–1661—An East Anglian Oligarchy in the New World," *Journal of Social History* 1 (June 1968): 351–70. See also Wall, "The Membership of the Massachusetts General Court."
4 Winthrop's Journal, 2 : 271.
5 *Mass. Col. Rec.*, 3 : 22.
6 Winthrop's Journal, 2 : 272.
7 *Mass. Col. Rec.*, 3 : 19-22.
8 Winthrop's Journal, 2 : 272, 273.
9 Ibid., p. 288.
10 Ibid., pp. 273-74.
11 Ibid., p. 274.
12 John Child, *New England's Jonas Cast Up at London* (London, 1647), in *Collections of the Massachusetts Historical Society*, 2d ser., vol. 4 (1816), pp. 108-09 (hereafter cited as *Jonas, MHSC*).
13 Winthrop's Journal, 2 : 319.
14 Samuel Deane, *History of Scituate* (Boston, 1831), pp. 61-84.
15 Edward Winslow, *New England's Salamander, Discovered* (London, 1647), in *Collections of the Massachusetts Historical Society*, 3d ser., vol. 2 (1830), pp. 114-15 (hereafter cited as *Salamander, MHSC*).
16 Ibid., 2 : 115.
17 Winthrop's Journal, 2 : 257.
18 *Mass. Col. Rec.*, 3 : 17-18.
19 Winthrop's Journal, 2 : 274.
20 Ibid., p. 275.
21 Ibid.
22 Ibid.
23 Ibid., pp. 275-77.
24 Ibid., p. 277.
25 *Mass. Col. Rec.*, 3 : 18.
26 Ibid., p. 23. The laws the magistrates are referring to can be found in ibid., 1 : 183, 187. Apparently, the towns were complying with these laws; cf. Forbes, *Winthrop Papers*, 4 : 106-07.
27 These exchanges between the deputies and the magistrates can be found in *Mass. Col. Rec.*, 3 : 19-23.

28 The session opened on May 14. The date of the magistrates' document suggesting fines is June 28. Ibid., pp. 23–24.
29 Ibid., p. 24.
30 Ibid., pp. 24–25.
31 Winthrop's Journal, 2 : 278.
32 *Mass. Col. Rec.*, 2 : 114, 3 : 26.
33 Winthrop's Journal, 2 : 280.
34 Ibid.
35 Ibid., pp. 280–81.
36 Ibid., p. 281.
37 Ibid., p. 279.

CHAPTER 4

1 For the story of Gorton's Plymouth troubles, see Edward Winslow, *Hypocrisie Unmasked* (London, 1646), pp. 66–68; and Nathaniel Morton, *New England's Memoriall* (Cambridge, Mass., 1669), p. 108.
2 Gorton's activities in Rhode Island can be traced in *The Records of the Colony of Rhode Island and Providence Plantations in New England,* ed. John Russell Bartlett, 10 vols. (Providence, 1856–65), 1 : 70 (hereafter cited as *R.I. Col. Rec.*). See also Winslow, *Hypocrisie Unmasked,* pp. 54–55. Winslow apparently received his information directly from Gov. Coddington of Rhode Island as can be seen in the letter "William Coddington to John Winthrop, 11 Nov. 1646," *New England Historical and Genealogical Register,* 4 (1850) : 221 (hereafter cited as *NEHGR*). One should also consult *Plain Dealing, MHSC* (1833), 3d ser. 3 : 96.
3 "Roger Williams to John Winthrop, 8 mo. 1640 [*sic*]," *NEHGR,* 4 : 216. The letter quoted above is from an unpublished manuscript form of Winslow's *Hypocrisie Unmasked.* The published version is identical, except that the date of the Williams's letter is given as "8 1st 1640"—or 8 March 1640/1." The authenticity of the letter has been questioned by some, including Kenneth W. Porter, in "Samuel Gorton, New England Firebrand," *New England Quarterly* 7 (September 1934) : 418. Yet I am inclined to accept it as authentic. The original is not to be found in the *Winthrop Papers,* but is it not likely that Winthrop gave Winslow the original to take to London with him for use against Gorton? Williams was the darling of English Independents at this moment and also a willing combatant in printed debate. Winslow would have been a fool to attempt to use Williams's name against Gorton unless he had absolute foolproof evidence in hand. Winslow was so confident he knew Williams's opinion of Gorton that he printed the text of the 1641 letter in his anti-Gorton pamphlet, *Hypocrisie Unmasked,* in 1646 and then printed it a second time in 1648 in a new edition of the same work. Neither printing drew a response from the polemicist Roger Williams. John Russell Bartlett, et al., ed. *The Complete Writings of Roger Williams,* 7 vols.

(New York, 1963), 4 : 141, reprints the letter, but wrongly, giving the date as "8th 1st 1646."

4 Winthrop's Journal, 2 : 71; Samuel Gorton, *Simplicity's Defence against Seven-Headed Policy* (London, 1647), in *The Rhode Island Historical Society Collections*, ed. William R. Staples (1835), 2 : 191–93 (hereafter cited as *Simplicity's Defence, RIHSC*).

5 "William Arnold to the Selectmen of Providence, 25 May 1641," in *NEHGR*, 4 : 216–18.

6 Morton, *New England's Memoriall*, pp. 108–09; *Simplicity's Defence, RIHSC*, 2 : 191; Archives of the State of Massachusetts, bound MSS in the State House, Boston, 2 : 2. The 13 men were William Fields, William Harris, William Carpenter, William Wickenden, William Reynolds, Thomas Harris, Thomas Hopkins, Hugh Bewitt, Joshua Winsor, Benedict Arnold, William Man, William Hunkings, and Robert West.

7 *Simplicity's Defence, RIHSC*, 2 : 193.

8 Winthrop's Journal, 2 : 69.

9 *Mass. Col. Rec.*, 2 : 26–27; for Gorton's opinions of these men see *Simplicity's Defence, RIHSC*, 2 : 50–52.

10 Winthrop's Journal, 2 : 102.

11 *Simplicity's Defence, RIHSC*, 2 : 47–49.

12 Winthrop's Journal, 2 : 102.

13 *Mass. Col. Rec.*, 2 : 26–27; *Simplicity's Defence, RIHSC*, 2 : 53.

14 *Simplicity's Defence, RIHSC*, 2 : 68.

15 Ibid., 2 : 63–71, 87–92.

16 Winthrop's Journal, 2 : 145n., 146n.; also *RIHSC*, vol. 2, App. 13, pp. 253–54, and Winslow, *Hypocrisie Unmasked*, p. 2.

17 Winthrop's Journal, 2 : 144–45; Winslow, *Hypocrisie Unmasked*, pp. 2–3; Edward Johnson, *Wonder-Working Providence of Sions Saviour in New England, 1628–1651*, ed. J. Franklin Jameson (New York, 1910), p. 223.

18 *Mass. Col. Rec.*, 2 : 38.

19 Winthrop's Journal, 2 : 148.

20 *RIHSC*, 2 : 213.

21 Winthrop's Journal, 2 : 146; Winslow, *Hypocrisie Unmasked*, p. 3; *Mass. Col. Rec.*, 2 : 35.

22 *Simplicity's Defence, RIHSC*, 2 : 95–96.

23 Winthrop's Journal, 2 : 165; *Mass. Col. Rec.*, 2 : 41.

24 *RIHSC*, 2 : 262.

25 Ibid., p. 265.

26 Ibid., pp. 265, 268.

27 Ibid., pp. 264–65.

28 Ibid., pp. 266, 268.

29 *Mass. Col. Rec.*, 2 : 44; also Johnson, *Wonder-Working Providence*, p. 224, and *Simplicity's Defence, RIHSC*, 2 : 101.

30 The story of the "Battle of Shawomet" can be found in *Simplicity's*

Defence, RIHSC, 2 : 98–119; Winthrop's Journal, 2 : 158, 168–69, 171–73; Winslow, *Hypocrisie Unmasked*, pp. 4, 5, 74–75; and Johnson *Wonder-Working Providence*, p. 224.

31   *Simplicity's Defence, RIHSC*, 2 : 120–21; Winslow, *Hypocrisie Unmasked*, pp. 5–8; Winthrop's Journal, 2 : 173–77.

32   Winthrop's Journal, 2 : 174.

33   *Mass. Col. Rec.*, 2 : 51.

34   *Simplicity's Defence, RIHSC*, 2 : 123, 124, 125.

35   Ibid., p. 123.

36   Winthrop's Journal, 2 : 175.

37   *Simplicity's Defence, RIHSC*, 2 : 125, 126, 127; see also p. 79.

38   Winthrop's Journal, 2 : 176.

39   Ibid., p. 177.

40   In *Simplicity's Defence*, Gorton writes:

"Old Mr. Ward, once lecturer in St. Michael's in Churchill, London, came to the prison window, and called to him, one of our society, namely Richard Carder, who had once lived near together in Essex. Mr. Ward seemed to be much affected, being a man knows how to put himself into passion, desired the said Richard, that if he had done or said anything that he could with good conscience renounce, he desired him to recant it, and he hoped the Court would be very merciful; and saith he, it shall be no disparagement unto you; for here is our reverend elder, Mr. Cotton, who ordinarily preacheth that publicly one year, that the next year he publicly repents of, and shews himself very sorrowful for it to the congregation; so that (saith he) it will be no disgrace for you to recant in such a case" (*RIHSC*, 2 : 122n).

The story is accepted by the biographer of Cotton, Larzer Ziff, and it sounds like something the witty Ward might say (Larzar Ziff, *The Career of John Cotton* [Princeton, 1962], pp. 206–07). Cotton was not yet free from the stigma attached to his "switching sides" in the Antinomian debates. Yet Ward himself denied ever saying anything so ironic and pays much tribute to Cotton:

"Samuel Gorton having made mee a margent not in the 53 page [orig. ed.] of his booke, I hold my self called to make this answer to it; I cannot call to minde that ever I knew or spoke with such a man as Richard Carder, no that ever I had any speech with a prisoner at a windowe nor should I need it in New England, where there is liberty enough given for conference with prisoners in more free and convenient places. This I remember, that one Robert Potter who went in the same ship with mee into New England, and expressing by the way so much honesty and godlinesse as gained my good opinion and affection toward him. I hearing that hee was affected with Samuel Gorton's blasphemous conceits and carriages and therefore now imprisoned with him, I went to visit him and having free speech with him in the open prison yard, who shedding many tears might happily move me to expresse my affection to him, which Samuel

Gorton calls passion. After some debate about his new opinions, I remember I used a speech to him to this effect. That hee should do well and wisely to make such acknowledgement of his erros as his conscience would permit, telling him that Mr. Cotton who hee had so much reverenced in Old England and New had given him a godly example in that kinde, by a publique acknowledgement upon a solemne Fast day with many tears; that in the time when errours were so strong God leaving him for a time, he fell into a spiritual slumber and had it not been for the watchfulness of his brethren the Elders etc. hee might have slept on and blessed God very cordially for awakening him and was very thankful to his Brethren, for their watchfulnesse over him, and faithfulnesse towards him; wherein he honored God not a little, and greatly rejoyced the hearts of his hearers; and therefore it would be no shame for him to do the like" (Nathaniel Ward, as quoted in Winslow, *Hypocrisie Unmasked*, p. 76.).

41 Winthrop's Journal, 2 : 178n. The Court's decision can also be found in *Mass. Col. Rec.*, 2 : 52, and *Simplicity's Defence, RIHSC*, 2 : 134–36.
42 Winthrop's Journal, 2 : 178n.
43 *Mass. Col. Rec.*, 2 : 53. Winslow (*Hypocrisie Unmasked*, p. 9) claimed that the cost to Massachusetts was over £160 and that the sale of the cattle did not cover the costs.
44 *Simplicity's Defence, RIHSC*, 2 : 136–37.
45 Ibid., pp. 103–05.
46 "Emanuel Downing to John Winthrop, 6 February 1643/4," in Forbes, *Winthrop Papers*, 4 : 439.
47 "John Endecott to John Winthrop, 22 April 1644," ibid., pp. 455, 456.
48 *Simplicity's Defence, RIHSC*, 2 : 122n.
49 Winthrop's Journal, 2 : 188, 178. Winslow is less than frank when he claims that the Gortonists were released out of sympathy for the sorry plight of their wives and children. See Winslow, *Hypocrisie Unmasked*, pp. 8–9.
50 *Mass. Col. Rec.*, 2 : 57; see also *Simplicity's Defence, RIHSC*, 2 : 148. A comparison of the official documents with the copies of them published by Gorton reveals a scrupulous care to reproduce them exactly, even at the risk of harming his own cause.
51 *Simplicity's Defence, RIHSC*, 2 : 149.
52 The text of this letter can be found in ibid., pp. 150–51.
53 Ibid., p. 152.
54 *RIHSC*, 2 : 11.
55 Winthrop's Journal, 2 : 332.
56 Ibid., pp. 148–49.
57 Ibid., p. 212; *Mass. Col. Rec.*, 2 : 85.
58 *Mass. Col. Rec.*, 3 : 51. Since the Downing petition was not discovered in the Massachusetts archives, the names of the other signatories remain a mystery.
59 Winthrop's Journal, 2 : 307.

60 *Mass. Col. Rec.,* 2 : 149, 3 : 64. This petition has survived and can be found in the Massachusetts Archives. See also Winthrop's Journal, 2 : 324 and note.

61 Weld had been in England since 1641. See Winthrop's Journal, 2 : 332; *Genealogical Dictionary,* 4 : 461.

62 *R.I. Col. Rec.,* 2 : 129.

63 Winthrop's Journal, 2 : 333.

64 Ibid., pp. 342–44, esp. p. 343.

65 Ibid.

66 Ibid., pp. 360ff.

67 Ibid., pp. 360–64, 363.

68 Morton, *New England's Memoriall,* pp. 108–10; *RIHSC,* 2 : 246–48.

69 *Mass. Col. Rec.,* 2 : 242–43.

CHAPTER 5

1 William Bradford, *Of Plymouth Plantation,* ed. H. Wish (New York, 1962), p. 203.

2 For the story of Vassall's efforts in Plymouth, see *Salamander, MHSC,* 3d ser., 2 : 137; *Records of the Colony of New Plymouth,* ed. Nathaniel Shurtleff and Daniel Pulsifer, 12 vols. (Boston, 1856–61), 1 : 81.

3 *Plain Dealing, MHSC,* 3d ser., 3 : 80.

4 The opinions of the two Newbury clergymen can be found in Thomas Parker, *True Copy of a Letter Written by Mr. T[homas] P[arker] . . . Declaring His Judgment Touching the Government Practised in the Chs. of N.E.* (London, 1644); and James Noyes, *The Temple Measured* (London, 1647).

5 Letter from an unnamed writer in New England to a minister in England, quoted in Walker, *The Creeds and Platforms of Congregationalism,* p. 138.

6 Parker, *True Copy of a Letter;* the date of the letter is 1643 and it was published in London in 1644. See Walker, *Creeds and Platforms of Congregationalism,* p. 138.

7 See Edmund S. Morgan, *Visible Saints* (New York, 1963).

8 Winthrop's Journal, 2 : 193, 321.

9 For an account of the second church of Scituate and Vassall's role in it, see Deane, *History of Scituate,* pp. 61–84.

10 Johnson, *Wonder-Working Providence,* p. 240. Winslow also points out the mixed religious veiws of the petitioners:
    "At a private conference with an eminent person (who well hoped to have satisfied them) hee demanded of the petitioners what church government it was they would have? One of them answered, he desired that particular government which Mr. John Goodwin in Coleman street was exercised in. Another of them said hee knew not what that was: But hee for his part desired the Presbyterian government. A third of them said hee desired the Episcopal government if it might bee, if not, the Presbyterian: and a fourth told me

himselfe that hee disclaimed any thing in the petition that was against the government of the Churches in New England" (Salamander, MHSC, 3d ser., 2 : 112).

11 Winthrop's Journal, 2 : 319.
12 Cf. Appendix for biographical sketches of the petitioners.
13 Hutchinson, Collection of Original Papers, p. 188.
14 Ibid., p. 189.
15 Winthrop reported that in Boston, early in 1646: "There fell out also a loathsome disease at Boston, which raised a scandal upon the town and country, though without just cause. One of the town [erased in the original] having gone cooper in a ship into [erased in the original], at his return his wife was infected with lues venerea, which appeared thus: being delivered of a child, and nothing then appearing, but the midwife, a skillful woman, finding her body as sound as any other, after her delivery, she had a sore breast, where upon divers neighbors resorting to her, some of them drew her breast, and others suffered their children to draw her, and others let her child suck them, (no such disease being suspected by any,) by occasion whereof about sixteen persons, men, women, and children, were infected, whereby it came at length to be discovered by such in the town as had skill in physic and surgery, but there was not any in the country who had been practised in that cure. But (see the good providence of God) at that very season there came by accident a young surgeon out of the West Indies, who had had experience of the right way of the cure of that disease. He took them in hand, and through the Lord's blessing recovered them all [blank in the original] in a short time. And it was observed that although many did eat and drink and lodge in bed with those who were infected and had sores, etc., yet none took it of them, but by copulation or sucking. It was very doubtful how this disease came at first. The magistrates examined the husband and wife, but could find no dishonesty in either, nor any probable occasion how they should take it by any other, (and the husband was found to be free of it). So as it was concluded by some, that the woman was infected by the mixtures of so many spirits of men and women as drew her breast, (for thence it began). But this is a question to be decided by physicians" (Winthrop's Journal, 2 : 315).

There is good reason to believe that the victims of the disease, with the probable exception of the anonymous cooper, were innocent of any wrongdoing. Oral contact with open lesions is atypical, but by no means rare, in the contracting of syphilis. It would be wrong to conclude that this occurrence was indicative of any moral breakdown this early in the history of the Puritan colony. It is also wrong to conclude that the solid front presented by the infected in their claims of innocence was a sinister plot indicating contempt for the magistrates on the part of the common folk of Boston.

One aspect of the case which deserves further study (but more properly by a historian of medicine) is Winthrop's assertion that a West Indian physician cured the infected parties. How this was accomplished in the seventeenth century is not at all understood. Syphilis apparently has a very high spontaneous recovery rate. The infected parties may have been lucky, in good health, and hit with only a small infecting dose. It may also be true that some were not cured at all but that merely their symptoms temporarily disappeared only to recur later on. The author is indebted to Barry Gault, M.D., of Boston, for the expert medical judgments given in this note.

16 Hutchinson, *Papers*, p. 190.
17 Ibid.
18 Ibid., p. 192.
19 Ibid.
20 Ibid., p. 193.
21 Ibid., p. 194.
22 *Salamander, MHSC*, 3d ser., 2 : 112.
23 Hutchinson, *Papers*, pp. 195–96.
24 Winthrop's Journal, 2 : 320, 321.
25 *Salamander, MHSC*, 3d ser., 2 : 116.
26 *Jonas, MHSC*, 2d ser., 4 : 111.
27 "Samuel Symonds to John Winthrop, 6 January 1646/7," in Forbes, *Winthrop Papers*, 5 : 125–27.
28 Winthrop's Journal, 2 : 321.
29 This call for a synod was much debated in the General Court and in the churches of the colony. The deputies and many of the faithful objected to the civil arm ordering the churches to meet. See ibid., pp. 323–24, 329, 332; *Mass. Col. Rec.*, 2 : 154–56, 196.
30 The story of the first session of the Cambridge synod can be found in Winthrop's Journal, 2 : 329–32.
31 *Mass. Col. Rec.*, 2 : 196.
32 Ibid., p. 162.
33 The text of this document can be found in Hutchinson, *Papers*, pp. 196–218.
34 Ibid., p. 197.
35 Ibid., p. 200–07.
36 Ibid., p. 204.
37 Ibid., pp. 204, 205.
38 Nathaniel Ward, "Body of Liberties," in *Puritan Political Ideas*, ed. Edmund S. Morgan (Indianapolis, New York, and Kansas City, 1965), p. 198.
39 Winthrop's Journal, 2 : 190–91, 305–06.
40 Hutchinson, *Papers*, p. 214.
41 Ibid., pp. 211–12.
42 Winthrop's Journal, 2 : 346–47.
43 "John Winthrop to John Winthrop Jr., 16 November 1646," Forbes, *Winthrop Papers*, 5 : 119.

44 *Mass. Col. Rec.,* 3 : 88, 89.

45 Winthrop's Journal, 2 : 347ff.

46 *Mass. Col. Rec.,* 3 : 88–89; and Winthrop's Journal, 2 : 347ff.

47 *Salamander, MHSC,* 3d ser., 2 : 124.

48 Ibid., p. 126. Winslow states that he also checked with others present at the sermon to check his account for accuracy. He claims that Thomas Peter, William Codling, Herbert Palham, Capt. William Sayles, Capt. John Leveret, Capt. Harding, and Mr. Richard Sadler all verified his account of Cotton's preaching (ibid., p. 130).

49 Ibid., pp. 128–29.

50 Ibid., p. 130.

51 The two sources of this story are *Jonas, MHSC,* 2d ser., 4 : 114–16; *Salamander, MHSC,* 3d ser., 2 : 130–33.

52 Winthrop's Journal, 2 : 348–50; *Mass. Col. Rec.,* 3 : 90–91.

53 Winthrop's Journal, 2 : 351–55.

54 *Mass. Col. Rec.,* 2 : 145–46, 3 : 61–62, 94; Winthrop's Journal, 2 : 356.

55 John G. Palfrey, *History of New England,* 5 vols. (Boston, 1856–90), 2 : 175n.

56 Winthrop's Journal, 2 : 376.

57 Ibid., p. 340.

58 Ibid., pp. 340ff. A "young fellow," Thomas Joy, was a Boston carpenter who became active in the cause of the Remonstrance. At a later date Joy was to question publicly the validity of action of the General Court. He was arrested and kept in irons for 4 or 5 days. When brought before the authorities, he confessed what he knew of the activities of the petitioners, admitted his guilt in involving himself in matters which were none of his business, and blessed God for the irons on his legs. He was released. Shortly after this, the publicly converted Joy moved his wife and 4 children to Hingham, where he built and operated the town mill (ibid., 2 : 359, 359n.). The selection of Hingham as his new home was significant. Joy may have admitted his guilt, but in Hingham there were others who thought like he did, and perhaps in Hingham he could question the validity of the magistrates' actions and not end up in irons for his efforts.

59 *Mass. Col. Rec.,* 3 : 94.

60 Winthrop's Journal, 2 : 355–56; *Mass. Col. Rec.,* 3 : 94.

61 Winthrop's Journal, 2 : 29, 30.

62 Ibid., pp. 340–45; *Salamander, MHSC,* 3d ser., 2 : 123–24.

63 Winthrop's Journal, 2 : 346.

64 *Mass. Col. Rec.,* 2 : 162.

65 Bradford, *Of Plymouth Plantation,* p. 227; Morton, *New England's Memoriall,* pp. 123, 124; Winthrop's Journal, 2 : 359.

66 *Mass. Col. Rec.,* 2 : 79.

67 Winthrop's Journal, 2 : 359; *Mass. Col. Rec.,* 3 : 79.

68 Winthrop's Journal, 2 : 364.

69 Ibid., pp. 366–67. For the Commission and secret instructions, see ibid., 2 : 365–66.

70   Ibid., p. 356.
71   Ibid., pp. 357–58.
72   Ibid., p. 357; Thomas Hutchinson, *The History of the Colony and Province of Massachusetts Bay*, ed. Lawrence Shaw Mayo, 3 vols. (Cambridge, Mass., 1936), 1 : 127.
73   Winthrop's Journal, 2 : 358.
74   Ibid.
75   Ibid., pp. 356–57.
76   Ibid.; *Salamander, MHSC*, 3d ser., 2 : 124.
77   Winthrop's Journal, 2 : 358.
78   Ibid., pp. 358–59; *Jonas, MHSC*, 2d ser., 4 : 120.
79   Winthrop's Journal, 2 : 367.
80   Winthrop states that the trial was postponed to the General Court because it was of such great importance. It may also have been postponed to stall for time and give Winslow a chance to work in England without Child to oppose him. See Winthrop's Journal, 2 : 367.
81   Ibid.; "Robert Child to John Winthrop, Jr., 15 March 1646/7," in Forbes, *Winthrop Papers*, 5 : 140–41, 160, 181; and *Mass. Col. Rec.*, 2 : 199. We know little about Child's confinement except what he wrote to his friend, the younger Winthrop on March 15, 1646/7, and May 14, 1647, in which he asks Winthrop to pay him the £40 he owed him in order to pay off his £50 fine. This was finally paid by Winthrop in September 1647. The General Court eventually seized £50 of Child's holdings in the Lynn ironworks to pay for his fines.
82   Winthrop's Journal, 2 : 374–75; *Mass. Col. Rec.*, 3 : 105.
83   Winthrop's Journal, 2 : 376; *Mass. Col. Rec.*, 3 : 113.
84   *Mass. Col. Rec.*, 3 : 114.
85   Winthrop's Journal, 2 : 359.

CHAPTER 6

1   Thomas Edwards, *The Second Part of Gangraena: Or The Fresh and Further Discovery of the Errors . . . of the Sectaries of this Time . . .* (London, 1646), p. 175.
2   Winthrop's Journal, 2 : 387–88.
3   "George Fenwick to John Winthrop, 6 April 1647," in Forbes, *Winthrop Papers*, 5 : 141–42.
4   Winthrop's Journal, 2 : 333, 342–44, 390; D. Brunton and D. H. Pennington, *Members of the Long Parliament* (London, 1954), pp. 225–45.
5   *Salamander, MHSC*, 3d ser., 2 : 110–11, 135–36, 120–22, 125.
6   Ibid., p. 139.
7   Ibid., pp. 140, 124, 144.
8   Ibid., pp. 123–24.
9   Winthrop's Journal, 2 : 389–90.
10   "Herbert Pelham to John Winthrop, 14 July 1648," in Forbes, *Winthrop Papers*, 5 : 237.

11   Winthrop's Journal, 2 : 391–92.
12   "Robert Child to John Winthrop, Jr., 13 May 1648," in Forbes, *Winthrop Papers*, 5 : 221–23.

EPILOGUE

 1   See Samuel E. Morison, *Builders of the Bay Colony* (Boston and New York, 1930), pp. 260–61
 2   *Jonas, MHSC*, 2d ser., 4 : 120; Winthrop's Journal, 2 : 382.
 3   *Plain Dealing, MHSC*, 3d ser., 3 : 80.
 4   Winthrop's Journal, 2 : 376.
 5   Ibid., pp. 402–03; *Mass. Col. Rec.*, 2 : 200.
 6   *The Cambridge Platform of Church Discipline*, quoted in Walker, *Creeds and Platforms of Congregationalism*, p. 205.
 7   Ibid., pp. 205–06, 221–22.
 8   Ibid., pp. 210, 215.
 9   Ibid., pp. 229–30.
10   *Mass. Col. Rec.*, 2 : 197, also 3 : 109, 110. This is the volume 3 version.
11   Italics mine. This conclusion has been substantiated by Timothy H. Breen in "Who Governs, the Town Franchise in Seventeenth Century Massachusetts," *William and Mary Quarterly* 27 (1970): 460–74.
12   *Mass. Col. Rec.*, 2 : 217–18; Max Farrand, *The Laws and Liberties of Massachusetts* (Cambridge, Mass., 1929).
13   *Salamander, MHSC*, 3d ser., 2 : 139.

APPENDIX

 1   *Salamander, MHSC*, 3d ser., 1 : 117.
 2   "Hugh Peter to John Winthrop, Jr., 23 June 1645," in Forbes, *Winthrop Papers*, 5 : 30.
 3   *Salamander, MHSC*, 3d ser., 2 : 111, 118.
 4   Ibid., pp. 112, 117.
 5   Winthrop's Journal, 1 : 32n., 33n.
 6   George Kitteridge, "Dr. Robert Child the Remonstrant," *Publications of the Colonial Society of Massachusetts—Transactions* 21 (1919): 23–24. See also Hutchinson, *Collection of Original Papers*.
 7   Hobart's Journal.
 8   Hutchinson, *Papers*, p. 211; II Samuel 15:11.
 9   *Salamander, MHSC*, 3d ser., 2 : 118–19.
10   *Genealogical Dictionary*, 2 : 97.
11   Hutchinson, *Papers*, p. 211.
12   *Salamander, MHSC*, 3d ser., 2 : 112; for information on the Reverend Mr. Goodwin, see Walker, *Congregationalism*, pp. 137, 172, 310, 342, 344, 345, 349, 350. See also Ralph Young, "Good News from New England" (Ph.D. diss., Michigan State University, 1971).
13   Hutchinson, *Papers*, p. 212.
14   *Mass. Col. Rec.*, 2 : 241.

Bibliography

PRIMARY SOURCES

Many of the basic primary sources for research in the history of 17th-century Massachusetts can be found in print. Absolutely essential for my purposes were Nathaniel Shurtleff, ed., *Records of the Governor and Company of the Massachusetts Bay in New England*, 5 vols. (Boston, 1853–54); John Winthrop, *The History of New England from 1630 to 1649*, ed. James Savage, 2 vols. (Boston, 1853). The Savage edition of Winthrop's Journal is particularly useful because of the Savage notes. Also essential were Allyn B. Forbes, ed., *Winthrop Papers*, 5 vols. (Boston, 1929–47); William H. Whitmore, *The Colonial Laws of Massachusetts* (Boston, 1889); Thomas Hutchinson, *Collection of Original Papers* (London, 1769). *The Collections of the Massachusetts Historical Society* contain several pamphlets of prime importance such as John Child, *New England's Jonas Cast Up at London*, in *MHSC*, 2d ser. (1816), vol. 4; Thomas Lechford, *Plain Dealing or Newes from New England*, in *MHSC*, 3d ser. (1833), vol. 3; and Edward Winslow, *New England's Salamander, Discovered*, in *MHSC*, 3d ser. (1830), vol. 2. *The Rhode Island Historical Society Collections* (1835), vol. 2, contain Samuel Gorton's *Simplicity's Defence against Seven-Headed Policy*. Another important pamphlet is Edward Winslow, *Hypocrisie Unmasked* (London, 1646). Very useful, especially in dealing with the Gorton controversy, were John Russell Bartlett, ed., *The Records of the Colony of Rhode Island and Providence Plantations*, 10 vols. (Providence, 1856–65); Nathaniel Morton, *New England's Memoriall* (Cambridge, Mass., 1669); William Bradford, *Of Plymouth Plantation*, ed. Harvey Wish (New York, 1962); Edward Johnson, *Wonder-Working Providence of Sions Saviour in New England, 1628–1651*, ed. J. Franklin Jameson (New York, 1910); Nathaniel Shurtleff and Daniel Pulsifer, eds., *Records of the Colony of New Plymouth*, 12 vols. (Boston, 1856–61). Useful for the documents printed in them are: Cotton Mather, *Magnalia Christi Americana*, 2 vols. (Hartford, 1855); Thomas Hutchinson, *The History of the Colony and Province of Massachusetts Bay*, ed. Lawrence Shaw Mayo, 3 vols. (Cambridge, Mass., 1936); Samuel Deane, *History of Scituate* (Boston, 1831); and Williston Walker, *The Creeds and Platforms of Congregationalism*

(New York, 1893). *The New England Historical and Genealogical Register* contains articles of use.

Important primary sources which have never been published are the holdings of the Archives of the State of Massachusetts in the State House, Boston. Also imperative in helping overcome the topical arrangement of the State Archives are the chronologically arranged photostat collection of the Massachusetts Historical Society.

The following are the county and town records, published and unpublished, which have been used in this study, especially in compiling the statistics found in Chapter 2.

ESSEX COUNTY

Essex Institute, *Records and Files of the Quarterly Courts of Essex County, Massachusetts,* 8 vols. (Salem, 1911–21).
Essex County Deeds, MSS in the Essex County Court House, Registry of Deeds, Salem.
Essex Institute, *The Probate Records of Essex County, Massachusetts,* 3 vols. (Salem, 1917).
The Probate Records of Essex County, Mass., MSS in the Essex County Court House, Probate Division, Salem. These records contain many wills and inventories for the period after 1683 when the published records end.

HAMPSHIRE COUNTY

Smith, Joseph, *Colonial Justice in Western Massachusetts, 1639–1702, The Pynchon Court Records* (Cambridge, Mass., 1961).
Hampshire County Deeds, MSS in the Hampshire County Court House, Registry of Deeds, Northampton.
The Probate Records of Hampshire County, Mass., MSS in the Hampshire County Court House, Probate Division, Northampton.

MIDDLESEX COUNTY

Middlesex County Deeds, MSS in the Middlesex County Court House, Registry of Deeds, Cambridge.
The Probate Records of Middlesex County, Mass., MSS in the Middlesex County Court House, Probate Division, Cambridge.

NORFOLK COUNTY

The Essex Records contain much Norfolk material, especially for the southern towns of old Norfolk County.
Bouton, Nathaniel, *Provincial Papers—Documents and Records Re-*

lating to the Province of New Hampshire, 10 vols. (Concord, N.H., 1867).

"Old Norfolk County Deeds," in *Historical Collections of the Essex Institute* (1913), vols. 49, 56–70.

Batchellor, Albert, *Probate Records of the Province of New Hampshire,* 3 vols. (Concord, N.H., 1907). Part of the State Papers series, vols. 31–33.

Probate Records of the Province of New Hampshire, MSS in the New Hampshire Historical Society, Concord, N.H.

SUFFOLK COUNTY

The Court Files of Suffolk County, Mass., MSS in the County Clerk's Office, Suffolk County Court House, Boston.

Colonial Society of Massachusetts, *Records of the Suffolk County Court,* 2 vols. (Boston, 1933).

Suffolk County Deeds, 14 vols. (Boston, 1880).

George, Elijah, *Index to the Probate Records of Suffolk County, Massachusetts, 1636–1893,* 3 vols. (Boston, 1895).

The Probate Records of Suffolk County, Mass., MSS in the Suffolk County Court House, Probate Division, Boston.

MISCELLANEOUS

Maine Historical Society, *Maine Province and Court Records,* 4 vols. (Portland, Me., 1928–   ).

Hull, John, *York County Deeds,* 12 vols. (Portland, Me., 1887).

Sargeant, William, *Maine Wills* (Portland, Me., 1887).

Manwaring, Charles, *A Digest of the Early Connecticut Probate Records, 1635–1700,* 3 vols. (Hartford, 1904).

Old Colony Probate Records (Plymouth Colony), MSS in the Plymouth County Court House, Plymouth, Mass.

Records of many of the Massachusetts towns and churches are extant. The list that follows includes all of the published and unpublished records used in this study. On occasion town histories, although secondary works, are included, particularly if they contain primary material which is no longer available.

ESSEX TOWNS

Andover

Abbot, Abiel, *History of Andover* (Andover, Mass., 1829).

The Records of the Town of Andover, MSS in the Town Clerk's

Office, Andover. These records have been transcribed, rearranged, and filmed by the North Andover Historical Society. Most useful were Land Grants, 1660–1713; Town Records, 1657–1708; Births, Marriages, and Deaths, 1650–1700; Records of the Town and County Tax Lists, 1670–1716.

Gloucester

Babson, John, *History of the Town of Gloucester, Cape Ann* (Gloucester, Mass., 1860).
The Records of the Town of Gloucester, 1642–1710, MSS in the City Clerk's Office, Gloucester.

Ipswich

Schofield, George, *The Ancient Records of the Town of Ipswich, 1634–1650* (Ipswich, Mass., 1899).
The Records of the Town of Ipswich, MSS in the Town Clerk's Office, Ipswich. These records have been filmed by the Ipswich Historical Society. Especially useful was Town Grants and Meetings, 1634–1757.

Lynn

Lewis, Alonzo, *History of Lynn* (Boston, 1844).

Manchester

The Records of the Town of Manchester, MSS in the Town Clerk's Office, Manchester—especially Town Records, 1640–1845, 1661–1720, 1636–1737.

Newbury

Coffin, Joshua, *A Sketch of the History of Newbury, Newburyport, and West Newbury from 1635 to 1845* (Boston, 1845).
Currier, John, *History of Newbury* (Boston, 1902).
———, *Ould Newbury—Historical and Biographical Sketches* (Boston, 1896).
The Records of the Town of Newbury, Mass., MSS in the Town Hall, Newbury. Some are found in the home of the town clerk.

Rowley

Blodgette, George, and Amos Jewett, *Early Settlers of Rowley, Massachusetts* (Rowley, Mass., 1933).
Mighill, Benjamin, *Records of Rowley, Massachusetts, 1639–1672* (Rowley, Mass., 1894).

The Records of the Town of Rowley, Mass., MSS in the Town Clerk's Office, Rowley. Especially useful were Town Meetings, 1648–1671; Births, Marriages, Intentions, and Deaths, 1639–1752; and Town Records, 1660–1712.

Salem

Essex Institute, *Salem Town Records, 1639–1691,* 3 vols. (Salem, 1868).
————, *Vital Records of Salem, Massachusetts,* 6 vols. (Salem, 1916–25).
Felt, Joseph, *Annals of Salem* (Salem, 1842).
Phillips, James, *Salem in the 17th Century* (Boston and New York, 1933).
Perley, Sidney, *The History of Salem, Massachusetts,* 3 vols. (Salem, 1926).

Wenham

Allen, Myron, *The History of Wenham, Civil and Ecclesiastical, from Its Settlement in 1639 to 1860* (Boston, 1860).
Pool, Wellington, "Extracts from the Town Records of Wenham Mass.," in the *Historical Collections of the Essex Institute,* vol. 19 (1882).
Wenham Historical Society, *Wenham Town Records, 1642–1706,* 2 vols. (Wenham, Mass., 1930).

HAMPSHIRE TOWNS

Springfield

Burt, Henry, *The First Century of the History of Springfield—The Official Records, 1636–1736,* 2 vols. (Springfield, Mass., 1898).

MIDDLESEX TOWNS

Cambridge

The Proprietors' Records of Cambridge, Massachusetts (Cambridge, Mass., 1896).
The Records of the Town and Selectmen of Cambridge, 1630–1703 (Cambridge, Mass., 1901).
Paige, Lucius, *History of Cambridge, Massachusetts, 1630–1877* (Boston, 1877).
Sharples, Stephen, *Records of the Church of Christ at Cambridge in New England, 1632–1830* (Boston, 1906).

Charlestown

Frothingham, Richard, *History of Charlestown, Massachusetts* (Boston, 1845).

Hunnewell, James, *Records of the First Church in Charlestown, Massachusetts* (Boston, 1800).

The Records of the Town of Charlestown, Mass., MSS in the City Clerk's Office, Boston—especially Town Records, vol. 1 (1629–61); also a microfilm of these records in the Boston Public Library, rolls 191, 192.

Whitmore, William, and William Appleton, *Reports of the Records Commissioners of the City of Boston,* 2d ed. (Boston, 1881–), vol. 3 (Charlestown Land Records).

Concord

Shattuck, Lemuel, *A History of the Town of Concord* (Boston, 1835).

The Records of the Town of Concord, Mass., MSS in the Town Clerk's Office—especially Ancient Records, 1635–1789, 1655–1784.

Medford

The Records of the Town of Medford, MSS in the City Clerk's Office, Medford, especially vol. 1 (1675–1718). The earliest records are lost.

Reading

Eaton, Lilley, *Genealogical History of the Town of Reading, 1639–1874* (Boston, 1874).

The Records of the Town of Reading, MSS in the Town Clerk's Office—especially Records of Death, 1659–97; Records of Births, 1637–1700; Records of Marriages and Intentions, 1653–1700; Town Rates, 1663–81; Town Meetings, 1644–1773; Town Meetings, Lands and Ways, 1638–1814.

Sudbury

The Records of the Town of Sudbury, Mass., MSS in the Town Clerk's Office, Sudbury. There is also a typescript of these records edited by Sumner Powell which is available to the scholar.

Watertown

Bond, Henry, *Genealogies of the Families and Descendants of Early Settlers of Watertown* (Boston, 1855).

Convers, Francis, *History of Watertown* (Cambridge, Mass., 1830).

Watertown Historical Society, *Watertown Records,* 5 vols. (Watertown, Mass., 1894–1919).

Woburn

Sewell, Samuel, *History of Woburn* (Boston, 1868).
The Records of the Town of Woburn, MSS in the City Clerk's Office, Woburn—especially Vital Statistics, 1641–1762; Town Records, vol. 2 (1673–1780); unfortunately, vol. 1 was missing from the vault and could not be located.

NORFOLK TOWNS

Hampton

Dow, Joseph, *History of the Town of Hampton, New Hampshire, 1638–1892,* 2 vols. (Salem, Mass., 1893).

Haverhill

Chase, George, *The History of Haverhill, Massachusetts* (Haverhill, Mass., 1861).
The Records of the Town of Haverhill, Mass., MSS in the City Clerk's Office, Haverhill. Especially useful were Bk. 1, Births, Marriages and Deaths, 1644 to 1664; Town Records, 1651 to 1800; Bks. 2 and 3, Births, Marriages and Deaths, 1664 on; Town Meetings, 1642–1724.

Salisbury

Hoyt, David, *Old Families of Salisbury and Amesbury, Massachusetts,* 3 vols. (Providence, 1897).
Merrill, Joseph, *History of Amesbury* (Haverhill, Mass., 1880).
Upham, William, "Records of the First Church at Salisbury, Massachusetts," in the *Historical Collections of the Essex Institute,* vol. 16 (1879).
The Records of the Town of Salisbury, Mass., MSS in the Town Clerk's Office, Salisbury. Especially useful was Town Records, 1638–1873.

SUFFOLK TOWNS

Boston

Pierce, Richard, *Records of the First Church in Boston, 1630–1868,* 3 vols., in the *Publications of the Colonial Society of Massachusetts,* vols. 39–41.

Robbins, Chandler, *History of the Second Church or Old North Boston* (Boston, 1852).

Seybolt, Robert, *Town Officials of Colonial Boston* (Cambridge, Mass., 1939).

Whitmore, William, and William Appleton, *Reports of the Records Commissioners of the City of Boston,* 2d ed. (Boston, 1881–), vol. 1 Town and Selectmen's Records), vol. 2 (Boston Tax Lists).

Braintree

Bates, Samuel, *Records of the Town of Braintree* (Randolph, Mass., 1886).

Pattee, W. S., *History of Old Braintree and Quincy* (Quincy, Mass., 1878).

Dedham

Hildreth, H., et al., *A Plan of Dedham Village* (Dedham, Mass., 1883).

Hill, Don, *Dedham Records,* 6 vols. (Dedham, 1886–1936).

Mann, Herman, *Historical Annals of Dedham, Massachusetts, 1635–1847* (Dedham, Mass., 1847).

Dorchester

Blake, James, *Annals of the Town of Dorchester* (Boston, 1846), in the *Collections of the Dorchester Antiquarian and Historical Society,* vol. 2.

Clap, Eben, *The History of Dorchester* (Boston, 1859).

Records of the First Church of Dorchester (Boston, 1891).

Whitmore, William, and William Appleton, *Reports of the Records Commissioners of the City of Boston,* 2d ed. (Boston, 1881–), vol. 4 (Dorchester Town Records).

Hingham

Records of the Town of Hingham, Mass., MSS in the Town Clerk's Office, Hingham—especially Town Records, 1635–1825; Vital Statistics, 1665–1780; Hobart's Journal.

History of Hingham, Massachusetts, 4 vols. (Hingham, Mass., 1893).

Lincoln, Solomon, *History of the Town of Hingham* (Hingham, Mass., 1827).

Roxbury

Ellis, Charles, *History of Roxbury* (Boston, 1847).

The Records of the Town of Roxbury, 1648–1730, MSS in the City

Clerk's Office, Boston; also a microfilm of these records in the
Boston Public Library, especially rolls 204, 205.

Whitmore, William, and William Appleton, *Reports of the Records
Commissioners of the City of Boston*, 2d ed. (Boston, 1884–), vol. 6
(Roxbury Land and Church Records).

Weymouth

The Records of the Town of Weymouth, Mass., MSS in the Town
Clerk's Office, Weymouth—especially Town Meeting Records,
1643–1772; The Proprietors' Allotments, 1642–44.

Weymouth Historical Society, *History of Weymouth, Massachusetts*,
4 vols. (Weymouth, Mass., 1923).

MISCELLANEOUS TOWN RECORDS AND HISTORIES—towns founded after
the date of this study, but whose records helped in calculating the
populations of the parent towns.

Billerica

Hazen, Henry, *History of Billerica* (Boston, 1883).

The Records of the Town of Billerica, Mass., MSS in the Town
Clerk's Office, Billerica. Most useful was Town Records, 1658 on.

Boxford

Perley, Sidney, "Boxford Town Records," *Historical Collections of
the Essex Institute*, vol. 36 (1898).

————, *The History of Boxford* (Boxford, Mass., 1880).

Bradford

The Records of the Town of Bradford, Mass., MSS in the City
Clerk's Office, Haverhill, Mass. Especially useful were Births, Marriages, and Deaths, 1670–1796; and Town Records, 1668–1742.

Chelmsford

Allen, Wilkes, *History of Chelmsford, Massachusetts* (Haverhill,
Mass., 1820).

The Records of the Town of Chelmsford, Mass., MSS in the Town
Clerk's Office, Chelmsford. Especially useful were the Proprietors'
Records and Town Records.

Dover

Quint, A. H., *The Charter and Ordinances of Dover, New Hampshire* (Dover, N.H., 1891).

Quint, A. H., *Historical Memoranda of Ancient Dover, New Hampshire* (Dover, N.H., 1900).
Wadleigh, George, *Notable Events in the History of Dover, New Hampshire, 1623–1865* (Dover, N.H., 1913).

Groton

Butler, Caleb, *History of Groton* (Boston, 1848).
Green, Samuel, *The Early Records of Groton, 1662–1707* (Groton, Mass., 1880).

Hadley

Judd, Sylvester, *History of Hadley, Massachusetts* (Northampton, Mass., 1863).
Proprietors' Records of the Town of Hadley, MSS in the Hampshire County Court House, Registry of Deeds, Northampton, Mass.

Lancaster

Nourse, H. S., *Early Records of Lancaster, Massachusetts* (Lancaster, Mass., 1884).

Malden

Corey, Deloraine, *History of Malden* (Malden, Mass., 1899).

Marblehead

Roads, Samuel, Jr., *The History and Traditions of Marblehead, Massachusetts* (Marblehead, Mass., 1897).

Marlborough

Hudson, Charles, *History of the Town of Marlborough, Massachusetts, 1657–1861* (Boston, 1862).

Medfield

Tilden, William, *History of Medfield, Massachusetts* (Boston, 1887).
The Records of the Town of Medfield, Mass., MSS in the Town Clerk's Office, Medfield. Especially useful were Town Records, 1652–65; Town Records, 1665–1742; Town Proprietors' Records, vol. 1 (1649–1742); Birth, Marriages, and Death, 1651–1723.

Milton

Teele, A. K., *History of Milton, Massachusetts, 1640–1887* (Milton, Mass., 1887).

Northampton

Trumbull, James, *History of Northampton, Massachusetts,* 2 vols. (Northampton, Mass., 1898).
Proprietors' Records of the Town of Northampton, Mass., MSS in the Hampshire County Court House, Northampton.

Topsfield

Dow, George, "The Early Records of the Town of Topsfield," in the *Collections of the Topsfield Historical Society,* vol. 3 (1897).
Topsfield Historical Society, *Town Records of Topsfield, Massachusetts, 1659–1739* (Topsfield, Mass., 1917).

SECONDARY SOURCES

There are several general histories of New England and of Massachusetts Bay in particular which are still of use. C. M. Andrews, *The Colonial Period of American History,* 4 vols. (New Haven and London, 1934–38), is still a very reliable general account. J. G. Palfrey, *History of New England,* 5 vols. (Boston, 1858–90), despite its pro-Puritan bias, is still useful to the historian. Brooks Adams in his *Emancipation of Massachusetts* (Boston, 1887) suffers from the opposite bias, but his is nevertheless the most insightful study of this period. Unfortunately, many of Adams's opinions have been dismissed because of his dislike for the rulers of 17th-century Massachusetts.

Important recent studies usually of a more specific nature include Bernard Bailyn, *The New England Merchants in the Seventeenth Century* (Cambridge, Mass., 1955); Loren Barlitz, *City on a Hill* (New York, 1964); Emery Battis, *Saints and Sectaries* (Chapel Hill, 1962); Daniel Boorstin, *The Americans, the Colonial Experience* (New York, 1958); B. Katherine Brown, "A Note on the Puritan Concept of Aristocracy," *Mississippi Valley Historical Review,* 51 (June 1954): 105–12; Richard Dunn, *Puritans and Yankees, The Winthrop Dynasty of New England, 1630–1717* (Princeton, 1962); G. L. Haskins, *Law and Authority in Early Massachusetts* (New York, 1960); George Langdon, Jr., *Pilgrim Colony, A History of New Plymouth, 1620–1691* (New Haven, 1966). The works of Edmund S. Morgan dealing with this period: *Puritan Family* (Boston, 1944), *The Puritan Dilemma* (Boston, 1958), *Visible Saints* (New York, 1963), and *Roger Williams, The Church and the State* (New York, 1967) are invaluable aids to the scholar. Samuel E. Morison's *Builders of the Bay Colony* (Boston, New York, and Cambridge,

Mass., 1930), *The Founding of Harvard College* (Cambridge, Mass., 1935), and *Harvard in the Seventeenth Century*, 2 vols. (Cambridge, Mass., 1936), should be consulted. But still the most influential and insightful of the scholars of New England and of Puritanism is Perry Miller. His *Orthodoxy in Massachusetts, 1630–1650* (Cambridge, Mass., 1933) *The New England Mind: The Seventeenth Century* (New York, 1939), *The New England Mind: From Colony to Province* (Cambridge, Mass., 1953), and *Errand into the Wilderness* (Cambridge, Mass., 1956) are the standard treatises on Massachusetts political and intellectual history. Williston Walker, *The Creeds and Platforms of Congregationalism* (New York, 1893) is excellent. The scholar should also consult Larzer Ziff, *The Career of John Cotton, Puritanism and the American Experience* (Princeton, 1962), Darrett B. Rutman's excellent *Winthrop's Boston* (Chapel Hill, 1965), and Timothy Breen, *The Character of the Good Ruler: Puritan Political Ideas in New England, 1630–1730* (New Haven, 1970).

In recent years there have appeared careful studies of the local communities within Massachusetts Bay, which have aroused a lively debate concerning social, religious, economic, and political structures. Among the best are Rutman's study of Boston, mentioned above, and Sumner C. Powell's *Puritan Village* (Middletown, Conn., 1963). See also the significant studies by Kenneth Lockridge, *A New England Town: The First Hundred Years* (New York, 1970), and Philip J. Greven, Jr., *Four Generations* (Ithaca, N.Y., 1970). Much of the publication concerning these arguments has been in the scholarly journals and has appeared in the form of the "case study." The beginning of the argument concerning whether Massachusetts Bay was an "aristocracy" or a "democracy" can be traced to B. Katherine Brown's very important article "Freemanship in Puritan Massachusetts," *American Historical Review* 50 (1954): 865–83. Mrs. Brown continued her research in a series of case studies of Massachusetts towns: "Puritan Democracy, A Case Study," *Mississippi Valley Historical Review* 50 (1963): 377–96; and "Puritan Democracy in Dedham, Massachusetts: Another Case Study," *William and Mary Quarterly* 24 (1967): 378–96. For differing views on this subject one should consult Stephen Foster, "The Massachusetts Franchise in the Seventeenth Century," *William and Mary Quarterly* 24 (1967): 613–23; Stephen Foster, *Their Solitary Way: The Puritan Social Ethic in the First Century of Settlement in New England* (New Haven, 1971); Kenneth A. Lockridge and Alan Kreider, "The Evolution of Massachusetts Town Government, 1640 to 1740," *William and Mary Quarterly* 23 (1966): 549–74; Richard C. Simmons, "Freemanship in

Early Massachusetts; Some Suggestions for a Case Study," *William and Mary Quarterly* 19 (1962): 422–28; his "Studies in the Massachusetts Franchise, 1631–1691" (Ph.D. diss., University of California, Berkeley, 1965); and his "Godliness, Property, and the Franchise in Puritan Massachusetts: An Interpretation," *Journal of American History* 55 (1968): 495–511; Robert Emmet Wall, Jr., "A New Look at Cambridge," *Journal of American History* 52 (1965): 599–605; and his "The Massachusetts Bay Colony Franchise in 1647," *William and Mary Quarterly*, 26 (1969): 136–44; and John J. Waters, "Hingham, Massachusetts, 1631–1661: An East Anglian Oligarchy in the New World," *Journal of Social History* 1 (1967–68): 351–70.

Index

Absalom, 181, 237, 238

Acadia, 48, 65, 67, 68, 144

Adams, Henry, 29

Adams family, 29

Adultery, 178, 179; persons charged with, 237

Agriculture, scientific: Robert Child interested in, 235

Aldus, John, 29

Allen, Bozoan, 96, 104, 108, 110, 111, 195; friend of Rev. Peter Hobart, 93; chosen captain of Hingham militia and presented to magistrates for approval, 95; militia company asks him to assume command, 97; elected to General Court, 105, 194; accuses Winthrop of misdeeds, 106; fined by General Court, 115–16

Allerton, Isaac, 69

Allin, Bozoune. *See* Allen, Bozoan

Allin, Francis: member of Commission for Foreign Plantations in 1646 and 1647, 216

America, 226

Anabaptists, 33, 148, 149, 225. *See also* Baptists

Andover, Massachusetts; adult male population and number of freemen in 1647, 39

Anglican church, 33, 213, 219, 237. *See also* Church of England

Antinomianism, 10, 13, 33, 250

Aquednick, 122. *See also* Rhode Island

Arbella (vessel), 2

Arbitrary government, 22, 48, 63, 81, 116, 166, 176, 190, 218, 232; defined by Winthrop, 5, 85–87; threat of, 15, 18, 41, 80

Aristocracy, 61

Army: of Massachusetts, invades Rhode Island, 134; of England, 226

Arnold, Benedict, 128; submits to Massachusetts jurisdiction, 125; requests Massachusetts intervention in Providence, 249

Arnold, William: submits to Massachusetts jurisdiction, 125

Arnold family, 126

Asia, 123

Assistants, 8, 47, 61, 79, 85, 141; to elect governor and deputy governor, 6; levy taxes, 6–7; request election of town representatives, 7. *See also* Court of Assistants; Magistrates

Atheism: Gorton accused of, 122

Atherton, Humfrey, 131; sent as envoy to Gorton, 130; army commissioner against Gorton, 134

Authority, 119

Baptism, 148

Baptists, 236, 238; banned in Massachusetts, 148–49; repression of, resented, 148–49. *See also* Anabaptists

Barbados, 220

Bare Cove: renamed Hingham, 93. *See also* Hingham, Massachusetts

Barney, Jacob: elected to lower house in 1647, 208; disagrees with verdict on remonstrants, 209

Bartholomew, Henry: disagrees with verdict on remonstrants, 193*n*; not reelected to General Court in 1647, 208

Beal, John: member of Hingham elite, 93

General Court (*continued*)
debates number of deputies per town, 14; appoints committee to study a code of laws, 17; adopts Body of Liberties, 17; number of, 27; number of towns which send deputies to, 27; hears sow case, 53–55; splits into two houses, 63–64; shall not commission Standing Council, 78; petitioned by Hingham men, 100–02; hears case against Winthrop, 107–19; appoints committee to state charges against Winthrop, 109; intervenes in Providence dispute, 124–26; hears appeals from Pumham and Socononoco, 129–30; sends envoys to Shawomet, 130; promises safe conduct to Gortonists, 130; intervenes in Shawomet, 134; trial of Gortonists before, 134–41; banishes Gortonists, 144–46; responds to petition against banning Baptists, 149; petitioned by Vassall, 158; of Plymouth, 158; takes steps to counter Remonstrance, 174–82; drops franchise bill of 1645, 175; calls for synod, 175–76; appoints committee to compose book of laws, 176; appoints committee to respond to Remonstrance, 176; publishes answer to Remonstrance, 177–82; hears charges against Fowle and Smith, 183–85; presses charges against remaining remonstrants, 189–96; convicts remonstrants, 191–96; orders funds raised, 199; instructs Winslow, 199–200; remonstrants appeal ruling of, 201; grants pardon to John Dand, 220. *See also,* Court of Assistants; Deputies; House of Deputies; Lower house; Magistrates

Gibbons, Edward: Boston merchant, 67; led Boston merchants wishing to aid La Tour, 68

Gloucester, Massachusetts, 35, 36, 242; pre-1647 selectmen in, 25; adult male population and number of freemen in 1647, 39

Glover, John: deputy from Dorchester, 77

God, 82, 132, 133, 139, 166, 186, 189, 190, 198, 200, 219, 251, 253, 255

Gold, Edmund, 111; fined, 115

Gold, 200

Goodwin, Rev. John, 239, 252

Gorges, Thomas, 246

Gorton, Samuel, 48, 120, 121, 125, 129, 134, 136–40 passim, 143, 145, 147, 148, 152, 153, 156, 170, 182, 194, 196–99 passim, 211, 213, 217, 219, 223, 248, 250, 251; arrives in Boston, 122, experiences in Portsmouth, R.I., 122; moves to Plymouth colony, 122; condemned by Roger Williams, 122–23; attacks Massachusetts intervention in R.I., 126–28; leaves Providence, 126; moves to Shawomet, 128; buys Shawomet from Indians, 128; receives envoys of General Court, 130; denies Massachusetts claim to Shawomet, 130–31; brought back to Massachusetts, 134; trial of, 134–41; claims his trial is persecution, 135; will appeal case to England, 136; confined at Charlestown, 142; returns to Shawomet, 146; leaves Shawomet for Portsmouth, R.I., 146–47; appeals to England, 147–48; appeals to Commission for Foreign Plantations, 150–51, 211, 219, 220; establishes precedent of Appeal, 152; remains in England, 154; writes *Simplicity's Defence against Seven-Headed Policy,* 155, 211; arrives in Boston, 155, 156; influences Remonstrance, 157, 212, 224; attacked unsuccessfully by Winslow, 211, 212; has support of English Independents, 211

Gortonists, 130, 131, 135, 136, 148,

Magistrates (*continued*)
tear democracy, 10; majority disapprove Newtown petition, 11; disagree with deputies and lesser gentry on negative voice and Standing Council, 11, 12, 13, 22, 42, 74, 78, 80, 81, 82, 84; some receive life tenure, 14; oppose a published code of laws, 16; receive support of elders on fundamental issues, 34; their role in God's scheme, 34; of Essex county, 38, 72; two newcomers elected in 1643, 50; veto Essex plan, 78; called together to discuss La Tour problem, 83; question elders about need for fixed laws and penalties, 91; and the command of Hingham militia, 95; request elders to mediate in Hingham church, 98; and Hingham charges against Winthrop, 106–07; contend with deputies on the issues in Hingham case, 109–13; triumph in Hingham case, 117; of Plymouth Colony, 122, 158; challenge sale of Shawomet, 128; attacked by Holden, 133, 134; all but three vote to execute Gorton, 139; grant safe conduct to Holden, 152; campaign against Remonstrance, 171; vote to convict remonstrants, 191, 206–07; determine to send agent to England, 196–200; confer with elders on relationship with England, 197; determine to halt Child, 204; judicial powers of, 231; dispute with deputies settled on their terms, 232. *See also* Assistants; Court of Assistants; Upper house
Magna Charta, 177, 178
Maine, 65
Major General, 110, 112
Malden, Massachusetts, 208
Man, William: asks Massachusetts to intervene in Providence, 249

Manchester, Edward Montague, Earl of: member of Commission for Foreign Plantations, 215, 216
Manchester, Massachusetts, 36; adult male population and number of freemen in 1647, 39
Marblehead, Massachusetts, 35, 36; involved in Williams case, 38; fishermen of, sign petition for general governor, 202
Marlorat, Augustin, 66
Mather, Richard, 62
Mattapan: renamed Dorchester, 4
Maverick, Samuel, 177, 181, 184, 202, 206; signs Remonstrance, 164; fined 195, 209; commissioner for conquest of New Netherlands, 237; biography of, 237
Meadow, 37
Medford, Massachusetts, 4, 40n
Merchant Adventurers, 52
Merchants, 222, 236, 238; aid La Tour, 67, 68
Merrimack River, 35, 36
Miantonomo: sachem of Narragansetts, 48, 128, 129
Middlesex County, Massachusetts, 36, 37, 42, 43, 48, 64, 66, 68, 69, 72, 74, 75, 175, 203, 204, 208, 222, 223, 230, 242, 243; residents of, serve in General Court for remoter towns, 27; differ from Essex-Norfolk, 35–39; adult male population and number of freemen in, 39
Midwife, 253
Miller, Perry, 47
Ministers, 47, 57, 64, 127, 170, 174, 182, 227; again mediate negative voice dispute, 60; berated by Endecott, 82–84; campaign against Remonstrance, 171. *See also* Clergy; Elders
Ministry: attacked by Holden, 133, 134
Moody, Lady: becomes a Baptist, 148

Winslow, Edward (*continued*)
chusetts agent, 153–54, 198–99;
writes *Hypocrisie Unmasked*, 155;
close supporter of Bradford, 159;
warns Winthrop about Vassall,
159; claims Vassall authored *New
England's Jonas*, 189n; receives
instructions from General Court,
199–200; fails to reverse pro-
Gorton decision, 211; attacks
Gorton in *Hypocrisie Unmasked*,
212; refutes charges of Child and
Vassall, 217–19; tries to associate
Child with Catholicism, 235–36
Winsor, Joshua: asks Massachusetts
to intervene in Providence, 249
Winthrop, John, 1, 2, 3, 15, 21, 28,
30, 32, 37, 45, 50, 53, 55, 57, 65,
67, 69, 70, 75, 78, 83, 90, 98, 99,
104, 106, 108, 111, 113, 115, 119,
120, 122, 123, 131, 135, 136, 138,
139, 142, 144, 145, 147, 152, 153,
166n, 171, 179, 183, 184, 185, 192,
193, 194, 196, 198, 202, 205, 206,
218, 223, 237, 246, 248, 254, 256;
preached to settlers, 2–4; establishes Boston, 4; on arbitrary
government, 5, 85–87, 87–89; refuses to move to Newtown, 7–8;
acknowledges charter as fundamental, 8; meets with freemen,
8–9; Cotton preaches in his behalf, 10; elected governor, 10, 50,
207; not reelected governor, 10,
15, 105; on the negative voice,
11, 56–62; on Code of Laws, 16–
17; attempted impeachment of,

23, 89, 99–102, 106–19, 116, 157;
attacks Saltonstall's book, 44–45;
and the French in Acadia, 48,
64, 66, 70–72; on the sow case,
54; Bellingham refuses to recon-
cile with, 58; comments on power
of deputies, 62, 85; how he
could be defeated, 64; elected
deputy governor, 75, 105; pro-
tests election of commissioners to
United Colonies, 76; his break
with Endecott ended, 84; calls
Hobart a Presbyterian, 93; comments on Vassall, 102–03; speech
on liberty, 116–18; desires outpost
on Narragansett Bay, 125; and
Gorton, 137, 144–46; reports crackdown on heretics, 148; and Vassall, 159, 164, 176; addresses
elders, 194–95; as possible agent
to England, 198; promised support by George Fenwick, 214–15;
dies in 1649, 233
Winthrop, John, Jr., 221, 235, 256;
elected magistrate, 14
Winthrop family, 30
Witchcraft, 178
Woburn, Massachusetts: adult male
population and number of freemen in 1647, 39
Woodbridge, Rev. John, 53

Yale, David, 177, 181; signs Remonstrance, 164; biography of,
238
Yorkshire, England, 32